SOFTWARE PROCESS DESIGN

THE McGRAW-HILL INTERNATIONAL SOFTWARE QUALITY ASSURANCE SERIES

Consulting Editor

Professor D. Ince
The Open University

Other titles in this series

Practical Implementation of Software Metrics	Goodman
Software Testing	Roper
Software Metrics for Product Assessment	Bache and Bazzana

Related titles on software engineering are published in an accompanying series: The International Software Engineering Series, also edited by Professor Darrel Ince.

SOFTWARE PROCESS DESIGN
Out of the Tar Pit

Jacqueline Holdsworth

McGRAW-HILL BOOK COMPANY

London · New York · St Louis · San Francisco · Auckland · Bogotá
Caracas · Lisbon · Madrid · Mexico · Milan · Montreal
New Delhi · Panama · Paris · San Juan · São Paulo · Singapore
Sydney · Tokyo · Toronto

Published by
McGRAW-HILL Book Company Europe
Shoppenhangers Road, Maidenhead, Berkshire, SL6 2QL, England
Telephone 0628 23432
Fax 0628 770224

British Library Cataloguing in Publication Data
Holdsworth, Jacqueline
  Software Process Design. – (McGraw-Hill
  International Software Quality Assurance
  Series)
I. Title II. Series
005.1

ISBN 0-07-707842-x

Library of Congress Cataloging-in-Publication Data
Holdsworth, Jacqueline,
    Software process design / Jacqueline Holdsworth.
      p.   cm. – (McGraw-Hill international software quality
    assurance series)
    Includes bibliographical references and index.
    ISBN 0–07–707842–X   :
    1. Computer software–Development.   I. Title.   II Series.
  QA76.76.D47H65   1994
  005.1′068′5–dc20   94–18466
                                                        CIP

12345CL   97654

Typeset by TecSet Ltd, Wallington, Surrey
Printed in England by Clays Ltd, St Ives plc

All author royalties for this book are gifted to:

25 Beehive Place London SW9 7QR

CONTENTS

The Quality Forum is pleased to publish jointly with McGraw-Hill this book which covers topics pertinent to software quality assurance.

The aim of the organization is 'to help the member organizations improve the quality of their products and services through the exchange of information between members and with other organizations with similar interests'.

The Quality Forum has over 200 members, including organizations from all sectors of industry and commerce, as well as local and national government. While these organizations are predominantly based in the UK, this includes a growing number from other countries in Europe.

This series of books aims to provide an opportunity for authors to publish works which are both practical and state-of-the-art. In this way Quality Forum members and other organizations will benefit from the exchange of information and the development of new ideas which will further the cause of quality in Information Technology (IT).

The Quality Forum publishes these books with the aim of stimulating discussion in the software community so that the industry as a whole will move forward to improved products and services. It is proud to be associated with the series while not endorsing every single point of view in every book.

If you would like to know more about the Quality Forum, please contact:

Quality Forum
17 St Catherine's Rd
Ruislip
Middlesex HA4 7RX
UK
Tel: +44 (0) 895 635222
Fax: +44 (0) 895 679178

PREFACE

Throughout the last decade, I have seen a number of software producers thrashing around, trying to make sense of total quality management (TQM) programmes while coping with the massive reorganizational effects demanded by the economic switchback of the 1980s boom and the 1990s 'rightsizing'. I talk of recession, just as it appears that we are coming through the worst, and there is the opinion that I should not really dwell on something that is at once unpleasant and now rather passé, but who would have thought in the golden days of the 1980s there would ever be an end to the increasing demand for software personnel and their skills? Yet in the last few years I have seen massive staff redundancies, up to 40 per cent in some organizations. This is so unprecedented in the whole of our profession's short lifetime, that I shall always keep it in my mind. Even when the sun shines.

Total quality management has its good elements, but something definitely gets lost in all the expensive packaging. I feel that, on the whole, we as a profession deserve more than the empty cheer-leading which was being noised throughout the software industry. The problems software people experience have little to do in fact with their personal shortcomings or lack of quality. The source of quality problems is deep-seated. It springs from the way working relationships are organized and managed (or not organized and not managed, in some cases) at a much higher level. At one and the same time, individuals are being exhorted to improve the process, while the process is kept a dark, shifting mystery to the majority. Clearly there can be little hope of anything except superficial success.

Top management has always been blamed for lack of commitment. My experience is that top management do not, or are unable to, appreciate the need for their being involved in the active design and engineering of the processes by which they earn their daily bread, and upon which the daily bread of their employees depends. So, let us help them. It is time to stop protesting that top management has got it all wrong, or lacks commitment. You have the power, if you are willing to shoulder the responsibility, to stop being the filling in your hierarchical sandwich and to escape your functional fortress to collaborate with the other people in your organization. You must use this power to negotiate and make the improvements you need to carry out your clients' work as they would like it, effectively and professionally.

This book is for all those who care about and enjoy the creative challenge of software production. It is about understanding why we need to work on making our software delivery processes visible, and how we can take steps, at whatever the level of the organization we work, to create that visibility, and make lasting improvements for ourselves, and for others. To help you, I have arranged the book in three sections. The first informal section (Chapters 1–3) revisits the real problems you experience when there is no visible process and explains how process management will support you in your work. The second section (Chapters 4–10) is a step-by-step guide which will enable you identify, diagnose, and streamline your process and key operations. The third and final section provides you with resources which are complemetary to software process design strategies, such as training and tools.

I am indebted to all my clients who have put their trust in me and given me the opportunity and the platform to help them create the changes and improvements they wanted to make. I would like to remember the people who have worked for me in the past and from whom I learnt most of all the important things I know, among others: Jon Bloom, Phil Higham, Peter Woods, Ben Stevens, Martin Midgley, Antonios Philippides, Kim Tong Chai, Sayeed Islam, and Alison Rowe.

I am also grateful to all those who, over the years, have shared their enthusiasm for improvement with me, those who have challenged me to search for greater relevance, and particularly those whose criticism and cynicism have made me see beyond the looking-glass. In particular I have to thank my father, Ronald, who taught me to look; my husband, Richard, who taught me tenacity and patience; and my daughters, Melissa and Lucy, from whom I learnt empathy and fun.

Jacqueline Holdsworth

INTRODUCTION: OUT OF THE TAR PIT

I am even prepared to be told that when you paid the price of this book you were paying me to think for you. But is it prudent to let me impose my thoughts on you and make you believe they are your own? Beware of such short cuts!

Bernard Shaw
The Intelligent Woman's Guide to Socialism, Capitalism, Sovietism and Facism

In 1975, Fred Brooks used the words 'tar pit' in his book *The Mythical Man-Month* to describe the state of software projects. It was a description so true, that it continues to resonate with many software professionals, even today. Fred is right, software production is chaotic. But the natural world is chaos. We get up each day, go to work and are faced with messes. Russel Ackoff described messes as systems of problems. Tangled webs of knotty problems. Solve one and the rest get thicker. Our first job as leaders, managers and reflective practitioners is to work with those messes and to understand, harness and ride that chaos, for our own benefit and the benefit of others. Our next job is to create an environment within our organization in which some order appears and the laws of cause and effect appear to hold true. This environment cannot be obtained by problem-solving. It requires planning and work redesign to eliminate messes. The task requires considerable energy, but not necessarily activity, to stem and reverse disintegration and confusion. And that is exactly why we are hired and paid.

I read in software management books that as a manager I need answers to questions such as: How much will it cost? Will it be ready on time? How reliable will it be? This is absolutely right. But the questions the empowered manager should be asking right now are: How can we design a process to produce this software at a price which still represents value to our customers? What sort of process needs to be designed to ensure the software is available on 4 April 1995 so that our customer achieves a competitive response? What process do we need to support our customer's imperative to change and adapt business systems in response to the market? What process do we need to engineer the level of reliability required by our customer? It is time to move away from tweaking our introspective, conceptual models of software production, and time to begin tweaking the real world. I know that if the map does not fit the territory, you have to change the map, because raising mountains and creating rivers, in peacetime at least, requires a superhuman hand. But, in software production, we are not talking about massive tectonic upheavals. We are talking about the human practices of organization and process, of negotiation and evolution. Surely, in that environment, if our map does not fit the territory, then we can collaborate to change our territory?

The objective of this book is to enable those who are in the business of delivering software to design the framework and operations which are critical to their own business success. You will be provided with step-by-step guidance on how to identify the processes in your organization; how to gather and map all the excellent know-how that already exists; how to identify and weed out all the operations which add no value; how to choose and implement relevant and significant performance indicators; how to streamline; and how to eliminate unnecessary bureaucracy. You will be helped to build a framework in which the various demands of business process improvement, total quality management, quantitative management, and standards can be incorporated seamlessly into business as usual.

GETTING OUR BEARINGS

In spite of the increasing maturity of information technology, the business of delivering software still remains at a craft level. We should not beat ourselves into a terminal despair about this. How long after its invention was the motor car made reliable and customer-friendly? Who would have thought then that it was possible to have such control over car production processes, that the sound a car door makes when it is closed can be tuned precisely? In the 1950s they were still spitting on the steel as it came out of the rolling mills, to see if it was done. We have come a long way in the short time since the birth of the software industry. Just stop to consider some of the progress you have experienced in the last 10 years.

As you are aware, the last decade has seen many good and concerted attempts to put software production on a sound business footing, but most of us still have not found the way to that level of practice where smooth running and sanity is the norm. And it is no surprise. The path is thick with tools, techniques, methodologies and standards: TQM, SSADM, CASE, OO, PRINCE, PROMPT, BS 5750, ISO 9001, etc. and they continue to multiply, adding to, rather than alleviating, the bewildering complexity of our software production practices. Having begun to elbow ourselves out of the tar pit, it would be a pity to be sucked back into a bog of bureaucracy.

So far, too, our application of quantitative and qualitative approaches to software management, in line with the practices of other industries, has tended to reduce visibility rather than increase it. In recent years metrics programmes have followed on the tail of quality programmes. But in spite of some excellent work in the field, from the practical side, measurement is as frustrating as trying to take the temperature of the ocean, and managers still have few indicators, if any at all, to give them a clear indication of the direction in which they should be attempting improvement.

Managers are harassed on every side for their unwillingness to stride out into the jungle. Corporate management wants less pain and more results. Engineers are frustrated by seeing their best professional attempts thwarted by the 'system' or 'politics'. Clients are going sour on their traditional relationships and are shopping around. And the growing pack of hungry competitors is closing in, particularly the generics vendors who, at a stroke, can make some of our efforts over the last decade look like very expensive prototypes.

All this in a climate of recession and change. It is important now, as perhaps never before, that the software providers do not become the brakes on business improvement and response. The risks are at present very great. Think of how much software and automation businesses now have. How long are the lead and cycle times for changing systems in your organization? How high the costs? We have to increase efficiency, we have to increase effectiveness, we have to manage costs down. But where to start? Must we always have no alternative to chopping off an arm or a leg at random to lose weight and so risk bleeding to death? Or, could we, by developing some understanding of our metabolism and needs, seek out a more sensible and scientific slimming programme? Is there a practical regimen that can be adopted to achieve a healthy constitution, that will enable us to stay fit, athletic and flexible?

There is no one single cause at the root of all our problems. Software suppliers, because they address different markets and different targets for success, and because of their unique history and culture each require a specific diagnosis, treatment and fitness programme. However, before we can attempt a diagnosis, there has to be a visible body to examine. In the majority of organizations there is no visible body. There is no visible process for software product and service delivery. There is, of course, at least one process (if not many parallel and competing processes) in existence, otherwise no work would get done. But to all intents and purposes these processes are invisible; they are the private intellectual property of individuals in the organization. Because this is a knowledge-intensive industry, the knowledge of these processes and all the associated skills arrive like nomad tents when people are recruited, and vanish overnight when people leave. Often the organization suffers. Useful knowledge is rarely communicated, and processes rarely packaged so that previous successes can be repeated by others.

But is it possible that we can capture that knowledge, that expertise, those skills — the experience which transforms and creates value? How do we capture it? Can we bring all that knowledge and experience together into a coherent body so that all parts serve the needs of the organization in harmony? Can we then work on the body, measure its performance, eliminate destructive growths and make changes to improve performance? We have been in the business for many years of transforming other people's processes for them. I see no reason why we cannot now do the same for our own benefit.

A COOKERY LESSON

In his *Book of Five Rings*, Miyamoto Musashi teaches us that, 'The principle of strategy is having one thing, to know ten thousand things'. It is a teaching I have taken to heart. Throughout my career I have endeavoured to take learning from many fields, and to apply it successfully to software production problems. Somehow it seems to work well for me, so perhaps you might like to try it too. Dotted throughout this book you will find an occasional account of an event which occurred in a non-work situation and provided me with insight. Here is one of them.

Ask people what is the one, single talent they would like to have, and most reply that it is to have a musical talent. For some perverse reason, perhaps because my free time is so short, the one single, talent I have always most craved is to be able to cook. In my early days I bought cookbook after cookbook, slavishly following every recipe. Being constantly disappointed in my efforts, I blamed the cookbook, threw it away and bought another one. As time went on, it was the weighing scales that I found inaccurate, the mixing bowl that was of the wrong material. What I really needed was a gas oven, a fan-heated electric oven. And so it went on, until one day, I bought a new cookbook, sight unseen, from a catalogue. When I sat down to read it, I felt tremendously disappointed, cheated even, because its recipes were like this:

BOILED CAULIFLOWER
It can be mushy or crisp and crunchy. Pay attention and get it right . . . the way you want it.

| Cauliflower | boiling, salted water | possibly butter | pepper |

For this recipe, the cauliflower can be cut in big pieces, but again try to get them of basically uniform size. Boil, and try a piece after about five minutes. Butter the cauliflower and season to taste.

I felt so cross, I could hear myself muttering, 'What does it mean, pay attention? How much cauliflower? What sort of pepper? Possibly butter!' I had never thought about whether I wanted cauliflower crisp and crunchy or mushy. I usually just cooked it for however long the cookery book said. My conversion happened not on the road to Damascus, but at my local market in Cambridge. Suddenly, everywhere I looked, I saw cauliflowers. Tiers of creamy white-laced globes stacked in their greenery. I had never really appreciated ingredients before. They used to be just things that I cooked, and not too well. But that was when it all started, my love for working with beautiful ingredients, for paying attention, and creating food which now gives delight.

If this book could be described as a recipe book, then it is like this last kind. My hope is that, after reading it, you will become curious about how we really go about organizing ourselves to produce software, and instead of relying on other people to give you precise instructions for this or that method, or to use this or that special equipment, you will feel free to see with your own eyes, hear with your own ears, understand with your own mind, and act with your own intelligence in this period of work which, in the normal course of our careers, consumes around 64 000 hours of our lifetime.

Section 1

1

THE QUALITY IMPROVEMENT DILEMMA

People think that we're just administrators. That all we do is write procedures. That we do not do much. The truth is, we can only say, 'we think it is a good idea to do this or that . . . we have no mandate for action.' We have no teeth, and yet everybody is wanting to measure our performance by the number of teeth marks we leave behind.

Quality team member

We have been working with total quality management (TQM) programmes for a good decade now. In many companies the promise of success has not been realized. What has happened to the dream?

As one of the early dreamers it is hard not to feel betrayed. Now that I work with several organizations that are picking up the pieces after TQM, I find it difficult not to feel angry when I am confronted by the pain of professional and caring people who led their company's crusade for quality and believe they have failed. They have not failed. They took on trust the expensive glitzy packages of TQM which contained no more than the superficial shell of the 'Japanese success story', lacking the engine of decades of sound operations management practice.

In this chapter I want to look at some of the paradoxes of TQM which undermine success. First, from the outset we created a closed system for TQM in the organization by effectively blocking critics, isolating quality managers and creating a separate quality planning function. Second, the model of internal and external customer–supplier chains on which TQM is founded has four fatal flaws. This simplistic representation founders on the complexities of present-day organizational relationships which are the legacy of Adam Smith's division of labour practices, unless we have a clear understanding of process management. Thirdly, when TQM founders and starts to break apart we regress into creating lashings of standards, controls and procedures to tie it all back together again.

1.1 THE CAPITAL Q

I have spent the last, long 10 years working on software quality improvement. Before that I worked on software quality improvement like everyone else, but no one had yet invented the big 'Q'.

I was motivated to join the capital letter brigade of TQM because it made sense to come out of the closet. At least we could synergize our improvement efforts and establish some reasonable working conditions under which we first, would not have to sit and watch the major part of our creativity and ingenuity being continually band-aided or scrapped, and second, not feel continuously embarrassed in front of our customers.

In some companies TQM flourished; in some it floundered. In others, well, that was last year. Maybe the fact that it was free had something to do with it. In the early days it was like the old hippy 1960s of free love — a terrific feeling, until you got slowed down with the bulge and the accusations started. But I do not think we should throw out the baby with the bath water.

Many good things have been achieved as a result of TQM. Progress has been made. The main failure of TQM was that we were constantly exhorted to improve, to change. To improve what, exactly? To change what, exactly? No one seemed able to define in practical terms what had to be improved, or what had to be changed. Having spent some time trying to get the measure of software production, it became apparent that the size of the technical problems were relatively small when compared to the stultifying problems within the environmental and management framework in which everyone seemed to be locked, like flies in amber. I remembered Deming's dictum that workers were responsible for only 15 per cent of the problems, and management for the remaining 85 per cent, and certainly my experience bears that out.

There were other problems too. The cynics were out in full force. Just who was this quality manager who always looked crushed by the weight of the world? Look at all the paper! Plans for this and procedures for that — when would there be time for the real work? The customers said they did not want quality, just their software, please. They did not want to be saddled with the bill for all these standards, procedures, and bureaucracy. Where before we had been blissfully ignorant of who our internal customers were, now we were in no doubt: they were snarling and snapping at our heels, saying, 'I am your customer. Do it or else!' Worst of all, we were just told to 'improve Quality' — an affront if ever there was one. But, again, who could tell us just exactly what was meant by this Quality with a capital Q? It all sounded like just another management sell-out to hype, and guess who were the guinea pigs again?

As a software quality manager, this then was the situation with which I wrestled. This book is the result of my work and the efforts of many others to find practical solutions to the personal pain and the need to improve the business of software engineering. If I had not wrestled with the problems, this would be just another theoretical text. It would be as useful to you as giving you a manual on skiing when I had never crashed and bumped down the piste myself, when all I had studied were the physical and aerodynamic properties of snow, skis, vertebrae, and knee joints. That is not to say that theoretical study is trivial. It is not. Theory informs practice and practice informs theory. That is learning. And one without the other is like a bicycle with one wheel. It does not take you as far as it could.

1.2 HANDS-UP THE CYNICS

I trust that whoever you are, you judge yourself to be a fairly normal, balanced person by recognized standards. Please now list, in the space provided below, three occasions in the last month when you expressed doubts about some aspect of company policy. Keep to three — it is specific and keeps you focused.

```



```

If you have found one, hands-up, you are a cynic — in someone's estimation.

How can you soar like an eagle when you are surrounded by turkeys?

When a company takes TQM, improvement or major change on board, everyone is expected to be positively positive, or they are not playing the game. I always find it interesting that the one topic common to all the writing and teaching on the subject of 'quality' and change, is 'how to handle the cynics'. These prickly, sneering fault-finders (I am sure that you are not in this category of socially defective cynics) are the thorn in the foot of any organization wanting to stride out in new directions. According to the SIMCA in-house journal *Informations*, they are:

> The ones who give you sidelong glances, the moaners, the bad-tempered ones who take offence at the least little thing, those who do not give a damn, the ones who are always embittered, sarcastic, plaintive, jealous or bitter, the ones who always seem to be miles away or to have got out of bed on the wrong side . . . they're all poisoners; they poison the atmosphere, and destroy the team spirit which makes work more pleasant, easy and easier and lighter.

There are numerous strategies put forward for dealing them. Depending upon financial urgency and the managerial capacity for patience and tolerance, cynics are to be: outflanked; outsmarted; left out; or, in the extreme, put out. Given, then, their pariah status, you may ask why I am devoting so many words and so much of your time to discussing them. The simple answer is that cynics often have vital information not known to others which is critical to the success of a change programme. Please go back now and consider the doubts you listed earlier. You can recognize the positive intent behind those negative doubts, but could others? What information would other people need to have to share your concerns? How would you feel if you expressed those doubts to someone else and they just papered over the top of them?

Cynics are us

I have three reasons for giving the 'cynics' space. First, like it or not, cynics are us. We are all intent on self-protection and survival. I remember the cynics who crowded round to crow at 'quality' most vividly. They were among the most vocal members of staff, and encounters with them were frequently confrontational and painful. I felt, at a very personal level, they were intent on undermining not only my 'good works', but also the organization as a whole. However, at the same time, I knew these people to be the most passionate and caring about the organization, and among the most able. In some cases, their feelings were so strong they knowingly, and without being manoeuvred, put their jobs on the line. Second, in my experience the number of cynics is far higher than textbooks indicate. Let us be frank, it is too easy to label anyone 'cynic' who is not as positive as we are about change, or who is pushing for change in a different direction to ourselves. So you can see that, depending on who you are and on the amount of change afoot, the number of cynics in the organization fluctuates widely. The third and not least important reason is that when you are driving round a tight corner in a mist on an uncertain road, no one suggests you throw away the gearbox or the brake. Cynics are the brakes that stop organizational megalomaniacs running out of control and taking the company over the edge.

Treading in the footsteps of the cynics

After some months of failing to outflank and outsmart the TQM 'cynics', I saw there was a problem: my ego. What I had been experiencing as the cause of all the pain and frustration was purely and simply good old negative feedback. I had locked into a vicious cycle of ignoring, discounting and discrediting it. The greater my persistence, the worse the resistance became. In the end, I had no alternative but to change myself. From being involved and enthusiastic, selling and convincing, I adopted more of an 'I am just a curious fly on the wall around here' style. I started to hear without prejudice what the cynics were telling me. And, although it was as masochistic as sticking my tongue into an aching tooth, I asked for more. Then, I started to understand the positive intent of the negativity and how important this feedback was to our learning about systemic organizational barriers to change. Here are a few for you.

'Imposed change'

Imposition of change from the outside by people who did not know the demands and constraints of the job as the practitioners themselves knew them, was a major cause for concern. It seemed to those people who considered they did all the real work that, from time to time, pressures on senior management or changes to the senior management team caused the beast to wake and rattle the cage. It had happened in the past, it was happening now for a while, and would certainly happen again in the future. The senior managers thought that by rattling the cages they were demonstrating the required commitment — what more had they to do? Both groups were suffering from process deficiency: a process for engaging managers and staff in the same purpose, and for understanding that purpose.

'Fuzzy commandments'

The practicalities and operational detail of change, even an outline, was missing. What was read or passed down was a set of very high level policies. How were these to be translated for use? It seemed that senior management was willing to cheer from the trenches as the staff leapt over the top into no man's land without a map. Is it a wonder there was digging-in among the ranks? When asked, senior managers had expected the staff to prepare their own maps, to take the initiative. Something had gone wrong. The casualties in all ranks were due to there being no thought-out change management process.

'Funny rules'

Tightening-up, introducing controls, paralysing with procedures and choking with bureaucracy were seen to be the major items on the agenda. Past experience with standards and procedures had been painful. Granted, documentation had been poor in the past, but now things were going too far the other way. Staff were swamped with documentation and associated administrative tasks. Procedures and standards were needed to deal with standards and procedures. It was like having to hire more home helps to service the extra facilities required by your existing home helps.

Staff were happy to subscribe to quality as customer responsiveness, and being more competitive, but all this red tape seemed to negate that purpose. Where was the process for understanding the real needs of the software delivery process?

'The customers do not want quality'

Come to think of it, when some customers were asked, notably the in-house customers, they said they did not want quality! The customers were satisfied with what they had. They did not want to pay extra for a product that had been tested 100 times more than the previous products. They, too, had a hunch that any tampering with an unpredictable process, which no one seemed to have the power to control, would just make their lives even worse and their products even more expensive.

'The quality problem is over there'

Examining the way work was done was not seen to be bad or particularly threatening — staff acknowledged that there was always room for improvement, specifically with the red tape that already existed and the 'funny' rules and procedures imposed on them by other functional groups in the organization. Talking to groups that passed work and information between themselves, it seemed as though they operated from different planets. Individually, they considered what they were doing to be right and proper and in keeping with the objectives of the organization. It was always the other group that had interpreted the objectives wrongly. It was not that one group was right or the other wrong, simply that they were each working to a different set of purposes. They needed help at a higher level to make the purpose clear, and they needed the free resource to tackle the issues 'off-line', so that delivery of work in hand would not be delayed.

'But we are already doing quality'

There was great concern that no one seemed to recognize the quality work already being done. It was as if strangers driving tractors had been sent in to plough up their fields for some new 'super crop', flattening and crushing all the existing crops that they had been tending and nurturing. They were told that quality was the responsibility of everyone, but their responsibility was being diminished by the hour, with every wheelbarrow of new standards sent hurtling in their direction.

In many ways this was the most hurtful and aggressive act. It was seen to be tantamount to the removal by senior management of all trust and autonomy. Personal contribution, self-esteem and years of positive feedback from performance appraisals had just been obliterated. They perceived their jobs to be deskilled, the work was no longer the work to which they had aspired or for which they had joined the organization. In many cases, given the economic context of a major recession, it was also felt that there was more on the agenda than met the eye, and that jobs were seriously at risk. Who would have ever recognized the motivational benefits of TQM?

The value of cynics

Cynics are early warning systems. They are acting on information that others do not yet have, and it is important to discover the source of that information. If it is in their past experience, then it is important that it is brought to the surface and validated against current situations. If it is valid, so much the better for everyone. If it is a dark fear, then maybe there are some risks to be managed. If the current situation is really different to past situations, then it is helpful to make clear all the points of difference, for everyone to know.

1.3 THE QUALITY GHETTO

Quality, we are told, is the responsibility of everyone. I have never heard anyone yet take issue with that statement. In fact, the very opposite, everyone endorses and defends it most strongly. It is potentially the most motivating phrase of the TQM movement. I say 'potentially' because there are just two small questions to be answered. First, what is actually meant by 'quality'? Second, whose definition of 'quality' gets the votes? You might just like to jot down in the space provided what your answers would be, if asked.

```



```

In line with the requirements of TQM and quality standards, most organizations appoint a quality manager. This person is usually tasked with project-managing 'quality'. I have known many quality managers, some sad, some happy, usually capable, almost always severely frustrated. Here are some of the reasons they give for their frustration.

The secret life of the quality manager

Quality managers either inhabit large, empty offices in remote buildings, or are cramped in cupboards under the stairs. Only occasionally do they enjoy a desk and chair in the middle of the action. Many are stigmatized by the rumour that they were 'spare' or 'waiting for a job' when the managing director decided a quality manager was needed. At best they are seen as well-intentioned amateurs by front-line managers. Whether the organization is centralized, decentralized, project-oriented, matrix-managed or separated into functional divisions, it is the quality manager's task to 'make quality happen', or to 'make quality better'. How are they to do this? Not by leading or owning 'quality', because the leader and owner is the managing director. Not by doing 'quality', because that is everyone's job. Not even by example through their own line, because they usually have no or limited line staff. Just how can they do it when they have no mandate for action?

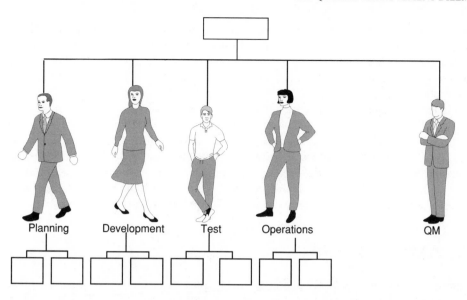

Figure 1.1 The quality ghetto. The position of the quality manager is at a tangent to the rest of the organization, with no responsibility for 'making quality', and no direct role in the process.

When asked, the reply, usually accompanied by a wry or apologetic smile, is 'by influence', 'by consensus-building', 'by being the conscience of the organization', 'by being living proof of management commitment to quality'. The quality manager's role is very much that of an internal consultant, and like any internal consultant, the organization prefers to have their advice backed up by, or have them shadowed by, an external consultant. So, not only have we succeeded in demotivating the staff by appointing a quality manager, we have also demotivated the quality manager. Have pity then for those quality managers quarantined in their organizational ghettos (Fig. 1.1), watching from lonely places the parade of organizational ills. Like Cassandra, capable of predicting trouble, but toothless to take action, doomed never to be believed. The question is, how could we have been either so pessimistic about the success of quality programmes, or so inhumane as to condemn these people to their role of organizational scapegoat? Should we go on doing it? If not, what alternative do we have? If you jotted some answers to the questions earlier, now is the time to look at them again. Would having a quality manager improve your answers?

The real quality expert is the customer

The customer gives quality meaning, and because the customer pays the money (which works first time) then they are the ones who get most of the votes. The reason I say 'most' as opposed to 'all' is explained in more detail in Sec. 1.5. This has nothing to do with the introspective acts of influencing, consensus-seeking, or conscience-prodding. This is about responding in an appropriate and accurate manner to the realities of the external world. Nothing less works. Quality is about tracking customers' key buying preferences with all the ingenuity, investment and persistence of a heat-seeking missile. It is integral to business success, or failure, and constitutes a prime process in the formulation of the organization's business strategy. The business strategy, supported by marketing and operational plans, provides a single source of customer focus and business intent. We shall look more closely at planning in Sec. 1.4, but it is important to say here that a separate quality plan, simply because it is separate, dilutes and confuses rather than strengthens the customer focus of the organizational mission.

Working from a single blueprint, one integrated process to communicate unambiguous operational definitions of customer key buying preferences to all staff is needed. This is the delivery process which works through the line and has no need for any intermediaries to intercept and slow the ball as it is being thrown from base to base. When this process is put into place, when project and development managers have been trained as process architects, and when staff have been trained to work skilfully with the process, to diagnose and correct process problems, then responsibility for quality is truly everyone's.

1.4 A PLETHORA OF PLANS

I have hinted at the problems of having a quality plan separate to the business plan, marketing plan and operations plan. Even with the best intentions in the world, plans devised by separate groups, at different times, for different purposes, create problems of consistency. In fact, they generate confusion among staff, and confusion is the biggest enemy in the workplace.

Plans produced in isolation create confusion

In the software industry, if we produce all the plans which are now being advocated, such as quality plans, project plans, configuration management plans, test plans, metrics plans, etc., the potential for confusion is magnified to the extent of all the combinatorial opportunities for inconsistency. Maybe you would like to make a list in the box below of all the separate plans of this nature that are produced by your organization. On the left-hand side write the name of the plan, and on the right-hand side the name of the group responsible for producing it. If you are able, you might also like to add whose interest the plan serves.

Personally, I have always rebelled against producing separate quality and project plans. This is because I have seen instances where the project plan was created by one group of people and the quality plan by another group, each one enshrining very different goals, and impossible for those working on the project to reconcile. When push came to shove, both were discarded. When policy requires a quality plan, there is no reason why it cannot be integral to a product or project plan. In this way mutual inconsistencies can be seen and resolved.

Looking again at the list you have just made, if you made one, how many plans did you note? What did you notice about the interests being served? What are people trying to do by creating all these plans? Can you identify an overall purpose?

Plans are our first attempts to define a process

I think there are two important aspects to all these plans. First, there is a growing awareness from different groups in the organization that the software delivery process needs to be and, most importantly, can be made more systematic. Secondly, the software engineers in their own discrete skill and interest groups are seeking to remedy the lack of overall process architecture. They are trying to obtain that bird's eye view of their own process which they have been in the business of obtaining for their clients. We just have to ensure that soaring for bird's eye views does not become an end in itself. When I look at all the plans, I see that a written process for delivering software is being attempted. However, there is a more straightforward, less confusing and less painful way in which we can perfect what has already been started. How we do this in practice is the central topic of this book.

1.5 THE CUSTOMER–SUPPLIER FRICTION BELT

One of the most powerful and lasting images of TQM is the *quality chain*, or *customer–supplier chain*. Through all the stages of production, the internal supply teams pass the product from helping hand to helping hand, rather like a relay baton, until when all production is complete, it is delivered into the hands of the final customer. At last, it seems, we have found the glue which will cement the diverse groups in the organization and bind them to a common goal — the customer. Not only will it provide the cohesion which we all need, but it will also become a means of empowerment. Staff will be able to negotiate, agree and improve their own internal customer–supplier requirements, and ensure they are kept relevant to the external customer's needs, without edicts from higher management. If you have had experience of the quality chain, then you may find it helpful to remember any difficulties you have encountered with this concept in practice before reading further.

The quality chain or ball and chain?

One of the first difficulties I can remember was an angry voice screaming at me on the telephone, 'I am your customer, I want it now!' This was someone from another functional group who was requesting non-standard (by established company policy) PC equipment. I did not feel empowered. I felt sandwiched in the middle of a lose–lose situation. Nor did this kind of relationship herald the bliss and teamwork TQM had promised.

Another interesting situation was the dispute that arose between a development team and a support team after the delivery to a very tight schedule of a major systems capability to an in-house customer. The customer was delighted to have the service available in the very narrow market window which had been specified. Development realized they had had to cut a few corners, but were generally euphoric. Support told a different story, one of having to provide extra manning to cope with all the difficulties of the cornerless software.

The support team felt that they were the unhappy customers of a time bomb which had just been lobbed into their court. They increased manning to cope with all the explosions. The situation was made even more interesting by the fact that the customer was currently pressuring the support team to cut manning, and measuring their efficiency in this dimension — any increase in manning was deemed to be due to support team inefficiencies! For me this was a very telling experience. What was happening at a fairly visible level was probably breaking out all over the organization, breeding resentment, confusion and suboptimization.

By the way, just who is the final customer? The commissioning client, an aviation authority, say? Or their staff, the airport controllers, who have to use the system? Or people who fly with the 'enhanced' systems? Or the families sitting in their homes under the flight paths who have no say in the decisions made and the products and services used?

I do not know how much these examples of the many difficulties I have experienced with the quality chain match yours, but I would expect to have mentioned a number of issues common, not just to ourselves, but to everyone. The TQM quality chain is a very useful model. However, it breaks down in a number ways: it is too simplistic; it is linear; it exists in the present tense only; and it is a model. It makes four fatal assumptions. Let me explain.

The four fatal assumptions of the quality chain

First, it assumes that those who pay the money get all the votes, unequivocally. This means that delighted farmers can continue to buy all the DDT they would like. It means that warriors can buy all the arms they like. And, closer to home, it means that software services which support the lives or livelihood of people who have no votes in this quality chain can be compromised by the selfish or corrupt cost and schedule-cutting practices of commissioning customers.

Secondly, it assumes that optimization of any one link is good for the chain as a whole. This means one functional group can reduce its overheads or improve its productivity very quickly by reducing or cutting operations which may be a critical requirement of the chain as a whole. Costs can be passed from one link of the chain to another, and it may be that this shifting of costs effectively doubles or triples overall costs. The best known scenario of this case applies to the error detection and correction costs at later and later stages of the development life cycle.

Thirdly, it assumes no future responsibilities. Are there none? I agree we have to stay in the business in the short term, for there to be any future. But will the next short-term fix be the one that makes the headlines and closes us down for good? I know in the long term we are either dead, or in a different company, or in a different job, so what does the future matter? But what if we are not quite dead, and there suddenly is no other job to go to, and we have no choice but to support the monster we created?

Last, and most important, it assumes that an ad hoc process has a coordinating intelligence of its own. Who is responsible for validating all the subtle improvements, to ensure that the business does not take a walk, and to ensure that the invitation for everyone to improve does not become a licence to kill?

The stakeholder model

So where do we go from here? As we have said, the quality chain is a useful model, but it is only a model. We require an operation to balance the needs of all stakeholders, of which there may be several, one of whom may be the commissioning client. An important stakeholder is the business itself. What investment is being made now to ensure that the business is more powerful, efficient and responsive in the future? It is not just investment in tools and techniques, but in product and service platforms, from which variants can be rapidly constructed that will match our customers' needs for fast response. Stakeholder management is a key operation which enables you to identify and resolve potential areas of conflict, to reduce complexity, and to rationalize the software delivery process itself. Without it the delivery process, if it exists, cannot be effective.

1.6 THE INVISIBLE MOUNTAIN

The road to quality is paved with continuous improvement, we travel along it one step at a time and it is a never-ending journey — so all the well-known stories go. I have also heard people ask whether it is yellow and brick, but I think they were cynics.

'Continuous improvement' is a more palatable slogan than 'quality', if we have to use slogans at all. It seems to acknowledge the fact that people might be already doing quality, and it is just a case of not resting on laurels, but of moving onwards, ever onwards. Onwards, to where? To better and more profitable things?

Goals and measures

In Sec. 1.7 I assert that managers need be concerned not only with the 'what', but also with the 'how'. But who wants to become involved in all that detail? Well, perhaps you might just concede it is a job for managers — but not for leaders. Leaders need to keep their eyes squarely on the stars, and not become bogged down in the gutters. For those of us in the gutter, it would be nice if someone were to give us some meaningful bearings, so that we might remove ourselves from the gutter and see the occasional star, too. The Japanese talk of *goals and measures*. 'Goals' I was fairly clear about. For a long time though, I mistook 'measures' to mean quantifiable targets. I suppose it was because I was doing most of my work on software measurement at the time, and to someone with a hammer, everything looks like a nail. Then I stumbled across the real meaning. 'Measures' meant the 'how to'. 'These are the measures we shall employ to reach our goals' or, 'These are the directions for getting out of the gutter, and along the road.' So, even a leader needs to give some thought to the 'how'. If not, the leader could turn round and find the followers have got lost.

There is another critical reason why the leaders need to have some concern for the 'how' — the problem of suboptimization. This arises when one function, group or team improves an operation, which is an admirable act, to the detriment of the business as a whole, which is not such a good idea at all. If there is any single reason for the senior management team to be committed to and involved in continuous improvement, it is this: only they have the big picture, only they can see the balance between the disparate groups, only they are empowered to make the necessary organizational and strategic changes to ensure the harmony and effectiveness of the whole. The management team alone know which mountain has to be climbed. Together, they have grouped and given assent to the assembly of teams to meet the challenge. They, alone, are capable of coordinating the overall logistics of the climb. If you are not convinced now that as a leader or manager you need to be concerned with the how, please pause to consider the scenario that follows.

You are attempting to climb K3 in the Himalayas. You have assembled a marvellous team. All consider this the chance of a lifetime. All are determined to complete the climb. Your team is composed of four functional groups. First, the forward scouts who know K3 and who will test the route for safety in advance of the main party and carry only enough food for themselves for each day. Secondly, the porters who carry the heavy loads of food, tents and backup supplies of oxygen. Thirdly, a small medical team who are skilled climbers who carry specialized resuscitation equipment and are trained in handling major emergencies. Finally, the main party, a macho bunch of skilled climbers who have never climbed K3. They carry some food, their own ropes and other climbing equipment, and painkillers and treatment for minor injuries. To succeed, you need to get all the main party to the top of K3. They and everyone else have to be returned, alive and safe, to base camp before the monsoon. Unfortunately, you were all stuck at base camp for six weeks because of severe gales before you could even make a start. You now need to reduce the team and make a quick ascent. The main party says they need only one scout, no medical team and half the porters, since they think they can manage without the oxygen. What do you say?

Of course, climbing mountains is easy — when you have climbed one, you have climbed them all! The process is crystal clear. When you decided what to do, did you compare the scenario to a standard process you already knew? Did you tailor a pre-existing standard process to fit the dynamics of the situation? Or did you have a lengthy session of enjoyable problem-solving to arrive at some new rules of thumb? If the latter, could you recycle your rules to help you cope with another mountain climbing problem? If only software could be like climbing mountains. But we say each project is different. That is the problem. How can you continuously improve your way of making software, when the software is always different, and the way of producing the different software is always different too? Can you answer this one? Some companies have managed to improve on the different ways of making different software. You can do it, too. Your mountain is over there. Off you go. I know you can make it. (If you think you might need help, take this book along with you.)

1.7 INFORMED EMPOWERMENT

This was written in March 1993, a few days after a visit to a large assurance company, where I was encouraged not to mention the word *empowerment* since it had already been picked clean by the organization. The half-lives of these words are shrinking at a phenomenal rate, which tends to reinforce my cynical view that we are gobbling up the diet plans, believing them to be the diet.

However, I do not feel shy about writing on empowerment since the concept and practice, where it is practised, is based on the sound, working principles used by every living organism since atoms discovered their valency. Here is your opportunity to fantasize. You are a single-celled organism, enjoying life, skulling around in the water, needing to keep your energy level up so that you can keep skulling around in the water.

When you have finished this fantasy, please write some answers to these questions in the box. How do you detect that there has been a change in your environment? How do you judge whether that change is better or worse for you? How do you decide what to do next? What can you do to enable you to spend more energy swimming, and less energy suffering panic attacks?

To survive, everyone needs to be able to manage change in their environment. As a complex, multicellular organism we delegate the detection of, and response to, many changes in the environment. We do not have to decide whether to sweat or shiver. Only when the environment changes beyond certain threshold limits do we consciously have to intervene and take action — take a cold shower or put on a coat.

Informed empowerment is not *laissez-faire* management

Employee empowerment is central to TQM, but is it not also how we have always been accustomed to running software projects? 'Just let me know if things go out of bounds, otherwise get on with the job yourself.' Our job, after all, is to manage the what and not the how. The staff are empowered and terrifically motivated, at least to start with. The problem is usually that no one tells us to put our coat on until we have caught the cold and morale has plunged below zero. So, what happens if there is a next time? We either hope for better weather, because after all, every project is different, or start to button up in anticipation — we legislate for all known weather combinations and arrange for measurements and reports and up-to-date predictions to be made at frequent intervals. What happens now? The staff take long lunch hours. When you ask about project progress, you are asked, not too kindly, what you think their priorities should be: giving you a reply, finishing a progress report or finishing the project.

Let us move on and consider another scenario. Your staff are working within your bounds of time and budget and reliability levels. They are delighting the customer by accommodating every change request. This time, the sun is shining, everyone is smiling. No one here ever looks at the design documents when projects are finished, so it does not matter that they were not reworked this time to reflect the changes made to the original design. Does it? So, what happens next time?

Empowerment is the organization's capability to detect change early

Empowerment is a wonderful concept. It means that the organization gives itself the degrees of freedom it needs to respond to changes in its environment in the most timely and appropriate way. The real value is that you do not need to legislate for every potential eventuality, nor wear garlic to stave off the unknown. Looking back to the insights you had when you were a single-celled organism, you will appreciate the disadvantages a large organization has compared to a single-celled organism when it is empowered to respond to a change in the environment. First, the number of 'sensors' who can detect change is huge. This is not bad in itself, but it is not good if the evaluation of news of a change differs across the organization, or if the news is kept local when it needs to be broadcast widely. Who decides what to do next? Is it the first one with their finger on the button? Talking recently to some senior managers about decision-making, their feelings were that they wanted the people working for them to take more decisions. They were concerned that they could not get on with their work because of all the decisions being referred up to them.

'Fine, so you do not want decisions referred to you?'

'No . . . well, only those we need to know about.'

I hope by now they have found their way up the invisible mountain.

The paradox of empowerment

The scenario I have quoted above is the very paradox of empowerment. Excellent in theory, but in practice problematic. We see some of the same problems creeping up in the customer–supplier friction belt. A process is needed by which decision-making can be delegated, safe in the knowledge that action is informed by the needs of all the relevant stakeholders, by which the swings of the pendulum between unharnessed freedom and rigorous control can be damped while staff motivation is maintained. This process informs or directs empowerment and requires the manager to be concerned not only with the what, but also with the how. In fact, the manager becomes the principal architect of the how process, assisted by a cross-functional team of associates, and the experience and wisdom of the software engineers working in the process.

1.8 THE STANDARDS MAFIA

At first sight it seems unfair to link the Mafia with standards. But my reasoning is that the Mafia was also concerned with protection. Over the last few years I have been very aware of the ambivalence towards software quality standards in our industry. Some managers think they should go for quality management standards accreditation, whatever their own feelings on the subject are. Their concern is that they will lose customers or competitive edge if they do not. Some also feel that it will provide a visible challenge for rallying all the troops. Other managers are very concerned about the potential for overdosing on an already burgeoning bureaucracy, and are not quite sure whether the quality management standards might not be a cul-de-sac branching off the main highway of continual improvement. The work of Watts Humphrey and the Software Engineering Institute's *capability maturity model* (Sec. 7.2) is also giving people cause for pause. The capability maturity model looks as if it genuinely applies to the software industry and, what is more, provides a staged route to improvement.

In my privileged position as a consultant, I am aware of the stages different companies have reached, not only as far as quality standards accreditation is concerned, but also in quality standards awareness. So I was interested to hear from one avionics software group that they had been told by their customer, another avionics group, that to stay on their list of suppliers they would have to be at level three of the capability maturity model. Interesting, because only a month or so before, I had been the first to explain to the customer's software team exactly what was the capability maturity model!

The need for standards

Let us focus for a while on standards, both in-house and external ones. What exactly is a standard? How do standards help? A standard is an exemplar. Its benefit to the world at large is to provide a coherent example or complete operational description of a product or service which has value to stakeholders and against which the same products and services can be benchmarked. I include the words 'has value', since this stops a proliferation of standards committees sitting to devise a standards equivalent of *The Guinness Book of Records*. In terms of value, a standard provides assurances on levels of risk, safety and reliability, it provides protocols for communication and interface, both geographically — from country to country, or team to team — and temporally, from the present to the future. Externally produced software quality standards provide neither of these benefits at present. They seek to bypass the end product or service, and to focus instead on the delivery process. The problem with this approach is that no one is quite sure, as yet, which processes provide reliable or consistent products and services. Instead, we are in the position of buttoning up without knowing what the weather will be like. We can say only that you will die more slowly in a blizzard if your coat is buttoned. Alternatively, you could be in for a lot of unnecessary heat and steam. I suppose, taking a more positive view, there will be the odd occasion when you feel just right.

Customer warranties and assurances

Given that deficiencies in durability and reliability can be covered by warranties and indemnification (a standard for these would be very useful), just who is being served by the quality standards? Is the customer being served? Well, does the supplier still undertake to provide warranties? Not to waiver personal liability? If buying on the basis of quality standards accreditation alone, I would say the customer is in a sticky position. If the customer has the warranties and there are steep penalties and indemnification for non-performance then I would say that the quality standard might be superfluous and an unseen charge on the bill. Is it the supplier who is being served, then? Well, only as much as he or she can stand on a bench too, as much as he or she has a periscope too. But how much does the supplier have to pay? Management and delivery processes have had to be constrained or overloaded. And these processes, second only to the human beings in your organization are the source of your competitive advantage.

Well, do people just dream up these standards for fun, then? Of course not. There are a lot of people trying to make the software industry better. There are people who judge their performance by the number of standards they can create in a month. There are people whose jobs depend on the demand for standards training, accreditation, auditing and consultancy. All of them cannot be bad.

1.9 A METHODOLOGY TOO FAR

I am not going to ask you to list all the methodologies you know. There are going to be far too many to fit into the box here. What you might like to do instead is to note any similarities and differences between 'methodology', 'system' and 'process' that you can think of.

Our role as methodology providers

We have spent the last 40 years or so of our professional lives imposing methodologies on other people. We may not have seen it that way, of course. We were delivering systems. Let us just stop and ponder this a moment because it is central to our problems. In the early days when we automated the payroll system, what did we do? We created a whole new way of working for the payroll staff and a whole new way of thinking and looking at work for the finance and human resource managers. When we created manufacturing resource planning software, we changed the way whole businesses went about their work and introduced disciplines which had previously been missing. We can probably still remember the impact and shock waves that resounded just after implementations, when the users found out that they had been systematized, that the way they used to do things had been drastically changed overnight. It was by having a disinterested bird's eye view of other people's processes that we were able to make them more systematic, methodical and simple. We made it possible for others to add value to their processes which had never been there before, and which would have been impossible without automation. One of the reasons for all the tweaks and changes after implementation was simply that people became creatively alive to the many different ways value could be added to their process. Of course, we did sometimes make the blind mistake of just automating what already existed — a bit like using a country ramble as a blueprint for a motorway — and extensive re-engineering had to be made.

Methodologies to drive the business or dictate the business?

The downside to this revolution is the amount of time now needed to change processes in response to business or market changes. At a time when agility and flexibility are at a premium, we often find that it is the software producer who is the bottleneck when change and innovation are needed. The competitive response of many businesses are now mortgaged to information systems departments or third-party software suppliers.

Because people had managed for 100 years or more without automating their business, who was going to be upset by a delay of a year or two when new systems were going in? Having a computer was a little like being a member of the privileged classes who could first afford a motor car. It did not matter that there was the odd splutter or puncture. You were only going at 15 miles an hour, but that was 5 times faster than most other people! But now the situation is radically changed. Even small delays and problems are crippling because we are propelling our businesses (or are being propelled) at tremendous speed. All future systems, changes and implementations need to be swift and reliable.

While we are in the business of supplying other people's methodologies, we are none too keen to have one imposed on us. We are creative. We are pioneers, after all. The lure of the frontier is inebriating. But now we have our backs to the mountains and the old slash-and-burn mentality has created many problems for us. We are all, desperately, and at great cost, casting around for solutions to help us out of our corner. Our biggest problem now is being a victim to the new methodologies. We are still applying old slash-and-burn techniques to the new methodologies, overriding any potential benefits we might have obtained from our careful understanding of them. 'Here it is today. Hands on everyone. Doesn't seem to work for us. What's next?' I have seen staff override a configuration management system so that several people could work on the same piece of software simultaneously, without pausing to examine the basic problem impelling them to play rugby with a grenade. How are we going to get the rewards of all the silver bullets we keep firing off, if we have no target process at which to aim? Every time we throw away a solution, we miss the valuable opportunity of taking our organization up a learning curve, which means that the next solution will have to be a silver cannon-ball, a silver Exocet or a silver intergalactic vaporizer — and that is a methodology, if not a metaphor, too far.

1.10 THE MISSING PROCESS

It is tempting to compare the quality improvement programmes sold to the West with an attempt at industrial espionage which went totally wrong. We were sent a photograph of a glossy, colourful, chic vehicle and were told to go off and replicate it. Which we did. The result of our work was a lovely chassis but, unfortunately, it just did not go — no engine. Not only did we not know what the engine looked like, but we did not even know it was supposed to have one. We were told that all we had to do was put our own shoulders to the wheel and push.

The engineering connection

It is interesting to think back to the 'sixties, when the Japanese were shipping cars from the West to Japan. No glossy photos, just a team of engineers with wrenches, ready to take the cars and engines apart bolt by bolt, to weigh and analyse each part systematically to determine its costs and scope for value improvement. We know now that this systematic study paid off.

The British and Americans led the world in systems thinking at the end of the Second World War. The British and the Americans had solid engineering disciplines. They understood processes, operations, value management, and statistical control. Their managers had engineering skills. Where are they now? I know of several excellent managers who employ these skills, but they are very much in the minority, and I see few managers coming through with those sorts of process-oriented, engineering skills. For the most part we are training our managers to appreciate photos — the case studies which are the building blocks of management training courses. This is not to say that case studies have no value, they do, but only when there is a sound appreciation of the designed and dynamic engineered process, if there is one, which drives the different organizations.

A defined process vs management mirage

When management build a process, it is there to be seen by the staff working on it. It provides a central focal point in day-to-day working. How we do things around here is clearly mapped out on the ground. It is not a management mirage. Change is made more understandable when it is linked to a visible process. Improvements to the process are captured in the process. They are 'wired in'. When there is no process, there is nowhere to save those improvements except in people's memories, or dusty standards manuals. TQM exhorts everyone to build a picture with their own few pieces of jigsaw puzzle, and everyone creates a different image that can join up with no one else's. Is it any wonder that, if instead of going forwards, we seem to fall behind? Only an informed understanding of our own processes can take us through the pain barrier of the quality dilemma.

2

WHY PROCESS MANAGEMENT?

Static quality patterns are dead when they are exclusive, when they demand blind obedience and suppress dynamic change. But static patterns nevertheless provide a necessary stabilising force to protect dynamic progress from degeneration. Although dynamic quality, the quality of freedom, creates this world in which we live, these patterns of static quality, the quality of order preserve our world. Neither static nor dynamic can survive without the other.

Robert M. Pirsig
Lola

In this chapter we shall examine the merits of having practical, on-the-ground processes as opposed to theoretical software development life cycles.

Process management, or *supply chain management*, is currently used in industry for designing and engineering business success. It is the visible game plan of the organization. Process design is carried out in conjunction with and complements product and service design. The process is designed specifically to deliver the quality characteristics demanded by the clients. A general process applied to a range of products and services without tailoring is inefficient and costly. The likelihood is that you miss out important functions, and more probably, that you overengineer your product or service. The test of a good process is that it ensures only those tasks which are necessary and sufficient are carried out. How do your life cycles and methodologies score on this test?

2.1 SUPPLY CHAIN MANAGEMENT

For most software managers and engineers the term *supply chain management* is likely to be unfamiliar. This is because in the software business we have coined our own specific terms, *systems development life cycle* being the best known. The purpose of the process expressed by both terms is fundamentally the same: to deliver software products and services. In Sec. 2.3 we shall examine in closer detail the similarities and differences between supply chain management and software development life cycles. But first, let us establish an outline understanding of supply chain management.

What is supply chain management?

Supply chain management is the overall process for designing and engineering your success by whatever value criteria you have been set by your market and stakeholders. It is the delivery pipe-line of the organization, providing a framework for consistent purpose and decision-making. The process is engineered at the same time as you are developing product or service design. It is assembled from a number of well-defined key operations, to provide a flexible, cost-effective vehicle for delivery. The process runs end to end, and is the critical path. Operations feed into it like tributaries feeding a river (Fig. 2.1).

Supply chain management embraces: market influence and education; new product or service exploration; requirements elicitation; development; delivery; product or service evolution; and finally, retirement, recycling, and safe disposal. In addition, all the operations required to define and support this process are included within its scope.

What is in a name?

The problems many people first encounter when presented with the phrase 'supply chain management' are to do with the words themselves. I have problems with the words also. I would much prefer to see simply *process management*, and for most of this book we shall be referring to 'process management' and the 'delivery process' instead. For most people, though, it is the manufacturing connotation which gives most difficulty. 'We don't build

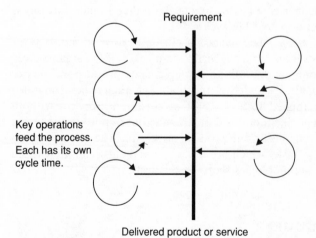

Requirement

Key operations
feed the process.
Each has its own
cycle time.

Delivered product or service

Figure 2.1 The process is assembled from a number of well-defined key operations to provide a flexible and cost-effective vehicle for delivery.

widgets here,' is one response which comes to mind. But when the reality is understood — that supply chain management is not a model, but is about real people managing the real world — then it becomes clear that supply chain management is less mechanistic, less rigid, less theoretic, and less bureaucratic than the life cycle models and standards with which they are currently trying to work.

What is special about process management?

Process management enables the flexibility, response to change, communication, and support needed for the real business. It is very much concerned with work on the ground, because this is where the real problems are, not in hypothetical models, and on the ground is where the business has to be improved. Rather than being focused upon internal activities for their own sake, it is concerned with real artefacts which can be valued, costed, assessed, and re-engineered. Costly hot spots can be located and worked on and significant and relevant performance indicators implemented. The important thing to remember is that the process is the message. If purpose and standards are not conveyed by the process itself, then no amount of standards' and procedures' manuals will ever succeed.

2.2 'I DON'T MAKE WIDGETS'

Supply chain management has been employed in manufacturing industries for many years. 'Fair enough,' you may say, 'but when has software development ever been remotely like manufacturing?' Never. And always! I say 'never', because building software has never been much like assembling widgets for most of us. If anything, our business is pure logistics, channelling knowledge and information this way and that. And I say 'always' because the delivery of goods and services in both manufacturing and software production presents very similar challenges, such as customer account management, scheduling, expediting, etc. So, to that extent, we can say there has always been supply chain management in software production in one form or another.

What do widgets have in common with software production?

Let us look first at the differences between software and widgets, and then the similarities. You might like to stop and think about those differences now and make some notes to which you can refer back as you read this section.

Unfortunately, I do not know how long you have been in the business of software production, so I am not sure how far back into your own personal experience I can reach. If you have been around for 20 years or so, then you will have noticed the slow but sure packaging of generic software 'widgets' or components.

In the early days when we used machine code, all reads, writes, buffers, and manipulations such as sorts were coded in great detail. With the advent of higher level languages such as FORTRAN and COBOL we no longer had to be concerned with the intricacies of specifying reads and writes and buffers etc., but we still programmed our own sort routines for a while. I could wax very nostalgic thinking of the heated discussions we used to have round the kettle, debating the merits of bubble, Fibonacci, and binary sort theory. However, time moves on.

We next had libraries of supplied subroutines and the debates turned to other more challenging topics. Now, just pause to think about what you have when you make use of a spreadsheet, or a database. These are very high level examples of packaged generics: all you have to do is to supply the interface that pleases you most and the data, and *voilà* . . ., your application is served. So, while we may not have been producing widgets, someone else has. This makes me ask myself if widget production is something done only by other people?

Widgets and reuse for creative people

It is usually very difficult for creative people to see the 'widgetness' in the fruits of their bared soul. But some very creative people have exploited just that widgetness. Homer, the poet of the *Iliad* and the *Odyssey*, employed reuse on a number of levels. He recycled many components, whether they were only single-phrase epithets such as 'the wine dark sea', or 'Poseidon, the earth-shaker', or whole sections, where bards sang well-known songs in the middle of his poems. I do not think we should feel bad at all about producing such components; it means that we can grow and stretch and reach out to other meaningful tasks which have been previously outside the range of our capability.

Toshiba recycles around 70 per cent of the components they develop. Just consider this in terms of value to their customers, and reduced waste of human effort. When I asked a member of the Toshiba production team if their staff were concerned about becoming deskilled as a consequence of using recycled components, I was met with bewilderment. Staff, it seemed, were very motivated by the high levels of productivity they were able to achieve.

Software project managers I have spoken to have said initially that their work was more akin to research and development, rather than manufacturing. At the root of this, when we explored the facts together, was a subtle confusion of product and process, which brings us back to the second point I made at the beginning when we talked about the fundamental similarities in the management of how we deliver products and services. Looking back at the notes you made earlier, can you see which of the similarities and differences you listed are product related, and which are process related? You see, even research and development has a process. Researchers may not know what the product is until they have built it, but there is among the R&D community a way of gathering information, testing out hunches and so on, which is acknowledged to be useful — a process, in fact.

The product–service spectrum

One final point, which is linked to both product and process aspects, needs to be mentioned. I expect on your list you will have mentioned the fact that software is intangible, maybe that it a 'bundled service' of sorts. It is because of a shift in our traditional market at this level that we are currently experiencing pain. Let me explain. When we examine outputs of processes, they can be categorized on something called the *product–service spectrum*. At one end, the service end, the output is purely a service, such as art valuation, on the other end of this continuum, the output is purely a product, often a commodity such as coal. The nearer your output is to the service end, the more your production process is esteemed and valued in financial terms by your customer. Unfortunately, the nearer the commodity end your output approaches, the less value the fruits of your production process can command.

As an example, consider this book. Does my process add value for you? Could I have bled more, sweated more, wept more, and asked you to pay extra? I doubt it. In high-class restaurants a premium is paid for the process which in some establishments is elevated to the point of ritual. In fast-food shops, on the other hand, the customer just wants a burger to go. The customer places no value on the baroquery of the process, only on its speed. This, I fear, is where the true source of our hurt lies. Customers for software are no longer placing a premium on our process. They want the software to go. They want widgets. And what are we doing in some cases? We are saying we are not in the business of making widgets.

So, a brief recap: we are in a business which, if not strictly classified as manufacturing, will tend to become more like manufacturing as time goes by. Look at how object-oriented techniques are changing the way we work. The tools we use and the raw materials of our trade are different to those used in cardboard box production, but the processes of management and delivery have many points of similarity.

2.3 WHAT'S NEW?

For those of you who are looking for a new software development life cycle model, here you are (Fig. 2.2). Be careful to cut only along the outline. You will need to score the dotted lines before folding. The test of your model is whether it can support your software delivery process. Do you think it can take the strain?

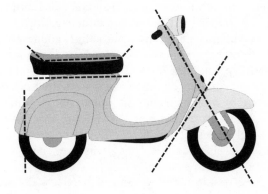

Figure 2.2 Your free life cycle model. Cut out the model and score along the dotted lines before folding.

Referring to the definition in Sec. 2.1 it looks as if supply chains could be very much like development life cycle models. There are requirements gathering activities, delivery activities, and so on. I am sure you noted many points of similarity, but there are also important differences.

Problems with life cycle models

Over the years, I have been struck by a number of problems with development life cycle models. The problems were to do with introducing the model to people in the development environment, with how the model coped in practice with day-to-day production issues, its ease of use, and its support for the business objectives. The problems were there whether we were using the Benington stage-wise model, the Royce waterfall model, the Boehm spiral model, or the 'V' process model, so I do not want to go into a lengthy discussion of the virtues or otherwise of one model over the others. What I saw in all the life cycle models was a worthy attempt by people to understand the confusion in their industry and to prescribe a logical method for finding a way through the woods.

The stage-wise model gave us a very simple set of stepping stones, which did not necessarily take us where we wanted to go, but we felt secure. The waterfall method gave us a two-lane path to allow us to retrace our steps when we got lost. The spiral model gave us the chance to bivouac en route; it did not mean that we necessarily ever got out of the woods, just that we could be more comfortable and visible while we were in them. Finally, the V model gave us a compass or homing device, but I am not sure we know how to use it yet.

Development life cycles lack integration with the business

The fact that they are 'development' life cycles highlights, for me, the introspectiveness and narrowness of their focus. It is almost as if the development process has become an art form in itself, unto itself, and its life is only important in so much as it coincides with the narrow boundaries of the development department. It has become disengaged from all those tedious but vital aspects of commercial life, such as costing, marketing, and tracking legislation. I would much prefer to talk about software delivery — at least it sounds as though we are contemplating getting something out of the door to the customer. If we talk of delivery, then the customer needs to be put squarely on centre stage rather than at the periphery, merely sending inputs and receiving outputs from our system. What we need then, is a Copernican revolution of sorts. 'The customer is King . . . Kong!' pronounced Professor Kanno who was heading up a delegation of Japanese software engineers and managers to Britain in 1992. Where in our development life cycles, whatever shape they are, is there any mention or accommodation of the customer?

How do the life cycle models fit into the business strategy and plans? How do they integrate with costing, decision-making, skills training, change management, product assurances, communication, market intelligence, reusability, and all the other functions of the business which are necessary for survival? The answer is they do not do it very well. They were never intended to go beyond the narrow confines of development. Well, it is time to open the doors, and see what is happening in the world.

Differences between life cycle models and process management

The difference between the development life cycle models and process management is that the models are models and process management is real people managing the 'here and how'. Starting with your market or customers, and the products and services they value, you design and engineer a process appropriate for managing product or service delivery. There is no map separate from the territory, because the territory is clearly signposted.

2.4 BACKING THE BUSINESS

One of the questions in Sec. 2.3 is, 'Can your life cycle model support your software delivery process?' Imagine you have to pick up a heavy load from the ground and raise it up above your head. How would you judge, first, that you could take the strain? How would you judge that you are taking the strain as you lift the weight? How would you know you were having problems? What would your responses be to those problems?

The software delivery process is like our backbone. Let us think about this. Our process has to be strong to support the body of our business. It needs to provide a secure attachment for the various operational limbs. It has to be flexible, so that it can bend, stretch, and reach on the occasions when bending, stretching, and reaching are necessary. It needs to be able to respond intelligently to different loads, expending just the right amount of energy and remaining in balance. When it flexes, our process has to stay connected — all the individual process components need to maintain contact, it must not fall apart or break. It has to be capable of movement and balance so that the business can change its situation for a more favourable one and not remain rooted to just one spot. It also has to house and protect a coordinated communications system. Finally, it needs to be capable of rapid self-healing. Is your life cycle model capable of all that? Or is it more of a body-belt: a corset which you use only occasionally for lifting abnormally heavy loads? Or is it a suit of armour which limits the growth of your business and weighs it down? Just run through another mental practice now as quickly as you can — imagine picking up your heavy load in a suit of armour. What did that feel like?

Is your life cycle strong enough to be the backbone of your business?

If a life cycle model is strong enough to support the business, we would have a general feeling of comfort and ease. I do not believe we have yet attained that state of comfort and ease, because I see people casting round trying to find new backbones, and I hear people asking me whether a new backbone would suit them better than the old one. I am also aware that the business as a whole is focused on the pain they are experiencing in this part of the organization.

Does the life cycle model support operational limbs? Does it support customer account management, resource management, skills management, costing, evolution, and growth? If it does, then all these functions will be found working in a reasonable state of harmony with the life cycle. If it does not, then I would expect to see all these functions behaving totally independently as if they had no relation to the life cycle model, and as if they did not care about its existence one way or another. And in most organizations this is precisely what I do see. In fact, it seems that some functions, like finance and customer account management, have been purposely amputated on health grounds. If the life cycle model helped us to stay connected, then we would not experience delays, interruptions, or a breakdown in understanding between one team on the process and another. Again, there would be a harmonious feeling of ease. Is there? Not that I have seen yet.

Is your life cycle flexible enough to allow change?

What about flexibility? Can the life cycle be made to reach and bend and consume energy at different levels depending on the service or the products to be provided? If the life cycle has this capability then we would expect to be able to fulfil all our contracts while remaining balanced — poised for more. We would expect to be fit and agile and not to respond at the pace of an arthritic patient. I see people engrossed in constructing 'small' systems life cycle models because the original model proved too cumbersome. But tell me, what is small, what is smallish, and what is medium, when it comes to software projects?

Is your life cycle responsive?

Does the life cycle allow the business to move, or does it nail it to the ground? Does the life cycle follow the movement of the business, or is it the life cycle which determines where the business can go? What happens when the business, out of necessity asks for changes to standards, procedures, methods, and organization? Is it told to go away because it is behaving in a non-standard way, that there are no procedures for handling such a request? Do six signatures have to be acquired for every change, and two standing committees to oversee the change? When the business can request change and obtain it within the time constraints that are decently available, and does not have to suffer a period of paralysis or falling over while this occurs, then the life cycle is backing the business.

Does your life cycle facilitate communication?

Communication and potential for self-healing have to be in the process, not superimposed. Information on the state of the process should flow with the delivery of services and products. Delays and problems should not require special sensory detection by control functions, taken off-line and reported asynchronously in weekly or monthly meetings. The delay is the message to the process as it occurs. The problem is the message to the process as it occurs. When problems or delays are encountered, the process, naturally, works to highlight and remedy the cause. Information about problems are automatically communicated to other parts of the system which may be affected.

You already have a process whether you know it or not — exercise it!

Some time ago, at a gathering of software quality professionals, the whole discussion ranged on the topic of life cycle models. There was a great deal of discussion on the lines of, 'I'll show you mine, if you show me yours.' But no one could say who had the best one. We were all different shapes, sizes, and weights and preoccupied with different targets for success. The point I want to make is that the process most suitable for your needs is probably the one you have. But it needs exposing, exercising, slimming, and educating.

2.5 A PURPLE PEOPLE EATER

A few years ago I came across an organization that was busily producing procedures and standards in line with the requirements of BS5750. There were a lot of words being written, consultative committees met to agree and reword standards in precise English, and inspection teams vetted the finished pages, quibbling over the use of this particular wording or that. The colour adopted by the quality department for the cover of their quality and standards manuals was a marvellous, imperial purple. This is why I nicknamed it the 'purple people eater'.

Standards do not change behaviour

I look at those manuals on people's shelves and think about all the dedicated consideration, heart-searching and human effort that went into their production, and I lament the waste, because rarely are they ever used. The people who worked on the manuals might have had all the intellectual understanding of what they wanted to achieve, and how it could be brought about. But the one thing they could not change was the sensation of comfort someone enjoys by continuing the activities of a lifetime. If you are a reformed smoker then you will know this for yourself. You may embrace totally all the logical, undeniable reasons for giving up smoking, but you cannot stop wanting to smoke. The habit is in the body and not the mind, and the body has a different reasoning which the mind knows not.

The problems with top-down standards

Let me tell you about some of my own bitter experience in this field. Several years ago I worked on the creation and implementation of a systems development life cycle. It seemed marvellous at the time. It had been commissioned by senior management, so I felt that there was every commitment to its implementation and its use. It was a very simple document, defining the life cycle stages: the major deliverables to be produced, by whom and for what purpose; the information required; and the methods which could be used for creating the deliverables. All the deliverables were standard and, I considered, straightforward: I had cribbed them from what we already had in place and from a wide range of literature on the subject. All in all, a neat, attractive computer-based document was produced. I had my first customer, a project manager who was willing to use it on his next project after the staff had had some training. What a disaster! It almost brought the project to its knees. The staff had immediate problems with the document deliverables which were to be completed. They had never had to create documents quite like this. What did they have to put in them? (An outline for each document had been included in the standards, but only at a fairly high level.) 'Well,' I asked in all patience and reasonableness, 'what does the person who reads the document need to know?' At this point a very glazed expression slid down between us. How foolish of me, no one knew who read the document after it had been produced, I should have included that information. But, when I stopped to think, I did not know. So I asked the project manager. He did not know either. The organization was too large for us to cry our wares and ask for a show of hands. We just had to go hunting. The treasure waiting for us was an intimate knowledge of how information moved around the organization. In the particular case I mentioned, the document was produced for visibility only, just something to show we had reached a milestone. I was tempted to order in some flags.

My efforts were well-intended, and I did the best I could with what information I had at the time, but I had created problems for other people at a time when they were under stress, and least likely to be open to change and learning. I learnt that you cannot just drop a process out of your head onto people's desks, even if it is the collected wisdom of many. If you do, then you have to reinvent a whole world, with all the cultural detail that the whole world requires. If the fine detail is missing, it will be asked for. If the fine detail is not appropriate then it will have to be changed, cycling through many change control procedures and committees. I learnt that even if you have all the fine detail, it will not be too helpful, because you will have created the book of life, and how do you find the right page in a crisis?

Criticality of information

I learnt about *information criticality* (see Sec. 10.4). This, for me, was the major breakthrough. All the work I had come across emphasized detailing as much information as possible in all the document deliverables. People creating the documents were concerned that they did not have all the information they thought they should have, and delayed releasing their documents. In fact, the receiver of the document usually did not need half the information, and could not find in all the words the few facts they really needed to get on with the job. I realized that we were second-guessing what information other people needed, not asking them. It was like throwing information over the fence, whether it was needed or not, whether it was going to the right person or not, whether the timing of the document was right or not. Now it was time to stop the information push, and look for an information pull. The only way that could be found out was by working from the end backwards, asking people what information they needed to do their job and when they needed it. That was a job of listening, not prescribing.

The next stage is building that information flow into the process itself, so that information is triggered when it is needed, in a form that is most accessible to the person who needs it. When people create their own templates to receive information, many document standards can be dispensed with. Not everyone is a natural reader, and not everyone can handle textual descriptions. What do you work best with? Do you have a preference for diagrams over text; for particular formats and layouts; for methods of access? Everyone is slightly different in this respect, but given that large numbers of software development staff spend their day thinking by manipulating diagrams and icons, the use of text for standards documentation and reference is questionable. The use of text which is out of step with the process is wasteful. Systems are now available for routeing documents, see Sec. 13.5.

2.6 THE EXPERIENCE BASE

Another interesting fact about books on quality is that a large number quote Petronius Arbiter, a Roman soldier who in 210 BC lamented famously the fact that every time they seemed to be getting their team together, someone would reorganize them because a new situation had presented itself. The Romans were for most of their history a very conservative nation. They went to great lengths to neutralize the risk to their status quo: Greece, Africa, Asia Minor, Germany, even grey Britain. They were able to put all that energy into buffering themselves from risk, because, like Homer, they had discovered reuse. They recycled other people's architecture, statues, religion, and slaves. They were excellent strategists, but could have done better on tactics. The Roman standards could not be held in skirmishes and guerrilla warfare. Petronius gives us part of the reason why — the soldiers moaned about change.

Reorganization and change

These thoughts, my own experiences of the six-month periods of turbulence which always followed reorganization, and Deming's dictum on constancy of purpose were very much at the forefront of my mind when I had my first occasion to tackle a Japanese manager on organizational change. I had a strong feeling that the Japanese would not be so foolish as to keep reorganizing their companies every year like we did. I was right, but wrong. This particular Japanese manager told me that in his company they were reorganized every six months. It was normal practice and there were no particular problems. If that had happened in my organization, we would have been in a state of total and perpetual turbulence with zero productivity as a result. There would have been at least three months of rumour before the change was officially announced. During this period people would be busy propagating and pondering the rumours, and pronouncing that there was no point starting anything new, because everything could change. And after the event there would, again, be another three-month period of dislocation while everyone tried to divine what the new organization signalled for them, everyone jostling for pole position at the same time.

Change and learning

It all made me think. How bitterly we were resisting all and any change, changes to requirements, changes to tools and techniques, changes to plans, and changes to the organization. It seemed very paradoxical. Where was that pioneer mindset now? Change has never been an accident in our profession. Rather we drive change. Why was it then that change was experienced so negatively? The reason was, we could not swallow it, literally. We had no way of assimilating change. We had no metabolism to support change. We were very good at blasting breakthroughs, but we had no way of clearing the rocks out of the way to progress along the possible path we had just created. As time went on I saw that we became more and more imprisoned in the debris. It was such a job to remember where all the rocks were, so as not to keep falling over, that if any were moved, or we had to change places, learning the terrain again was just too much for us to cope with. The maintenance people did the best they could, moving rocks from here to there and back again, but the problem would not go away.

Assimilation of change

Improvement comes in two forms. On the one hand it is effectiveness, the extroverted bold move forward, the paradigm shift, the breakthrough. On the other it is the methodical internalization of the new — conversion of the new into building blocks which can be refined and made more efficient, to support the next push forward.

When life cycles or standards are passed down to people, they usually suffer from one of two problems. The first problem occurs when they are simply textual directions on how to locate and bypass all the existing rocks. But if you precisely map all the rocks, what happens when the rocks are moved? Do you tell people not to move the rocks? Do you tell people not to accommodate new rocks? The second problem occurs when ideal standards and life cycle models are dropped down on the territory. The gorges and gullies we have to navigate at our peril are perceived only as an interesting ground texture by those with the distanced bird's eye view. This means that often standards and life cycles ask us to drive straight over the cliffs. If our response is, 'We can't do that', someone is chopped for not selling the standards and life cycles well enough. That way we confirm we are all victims of our landscape, and there is no favouritism.

All very well, but what are we going to do about the rocks? Are we going to bring up a bulldozer and clear them all away? This is what usually happens when someone changes jobs: 'There's going to be a whole new set of rocks around here.' This is not helpful. First, you need to check on the ground that the rocks have not been colonized by departmental groups or have not been built into any strategic architecture. In either case it is dangerous just to bulldoze them away. It needs careful re-engineering. You need to have an *inventory phase* (see Sec. 7.4) to map out exactly what you have, and then an *assessment phase* (see Sec. 7.5) to find out exactly what you need. Then you can set to re-engineering in earnest and safety; but do not just lose that information once you have it, it needs to be available for everyone to reference. This is your *experience base*. Rather than having knowledge dotted about the business in people's heads, notebooks, and top drawers, that information needs to be brought together and held on-line so that it can be used to provide balanced, organized process and product components which can be wheeled and turned to face the next challenge.

2.7 CYCLES, CHAINS, AND SEALING WAX

How does your software development life cycle map onto your other systems? Onto your quality management system? Onto your project management system? Onto your work breakdown structures? Onto your time recording systems? Onto your costing systems? Onto your job descriptions? Onto performance appraisal systems? Onto your system for recommending promotions?

Lack of integration in management systems

My experience has been that in most organizations few of the above systems mapped onto each other. It was not so much that people did not see the links, as much as they did not have the power to bring them all together, since each system was usually administered by a separate group for separate purposes. Did it matter, anyway? The project management system was the one that was being used. That could embrace all the others, could it not? Yes, indeed, but then why go to the bother of having all the other systems? Why, as we would ask our clients, operate with more than one set of books? Why create islands of information?

How does the development life cycle map onto the quality system? The quality system usually just says, 'We are using the development life cycle documented in such and such a document.' But, there is a lot more in the quality system; how to contract with suppliers for example. Where are suppliers and supply management in your life cycle model?

How about the map onto the project management system, then? Does the project management system follow the life cycle, or does it just reference it, like the quality system? If you are using a spiral life cycle for instance, is a finite number of iterations stipulated? Is your work breakdown system derived directly from your development life cycle? Is the work breakdown structure a finer level of detail of the life cycle, and could the fine detail be aggregated back to the various life cycle phases? Is your work breakdown structure activity or component based? The same as the life cycle? How do both handle such items as 'management overheads'? Do they do it the same way?

Can you find out from your time-recording system how much effort went into each phase of the life cycle? How about posting time to closed down phases of the life cycle? Are you allowed to record time against analysis activities or products when you are in the design phase? Strange as it may seem, I know organizations who cannot do this. This means that there is great difficulty and tweaking not only when costing the phases, but also for estimating projects the next time round. 'Can you remember how much analysis you did in design?' is the plaintive call of the new project manager.

Process roles instead of jobs

Where do people's jobs fit in? Are job responsibilities linked to roles in the development life cycle, or what I record time to? Is that the same as what I am actually doing? I have met people whose daily activities did not match their job descriptions, and certainly did not match the work breakdown codes they had been allocated. Who knew what was happening there? On what basis were decisions made? Was it to do what was necessary, the work detailed in their work codes, or their job descriptions? They did what was necessary and massaged the rest. Consider the waste involved in creatively managing not one set of books but three! On what grounds could their performance appraisals be conducted, against what measures and standards, other than some slight fiction? But that slight fiction made all the difference in the amount of increment earned each year, and on promotional prospects. No wonder the jobs start to take the business for a walk.

Each of the eight systems or structures I have mentioned conveys a separate purpose, urgency, set of priorities, and decision-making framework to members of staff, as well as all the administrative burden of following them and keeping them up to date. Each adds in its own way to disinformation and confusion, and in the organization, confusion kills.

Process management integrates all the systems

If your systems all map onto each other, then I would say you only need one, your 'here and how' work breakdown process. From it you can generate all the other information you need as a by-product. How much time has that saved you? If your systems do not map yet, then you will benefit greatly from bringing them together. When all the life cycle activities, quality activities, and project management activities are mapped onto a visible process, they can be lifted out to provide the higher level documents you need for planning and quality. Because you are using just one set of books, you are able to drill back down, and prove with work-related data from the process that the work is being done.

What people do is what they do, and if they are to be evaluated, it should be done honestly on what they have accomplished. If that is different from what someone had in mind when they composed work plans or job descriptions, then they need to walk the floor to understand the difference between their model and the real world, and the problems which are keeping the two apart. The process is the message.

2.8 SPOT THE HOT SPOTS

When we have one set of books, one integrated process, you can use it to help you manage the value and costs of your products. First, let me ask you how much would usability improvement cost you? How much is usability engineering currently costing you?

I have listened to many managers complain that using standards and standardized development life cycles increases project costs and schedules and adds little, if anything, of value to the customers. I ask them how they know this. They do not know, they just assess that there are more dubious documents to be produced, and intuitively feel that the costs will increase as a consequence. Maybe they will. Maybe not. All assessments to do with changing the course or content of projects are carried out in much the same way. This is because, in truth, over and above the total costs, effort, and duration of the project we know very little else in quantitative terms about our delivery process. We shall remain in the dark, while our competitors pass us by, until we actively do something different.

Opening up the money box

I had the wonderful opportunity in one job, of opening up the black box of a CASE tool to obtain function weights for some past projects. Function weights are a metric proposed by Tom DeMarco in his book *Controlling Software Projects*. Designed functions are decomposed to the lowest level where they are assigned a value depending upon the type of primitive operations being carried out by the function and the amount of data exchange between this function and other functions. This value can then be used as an indicator of the cost to produce the function. But, as with any other indicator, it needs to be calibrated within the environment in which it is being used, so that the information conveyed relates to the 'real world'. Since the organization had been recording time quite thoroughly for a number a years, the idea was to use this information to perform the calibration by relating the function weights to effort, doing some analysis, and then making some first-cut estimates for a new project coming along. The new project was like one of the old ones for which we had data, but without a database build. If we could only have found out how much effort went into that build, it would have been plain sailing. I say 'would have been', because as you have guessed there were problems. The way time had been recorded was totally inconsistent with extracting that sort of information. All time had been activity based, and not product or component based — and there was no way of tying up the activities to components or products.

While some may argue that we work with intangibles and invisibles in our profession, I would say the invisibles are only invisible until you have a means of isolating them from the background. A feasibility study is not invisible, neither is a requirements document, nor object class 'customer'. Identify these components and you are half-way home. Set up your process to gather information about the costs to build and assure each component and you are well on the way home.

Process-based costing

You can leave it up to individuals how they want to break out the activities to build these components, but you must be able to link all activities to a component or product. This helps you with at least four problems. First, you do not have to specify all the activities in advance from a position of ignorance. This means people will not have to massage activities when they do not fit your model. Secondly, if people start producing new components you will learn of it and be able to find out more about the exact need. Thirdly, components are allowed to span more than one life cycle phase which is a better match to the real world. Fourthly, when you know the component costs, you can work with your staff on the activities they used to produce a component as a basis for coaching and improvement. The current practice is to measure activities, testing, designing, and so on. But activity is not a virtue in itself — why encourage it? What is of value are usable and reusable components. What are the components? Who are the stakeholders interested in the component? What value do they place on the components? Here is your chance to find out how much all the components cost. Does it seem reasonable that they are costing what they do, considering the value they are adding? Are you surprised? Can you spot the costly hot spots? What, exactly, is making them expensive? Your standards, your staff, your process, or your poor communications? Could you make them a different way, more cheaply? Would automating improve the costs? If you automate the production of a component, are costs of any other components inflated or reduced? Can you understand now how you would tackle cutting costs in an emergency? How you would decide the best targets for investment? How you could monitor the return on investment?

Costing usability

So, back to the tough questions. How do you know how much usability engineering is costing and how much it would cost to improve? What is usability? Tom Gilb would give as an example, that it is the capability provided to a customer to handle, with the aid of the manual, all the new functions in an allotted time, incurring only a stated number of mistakes. (Given that the customer has completed a year at college, and a one-day standard training course in the use of the new functionality.) Working from this we can begin to identify the components of usability: the training course, manual, and user interfaces. These can all be developed and costed separately. How much do they cost to produce? How much will it cost to tailor them more closely to the customer's needs — to make them more tolerant and independent of the level of college skills? If you invest more in the training, can you bet on reducing the costs of the manual? If you improve the user interfaces can you bet on reducing the costs of both the manual and the training?

2.9 LUCKY NUMBERS

I do not know anything about gambling. All I know is that when I was a student in France, I once went to the races and bet on number 9, both ways in three different races, and won enough money to see me through the holidays. Can you tell me if my success was due to the language? The distance I had to travel to place my bets? The training of the horses? The power of '9'? My superb betting ability? The forces at work in the Universe? If your project comes in healthy, to budget and on schedule, is it due to the language you used? How far you had to travel between development sites? The skills of programmers one, two, or three? The power of your life cycle model? Your superb project management skills? The forces at work in the Universe? Is there a difference between the two scenarios? If I told you I had a computer model to increase my income from betting, would you want to buy one, too?

Estimating without a process

Estimation models have the religious power of oracles. But, the benefit of having them computer based is, if you do not like the answer they give you, you can knock again and pretend you are someone else, and they will give you a different answer. I met someone who had used an estimation model to assess the resources they really needed for all their on-going projects, found out they were overstaffed, and as a consequence reduced the numbers employed. Numbers are less important than patterns of behaviour when you want to know how long or how much some delivered product will be.

My novel use of these models is to use them as risk management tools. 'You mean you are going to inflate my schedule and budget by 20 per cent if my staff are not trained in this application? It seems like it would be cheaper to train my staff.' 'You're saying it's going to take so much elapsed time because my development staff are split over three sites? The heck it is! I'm bringing them all back under one roof.' 'You're telling me that because the application complexity factor is at that level, we will need to add more resource? We'll see about that — we can work on engineering that complexity down.' I feel more confident tweaking the real world, than tweaking models these days. It goes back to the time I looked at economic order quantity models. (The models helped you to optimize volume purchasing benefits against costs of inventory.) These were developed and refined over quite a considerable period of time by operations research people. Then someone asked the bright question, 'What would happen if we got rid of inventory altogether?' The just-in-time revolution cut through the Gordian knot of economic order quantity problems. The same thing is about to happen in our business, when we have a visible process, and process management.

Let us consider something else. The product assumed by estimation models, and by our life cycle models also, is lines of code, or in some organizations, *function points*. (Function points are values derived from high-level systems designs. For more information, read Paul Goodman's book *Practical Implementation of Software Metrics*.) But is this truly all we produce? It is time to look at some 'ilities'. Quality models tell us that we do not just produce functionality (which is rather more than neat lines of code or function points), they tell us that we also produce a number of 'ilities' such as portability, reliability, maintainability, usability, security, and so on. Are all these qualities inherent just in lines of code? What happens if we turn these 'ilities' into components? As we saw from the earlier example, usability has a number of non-code components: manuals, training, maybe a help desk service. How do we estimate for producing those? Maintainability requires plug-in compatible interfaces, an index of components, maybe a repository. Who estimates for these? Perhaps that is why we never build them, or if we do, they are skimped.

The value of process management is its proximity to reality

The most important message of this chapter which I would like you to remember is that our effort spent refining models has no impact at all on the real world. Our early models of circular planetary orbits around the sun had not the slightest effect on the elliptical march of Mars. If we become preoccupied with measurement models, then the risk is that all our learning will go into refining the models, rather than understanding our environment. And it is in the environment, in the delivery process where the delays and breakdowns occur and only in the delivery process, in the real world, where they can be fixed. We have talked a little about estimation models, but do you have a model of the estimation operation? Have you ever tracked what happens to an estimate in your organization? What is the cycle time for producing an estimate? What is the lead time? How much of the cycle time is actually devoted to sweating-out the estimate? How much to sitting in someone's in-tray? I strongly suggest you look. In one organization, the active time spent estimating in the estimation operation was 2 days out of a total cycle time of 23 days. If that sort of inflation occurs for every operation, then the time spent actually coding begins to pale into insignificance. What help are the models then? Will they help you to improve your bets on your next project? When we map the real process on the ground, we can identify quickly the bottlenecks and delays and re-engineer them. We can streamline and simplify. These are the actions which result in not only more competitive estimates, but also more competitive practice. The cost of delivering software products and services is not so much inflated by the widgets we produce but by the (lack of) organizational process glue that brings them together.

I remember many years ago being told by a project manager that a job takes as long as it takes, and that targets and deadlines just seemed to knock projects back. There is a certain amount of wisdom in this. A job will always take as long as it takes — until we do something different, until we move into another process system. That shift into another process system may be triggered by pressure of deadlines, but pressure of deadlines cannot change anything in themselves, except perhaps by jamming people's systematic behaviours. Pressure does not remove bottlenecks or delays. Only we can do that when we sit down to design and engineer our process.

3

WHAT HELP IS SOFTWARE PROCESS DESIGN?

Here is Edward Bear coming down the stairs now, bump, bump, bump, bump, on the back of his head behind Christopher Robin. It is, as far as he knows, the only way of coming downstairs, but sometimes he feels that there really is another way, if only he could stop bumping for a moment and think of it.

A. A. Milne
Winnie the Pooh

What help is software process design? The honest reply to this question has to be, 'We don't know.' This is because the majority of software developers do not actively design a process to deliver their software product or service. If there is a process at all, it is usually called something like 'the development life cycle', which is usually a fixed methodology applied to all production. For some organizations, there is not even that. But even though we do not actively design a process, a process nevertheless exists.

The main problem I have with writing this book is the propensity to put on weight. Writing has taken up the time I would normally devote to exercise. So, I have had to work on a diet for myself. Passing friends and colleagues ask me how my diet is going. I say, 'Fine. How's yours?' At which they look at me blankly. They have yet to become conscious of their eating patterns, they do not realize that they, too, are on a diet. The only difference is that I have a goal-oriented diet, which, I am happy to add, is now under statistical process control. In this chapter, let us focus our attention on what exactly constitutes a process, on how processes are linked to operations, and on how you can begin to think about controlling and improving operations. But, first, I want to review some of those unconscious processes we use to produce software.

3.1 THE FIRING LINE

One of the most powerful and enduring images of a supply chain is the human chain which forms to connect a source of water to a burning house. It is a spontaneous response to an urgent demand. Its purpose is to convey just one commodity, water, to a single destination. When that purpose is fulfilled or aborted, the chain fragments, and, no longer a collective whole, everyone goes their individual ways once more.

Project management and fire-fighting

In a number of ways this chain mirrors our project-based approaches to software delivery. If we pause to reflect on this a moment, here are some correspondences we might see. First, every demand for software tends to be treated as a one-off demand. Although there may have been fires and demands for software before, and there will certainly be fires and demands for software in the future, the supply chains have just a brief, episodic life. Secondly, a project team is formed to deliver one-of-a-kind software products and services to a single purchaser. Thirdly, the project team has a life of its own and does whatever is expedient to achieve its objective. Fourthly, at the end of projects, the teams are disbanded, and people move on to different projects, taking their individual experiences of the project with them. Lastly and importantly, nothing remains. Although individuals may be heard to grumble that something ought to be done to improve next time, no fire engines are built, no sprinklers are installed. Nothing is done which would make the approach to putting out fires any more efficient or effective in the future. In software supply, no product or process platforms are built which will provide a faster start to future projects. This is not an oversight of the project manager. The project is not set up to leave anything behind, except a smouldering waste.

Project management is not a process

Let us be clear on an important point. If you are hurrying for your train and you cannot reach the platform because of all the streams of people struggling between you and where you want to be, no matter how bad you feel, there is no point in becoming annoyed with the other people around you. They are not the problem. The problem is the design and layout of the station itself. So, as far as software development goes, there is nothing wrong with project managers, nor is there anything wrong with project management methods, but there is a problem with how we emphasize, exploit, and reward the project-based approach to software delivery. Project management is for monitoring and control, not for laying down business assets or for improving the software delivery process.

Project management engenders slash-and-burn approaches

By employing projects in a way in which, perhaps, they were never intended to be used, we have created the perfect culture for slash-and-burn approaches to software delivery. We have created the perfect process not only for starting fires, but also for keeping them burning, as we move on from project to project. We have used the strong individualism and enthusiasm of bright people to expedite software production. 'Just get the software out! Any way you can. Get it out. You hear me?' 'Yes, indeed.' And the fires blazed, and everyone got to feel the heat. Now, when projects form we make sure everyone has fire-fighting practice, is subjected to stringent safety controls, can handle buckets without spilling too much water, and has well-developed hand-over techniques. But this is like taking an aspirin for appendicitis. What are the underlying problems?

The four weaknesses of project management

The project-based supply chain is used for coordinating one-off complex jobs. It is designed to link one particular product with one particular customer, but there are four inherent weaknesses. First, the project needs to create a virtual production line, which is supplied by a number of contracting groups who can be either internal or external to the organization. This dynamic supply chain is usually supported by an inflexible sequence of protocols called a development life cycle, which is not chosen in response to the needs of the product, but exists as a de facto organizational standard.

Secondly, the project has to coordinate all the components from the supply groups. This requires very detailed early knowledge with precise designs and interface specifications. There is very little tolerance for the unknown. This is a tall order for a supply chain that has been set up, ostensibly, to cope with above-average delivery complexity. Without detailed designs, or with many unknowns, the project manager, who is the hub of the project, becomes an information log-jam. There is little opportunity for ad hoc head-to-head communication between the various contractors, and messaging tends to be highly bureaucratic, with each group behaving as though litigation were only just around the corner.

Thirdly, a project is a unique event. It cannot be compared to other events since the all-important environmental conditions are subject to the individual control of the project manager and vary depending upon their temperament and experience. The contracting groups, not expecting to repeat the work, have no vested interest in preserving any process tools which they might have created to help them in their job. So no, or little, organizational learning occurs. Although one might argue that the creation of new standards and controls by a central body in reaction to all the problems is a form of organizational learning, I would argue that it is learning of an inefficient type.

Fourthly, the project exists in the present tense only, but its products have the capability to put at risk the future of the organization and its clients. Usually, a standing group exists to provide maintenance and support for a variety of products and services once they have been delivered, and it is up to this group to stand proxy for the future. They can only go on past experience, and because past experience has been so bad, they button themselves up for every possible contingency, and impose substantial burdens of proof on the project.

Improvement is limited to project management operations only

While project managers within the organization may be able to work together and share experience from project to project, to save pain in the future, they only improve their project management operations; they are not empowered to improve the software production process as a whole. This is where there is more room for conflict, particularly in matrix-managed organizations. The project managers blame the development managers and the development managers blame the project managers when things go wrong, and somewhere in the middle of the crossfire are the staff who are trying to deliver the product or service. Because a project can spring into action quickly and be lean and mean, does not alter the fact that it is tied to a rigid development life cycle which fetters its responsiveness. Projects always have to start from the same production baseline, project after project.

They can never move further forward without direct investment in the delivery supply chain. Is it surprising there is such a high rate of burnout among project managers?

Why has project management had it so good?

The strengths of the 'one product to one customer' project-based supply chain are twofold. First, it is the devil most of us know and it has the apparent capability for dynamic response. Secondly, there are well-developed techniques and procedures to support project management. Project management tools sit on just about everyone's desks these days and most people have had project management training of some sort or another. But there is a difference between abstract work-planning and scheduling, and the actual process on the ground which delivers the goods.

3.2 CLIENT CENTRES

Most people are familiar with customer supply lines. Those of us who have spent some of their career in an in-house software delivery group will have focused their work on a single customer.

In the early days of software development, our supply chains were largely client focused. But not in the formal sense that anyone would say, 'We operate a customer-oriented supply chain here.' We had individuals or teams whose responsibility it was to serve solely either the needs of one customer in the organization, such as finance, personnel, or manufacturing, or, if we were a software house, external groups of clients, such as hospital administrators, bankers, local government officers, and so on. Teams were able to build up considerable client knowledge, if not respect, for their clients.

By and large this arrangement worked while the separate groups of customers worked independently and saw no benefits from integrating their information with that of others. In the late 'seventies, when the focus shifted from applications to data management, a wider view of the organization had to be taken and the customer supply line was dismantled. We started to be concerned with the total information needs of the organization as a whole. It became clear that, without a plan for an overall information infrastructure, everyone would be marooned on their own islands of information. It was at this point that many software supply teams were rearranged into functional groups. Planning groups, development groups, and operations groups were stitched together by the tenuous threads of the new project management methodologies.

The advantages and costs of client-focused supply chains

In addition to customer rapport, the advantages of this customer-focused supply chain lay in the very direct links between the customer and the software producing team. If there were any problems or need for change, then these were handled responsively without the weight of bureaucracy that the new functional groups would interpose. The problem this incurred was the ever-creeping goalposts. Small changes were constantly requested which held up the supply of new capability. Working with the unknown was a challenge to which this team could respond positively in that problems would be kept on the boil, discussed at every turn, and solved by the team and their customers collectively. But on the negative side was the determination to find 'just the right solution' which tended to get out of proportion to potential benefits in terms of time and effort consumed.

Few internal communication standards were needed when the team worked in close proximity. Because the development team was also, in the early days, responsible for maintaining the products and services they supplied, standards for communicating with the future did not have to be so formal. Only when developers started to change their jobs every two or three years, to increase their experience and earnings, did lack of documentation for maintenance become a big headache for managers.

Looking back, most people remember the days when they worked directly with customers as one of the highlights of their careers, such was the motivation it inspired. The customer-focused supply chain was capable of developing marvellous rapport with customers to the extent that it could, and did, in some cases, become a liability. Sometimes loyalty to the customer overrode loyalty to the business. Why was that a bad thing? Well, it was a form of suboptimization. We created many bespoke packages from scratch, unnecessarily. Our ties to our customers insulated us from other teams in our group and it was easy to get stuck in 'group think'. We did not look around to see if there were opportunities in the sum of what we had created for reuse. We were convinced that our customers' needs could not be served by mining the software created by other teams for their customers. Who would be willing to carry the infrastructure costs of creating objects for reuse in the first place? 'Not my customer.' In the end, the casualty of the client-focused supply chain was the customer. Each time they had to pay unnecessarily high costs for hand-crafted software. But, recognizing that difficulty, we could redesign that old model to reduce all the disadvantages while maintaining all the logistical benefits.

3.3 PRODUCTS ON PLATFORMS

As an alternative to client-focused supply chains you can choose to have a product- or service-based supply chain which just delivers products or services of a single or limited type. This may sound very 'widgety' to you, and in fact it is. But because you are not in the business of producing many copies of a single piece of software, its usefulness relies upon your being able to exploit the generic nature of related, one-of-a-kind software. Some people are better at spotting generic products than others. A useful test for identifying people in your organization who are able to identify and exploit generic solutions for simplifying and reducing costs is to give people two coins. You can give them an American dollar and an English pound, or any two coins out of your pocket. If you then ask for a description of the coins, comparing one with the other, those people who talk of the likenesses and similarities first are the ones with the skills to spot generic solutions. Those people who see the differences first are more likely to be the people who provide bespoke solutions, time after time.

Product platforms provide a basis for investment

In product- or service-focused supply chains, processes and teams are centred on product or service families such as financial, health care, stock control, resource planning or booking systems. The teams have the end-to-end accountability and capability required to deliver the product or service. Because of the scope of accountability, people are more motivated to stay with the process, to improve it, and to invest in it in terms of banking and exploiting reusable product components. The process itself is subjected to refinement and improvement, and it is this learning, which is constantly being built into the process, that is a tremendous asset. The team will package and automate procedures to the extent that little in the way of extra detailed standards and procedures will be required.

Every time a new development comes through, the team is not having to start from go, but moves to a more advanced position each time. In addition, there are distinct advantages from learning about the product or service and, instead of committing to oblivion the products which have been built, the team can recycle them. As well as routine maintenance and enhancement, the team is well placed to carry out preventive maintenance. This means that the reliability of the software components improves over time, rather than deteriorates. The core and components of products become business assets — by that I mean they provide platforms for proactively generating variants. Let me explain.

What exactly is a *product platform*? A platform is an existing product or service which can be enhanced and customized to provide a variant, so you do not have to go back to the drawing-board every time there is a new requirement for a similar sort of product. What is more, each platform can provide a springboard to reach new platforms faster.

Advantages and costs of product-oriented supply chains

Product-oriented supply chains develop excellent operations for rapid application development, incremental development, and prototyping. The whole team is able to work together on an existing product and process infrastructure. Again, like the customer-focused supply chain, the team is able to work with the unknown. It will break the standard rules for partitioning designs, and will put all the unknowns, or disposable parts, into a few modules. The danger is a tendency towards creeping elegance. But if that creeping elegance produces a better and better platform which can be reused many times, then perhaps there are benefits there.

As long as they work together as a coherent team, the need for cross-functional standards is reduced. The loyalty will tend towards the product or service they are providing, and the difficulty is if there is a major shift in customer values and preferences. The first reaction of the team will be to say that the customers do not know quality when they see it, and will tend to get defensive about their product. Problems will also occur when product or service platforms are retired.

Creating hybrid processes

When we free ourselves to design the most appropriate process for delivering software, as the software itself is being planned and designed, we can draw on the strengths of all these approaches. We can create our own hybrid processes, bringing together people with client expertise, product expertise, and asset management. If it appears that a new product in the pipeline has potential for future reuse, then we include operations to quarry out reusable components at the design stage. It does not mean that every product has the same treatment. If there are opportunities for client definition of requirements, then we establish joint application development operations with a strong client-focus . We are not tied to producing every product or service in exactly the same way, with the same burden of costs, whether the product is small or large. We just design whatever process is appropriate. In Fig. 3.1 the flowchart shows you how this fits into your chain of operations.

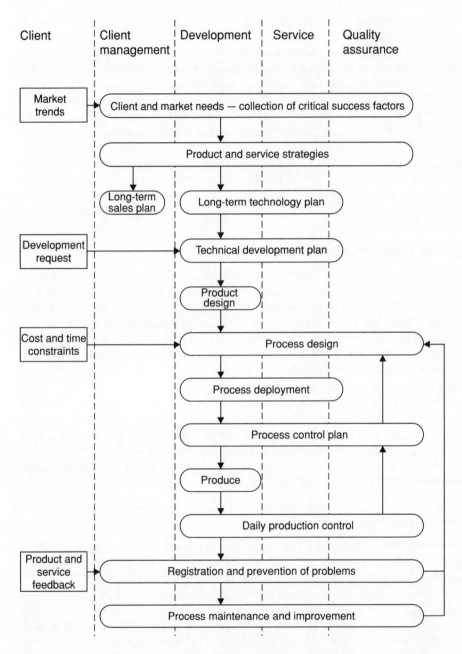

Figure 3.1 Product and process design are essential operations in the software delivery process.

3.4 SOFTWARE PROCESS DESIGN

In Sec. 2.1 the supply chain was described as the overall process for designing and engineering your success by whatever value criteria you have been set by your market and stakeholders. Let us look at 'process' in a little more detail.

Process is the backbone of software delivery management. It is the transforming flow of knowledge, understanding, and human effort into software solutions and services that are capable of governing, guiding, and supporting the lives and livelihoods of other people. A process can be an expensive six-lane parallel motorway, or a budget single track. But, most importantly, it is the critical path for transporting stakeholders and their unsatisfied needs to a point of satisfaction or even delight.

Four important characteristics of a process

The four important characteristics of a process are: its cycle time; its cost; its capability to add value for your stakeholders; and your capability to intervene, and design and engineer cycle time, cost and value to whatever level you would like them to be.

Process cycle time

Process cycle time is the elapsed time needed to travel the length of the process from start to the end. This does not mean that all cycle time is necessarily spent engaged in production. It may be that cycle time is consumed by internal delays, or other inefficiencies. It may be that cycle time is consumed unnecessarily by poor process synchronization. Our ideal is to reach a state where the cycle time equals the actual time to do the work, and then to start to improve or re-engineer the process, to reduce this even further.

Process cost

Process cost is linked to the number of lanes, or parallel streams, of the process. At one extreme if you want to build cheaply and time is not critical, then a single track is probably best; at the other extreme a six-lane motorway is more expensive but gets you to the end of the project in shorter time. Costs are also going to be linked to the inefficiencies you have in the process.

Process value-added

Process value-added is the capability of your process to provide value to your stakeholders at a price they are willing to pay. Again, you are likely to find that not all of your activity results in value for your stakeholders. It is important that you identify activity that adds no value, because there is a cost associated with that and your customer should not be burdened with it. Remember that stakeholder value includes value not only to your clients but also to your business. Take care that the right balance is found when you are engineering your process to obtain appropriate ratios between activities which add value for the clients, and activities which add value to the stakeholders but not the clients.

You can design costs and cycle times to be whatever value you want

This leads us to the fourth attribute: our capability to design and engineer our process. In many organizations people behave as though the process has a life of its own and nothing can be done whatever to alter its working. The evidence of this is in the recourse to standard estimation models for lucky numbers. What process does the model assume — does it assume yours? Some organizations have tried to compensate for this lack of control by imposing rigid life cycle methodologies and, by doing this, the process has been consciously removed from any possible design interventions and has been purposely given its own life. The acid test of whether a methodology is working for you or not is whether it will give you, first, cycle time, cost and value-added information, and secondly, whether the values meet the constraints of your stakeholders. Remember that the process you design is how you can differentiate your business. It can either be your competitive edge, your loss, or your mediocrity. While you may not actively design your process, a process will come together, but it certainly will not be efficient, and it may be totally ineffective.

Multiple processes

In Sec. 3.3 we read that you can have any number of processes depending on the different value criteria of your stakeholders. You may have one process to meet the requirements of a family of stakeholders with similar requirements, you may have another process for a different group. You could have different processes for different families of products or services. You design whatever is appropriate. Whether the processes are long or short, if they run from one end of the supply chain to the other then they are processes.

Operations defined

Operations are not cut-down processes. Operations are groups of coherent and distinct activities which have to be fulfilled, serially or in parallel, to progress the delivery of the software. An operation by itself is not sufficient to complete the software delivery. An operation can be performed wholly on the critical path, in which case it is internal to the critical path and adds to the process cycle time, or it can be performed externally, largely in parallel with the critical path, in which case additional resource may be required (Fig. 3.2). The benefits are that if you design parallel operations you can decrease cycle time and, as a consequence, the time to get your product or service to market and earning money.

What is an operation, then? An operation is a fundamental package of activities and tasks which is necessary to support the process. The activities or tasks taken together constitute the procedure or method for that operation. Procedures and methods can be standard or ad hoc. A standard procedure or method is the acknowledged best practice for completing an operation to the satisfaction of all affected stakeholders.

Usually ad hoc methods are employed either when an operation has not yet been quarried from the bedrock of all other organizational activity or, early on, when the operation is still being shaped and refined. Ad hoc methods are not excused by there being more than one way of carrying out an operation. When more than one way of carrying out an operation exists to provide cost and value alternatives, then there must be more than one standard procedure from which an informed choice can be made when the process is designed. The presence of ad hoc methods, apart from signalling immaturity and lack of definition, can also signal conflicting understandings of purpose or stakeholder demands. You can see this at work when one person carrying out the same operation as another, for apparently the same ends, denies similarity between the operations and uses very different methods.

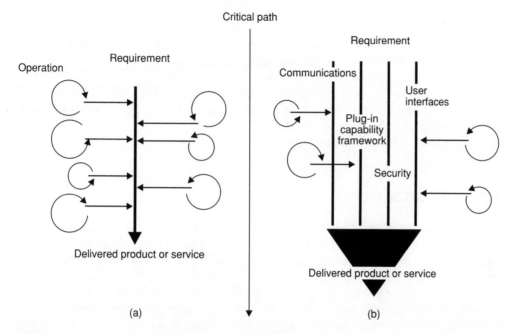

Figure 3.2 A process is a network of internal and external operations which progress delivery of your products and services. Processes can be (a) single track and sequential or (b) multi-track and parallel. It all depends on your delivery and design constraints.

Operations are frequently cyclical, by that I mean that there is a set sequence of actions which is triggered routinely. When the sequence is completed, the operation is ready to start again. Each operation has its own associated cycle time and cost, that is, the time and resource required to complete all the necessary activities.

Operations can be synchronous or asynchronous. Synchronous operations are those that can respond immediately to triggers without any increase to cycle time or costs. When organizations have uncoupled operations and marked them out as functional groups, it is likely that the operations have become asynchronous. The function, to maintain internal efficiencies, will probably seek to 'bus' triggers on either a daily, weekly or monthly basis, depending on the particular cycle times of their operations. This means there could be significant delays which will inflate the main process schedule, or demand for extra resources to respond to urgent requests which will, in turn, inflate costs. It is not necessarily just defined functions that operate in this way. Ad hoc groups, such as review bodies and management teams, all work asynchronously. They have set dates for meeting and considering process items, and if the process misses the bus, it has to stand down until the next meeting. It is important to be aware that management operations are as critical to the process as production operations. In fact, management operations have a greater potential for braking (or breaking) the process than production operations.

Uncoupled operations

Following the manufacturing line of thinking, that there are benefits to be gained from the division of labour and from mass production, we have 'uncoupled', or made external to the process, many important operations. These operations have polarized into organizational functions, such as finance, human resources, planning, operations, and so on. Most of our problems occur because we confuse 'process' and 'operation'. Each function mistakenly believes their operations to be, or to enshrine, 'the process' or even 'the right process'. This is suboptimization.

3.5 SUBOPTIMIZATION

Suboptimization is a misleading word. For one thing, I cannot find it defined in *The Concise Oxford Dictionary*, and for another it does not mean what it appears to mean — the conscious attainment of something less than optimal. The core meaning of the word is 'the conscious attainment of the optimal at a subgroup level'. The fact that these optimizing strategies might add up to something good or bad for the whole is neither here nor there. What the word has come to mean in the literature is optimization at the subgroup level which results in negative consequences for the whole.

Competing processes within the organization

What does this mean in practical terms? It means we have operational or functional groups working as separate islands, putting their heart, soul, and ingenuity into improving what they consider to be the process. It is in fact only their view of the process or local operations which are being tuned. Unfortunately, the result of their efficiencies is to throw the real process off balance, either because the improvement has led to a deterioration in the operations' relationships to the process, or because it has had a negative impact on another group or function working in the same process.

When both groups are driven by targets set from above, and both groups are fulfilling those targets to the detriment of others, it is easy to see how war breaks out in the organization. If the high command is 'go faster', then the various heads of planning, development, and operations, say, pass on the message to their teams to go faster. Here we have a direct, unadulterated communication of the original command. There is no communication problem. What is the problem, then? Just pause to contemplate this a moment and see what thoughts you have.

Each head has specified to their functional group, 'go faster'. So the planning group go faster and produce specification documents that are a bit sparse on some of the critical detail, because it would take too long to track down, and besides it will work its way out eventually. Development design and build as fast as they can go. They cut corners and expect a few problems, but they have gone fast, and the problems will turn up in operational testing anyway. When the software reaches the operations group, they just cannot believe what has hit them. Within the operations group, the test group go faster and get the software out of the door and just hope that their sister support group has no holiday booked for the next three months. What is the result? The purchaser is happy because they have the system quickly. The users of the system hate it. They cannot manage their workloads because the system keeps going down at critical times. The managers of the users have been told by their senior management — the purchasers — to reduce staff if they want their annual bonus. This means increasing existing staff workloads when the staff are on a learning curve — a situation exacerbated by the fact that the staff are doing so much fire-fighting they have not all had training yet. And, since it was expected that staff would have formal training early on, the planning group decided to go faster on the training, and not produce the user manuals until three months after installation. The users now hate their managers, their penny-pinching senior management, and the software producers — particularly if they are an in-house team, since their payroll only goes up and never down.

What else? There is war between the two groups in the operations function. The head of operations is thoroughly fed-up with his managers — when he said 'go faster', he did not mean behave like morons. He is not on the best of terms with the heads of planning and development to say the least. They are not that happy with him either and take offence at his sour mutterings about their lack of competence. He is thoroughly rattled by his manager when his annual bonus is reduced because of the high staff costs he has been forced to incur in his support team. His muffled criticism of his peers is not taken too kindly — they have done a splendid job, they have met their targets. He is sent on a team-building course in the wilds of the Highlands and has to subsist on snake and live in a dustbin liner for a week. His team-working skills, strangely enough, leave much to be desired upon his return.

This is not quite the end of the story — would that it were! After six months of putting up with the bad manners and rudeness of clerks processing their requests, which take even longer now they have those new-fangled computers, the client's customers decamp *en masse* to a welcoming competitor. The commissioning firm goes out of business. The software service groups taken on to support the customer are laid off abruptly because they are no longer necessary. The operations manager regains some of his smile, albeit lop-sided. History is ready to repeat itself once more.

'Politics' is lack of visible process

Let us not forget the soldiers carrying out orders on the front line. How do they perceive suboptimization? When they run into peers from the other groups, what happens? I know two groups, let us call them A and B. Group A has an activity code set up for 'Handholding B'; Group B has an activity code set to 'get group A out of their mess.' Who knows the amount of wasted effort which occurs at this level — for what? They call it 'politics', and nine out of ten software engineers agree that, 'I could do a much better job, if it wasn't for all the politics around here.' But it is not really politics at all. We do not hate and despise each other because we are inherently hateful and despicable. We just have not designed a process. If we do that, I would like to think of all the money and time we could save by not living on snake in dustbin bags in the Highlands — but that might upset the people whose living depends on breeding snakes and customizing dustbin bags.

The damage caused by lack of visible process

I hope this fairly simple example of suboptimization helps you to see how totally damaging it can be. Not only to the process, but also to the competitiveness and viability of businesses depending on the software produced. Not only to team-working and individual relationships, but also to the very livelihood of people associated with the delivered goods. So, what can be done? What can stop history repeating itself? What would your prescription be?

Let us look first at that original command — go faster. What was intended? Did the chief mean for everyone to behave like morons — or did he tell them to? If he had said, 'We need to reduce our delivery cycle time for this job, we have an urgent request and we could get a lot more business from this client if all goes well', would that have improved the situation? What if he had said, 'I don't care how much it costs, just get it done by 4 April', would that have been better? If he had sent his management team on the team-building course before the project and then said, 'go faster', would that have been an improvement? What about if he had gone along on the team-building course with his team?

Any or none of these alternatives might have worked better. It would all depend on whether they, as a team, had sat round the table and explored process options. They would have had to design a delivery process to meet all the constraints imposed upon them. They would have had to understand exactly how each could go faster, and identified and resolved the potential conflicts that lay in wait for them. It might have been that they would have had to go to their staff and ask them how they would go about it. The important thing is that they would have to stop to consider the process as a whole. By and large we do not do that. We tell our managers to go away and do something as if they were black boxes. We trust them to do their best. And they do. And this is the problem.

3.6 TRANSFORMER POWER

For some time it was quite fashionable to carry out cost-of-quality measurement exercises. Companies gathered and demonstrated year-on-year the costs of failure, appraisal, and prevention. Did you ever carry out this exercise? How successful was it? Were you able to identify resource consumption and waste? Could you attribute waste to a source, as opposed to unwitting accomplices? Did you change your process as a consequence?

Establishing costs of quality success requires a visible process

I have met people who have had considerable success with this exercise and have been able to establish year-on-year trends. The first year always looks bad; the second year looks appalling as we begin to discern more sources of wastage. The third year is an improvement on the second, and usually, if the exercise reaches the fourth year, senior managers lose interest. Why is that? You might like to note your reasons here.

When I asked people who could show success in pulling down their failure costs if they had changed their estimation models to take account of the leaner running, the answer was 'no'. So, what was different? Had cycle times been reduced? Had costs to the stakeholders been proportionately reduced? Had value-added been increased? Nothing tangible which had impacted the stakeholders could be positively identified.

The problem is that unless you are clear about what exactly your processes are, it is very difficult to get to grips with cost of quality or improvement exercises in general. It can be as frustrating as jumping up and down on the ocean to try and change the sea level. But if you know what the process is, then cycle times, value, costs, and waste can all be attributed to specific operations or their relationship to the process as a whole. But the problem is that the software delivery process is very complex and lengthy and trying to find the source or cause of anything is frustrating.

Designing a simpler more amenable process is within your control

Why is the software delivery process complex and lengthy? Does it have to be? Is that what we want? Does the software work better for the complexity and length? If it does, then better for whom? I have yet to meet a software manager who is pleased with life in the tar pit. Because a tar pit is what it truly has been. If we do not like it the way it is, what are we doing to get out of it? I do not think that we are afraid to be visible and accountable for problems. I do not even think we are looking to let the tar pit absorb all the blame. Perhaps it is just that we have not yet realized that we can get out of the tar pit — that we can transform ourselves and our situation. This is the true work of managers — to be transformers, of ourselves, our staff, our environment, and the process we work on.

It is a hard job. Sometimes it is like being in charge of the library when the whole town decides to change books on the same day, and you have not had time to finalize and implement the classification system yet. Your staff are running round trying to find books for people, mopping up the anger, and trying to avoid pain, totally unaware of all the other staff they are tripping up. So what do you do? Do you give in and look for another job? Do you make a feature of the chaos? Do you write learned papers on the inherent chaos in library systems? Do you write estimation models for book retrieval times from unclassified systems? Do you go to war with the authorities about lack of resources? Or do you sort the mess out?

Working with your staff to design a better process

I hope you opted for the last choice, because that is the only way out of your pain and the only way you are going to find some true job satisfaction. So, together with your staff, you design a way out of the tar pit. You share your understanding of the purpose and improve the total knowledge of your stakeholder needs, so that everyone can make evaluations and decisions based on those guiding success criteria. You look at what is happening now and begin to map your process, and how you are currently fulfilling the purpose. Not surprisingly, you find there is a lot of duplicated effort, much crossing over of activity, and a lot of confusing activities which would not be there, if there were no confusion to be sorted out.

You start to design a supply chain which will get the desired software into the hands of the customer (subject to stakeholder constraints) in time and in a state for it to be valuable to them and at a cost they are prepared to pay. You design or bring together a number of operations appropriate to and supporting your process. What customer account operations do you require for this specific customer? Can you create a separate operation just to handle user interfaces? Can you design test operations which, while remaining effective, are more external to the process and incur less critical path schedule?

When you have looked at your process options alongside your product or service options, and decided the operations you need, you can begin to work out costs based upon operational cycle time and resourcing. By going through this exercise, you will also have a clearer picture of which operations could impact your total process cycle time, and understand the risks involved and where they could come from. When you have the process defined at this level of detail, you have a chance of predictably repeating success and avoiding past failures which previously you did not have.

Now you can work on costs of quality, or process improvements. Not only will you be able to show the changes, but you will also be able to demonstrate their positive impact on the process, on cycle times, costs, estimates, and ultimately, your stakeholders.

Luck is not the lever for getting us out of the tar pit — design is.

Section 2

4

THE IMPORTANCE OF PURPOSE

Above all, you must be intent on cutting the enemy in the way you grip the sword. . . . Fixedness means a dead hand. Pliability is a living hand.

Miyamoto Musashi
A Book of Five Rings

Most TQM initiatives fail through lack of purpose. Not lack of purpose for the initiative, but, surprisingly, lack of purpose for the business. Unless there is a clear vision of the direction in which the organization is heading, then exhortations to improve quality will just result in everybody pulling in the direction they personally favour. The result is consistent with the laws of physics and all the effort cancels itself out.

Quality initiatives which do not concentrate on stakeholder expectations are doomed before they start. You may get some internal improvements in efficiency through all your procedure-writing, but your customers will have packed their bags and left by the time you can report the benefits back to them. It is vital that you make a start working from the outside in, by improving those operations which are in direct contact with your clients, and then working on the internal or 'back office' operations which support them. At every stage the test is whether you are applying appropriate leverage to obtain the results you want. You may not be focusing on the results you want, or you may be overengineering your response. This is where a clear definition of purpose, clearly communicated to all members of staff through regular planning mechanisms, gives you a clear lead.

Let us make a start in this chapter by looking at what happens if there is no clear purpose, then we can move on to ways of obtaining a purpose and, finally, we can look at how purpose can be woven into the fabric of the business.

4.1 CRACKING EGGS

Think of an egg — a hen's egg — like the ones you see on supermarket shelves. White or brown, it does not matter. Just call to mind an egg. As you think about the egg, consider what purpose it has.

Purpose is a point of view

From the egg's point of view, it has only one purpose — to recreate itself. But in your hands it can have many more purposes, all of which depend upon your individual design on the egg, which in turn depends upon your values, beliefs, likes and dislikes, your physical needs, your particular skills, and motivation to use your skills. You might believe the purpose of this egg is to become a chicken, so you incubate and nurture it. You might assume the purpose of this egg is to kill your hunger, and, depending on how you break it, you could poach, scramble, or meringue it. Then again, you might think the purpose of this egg is to provide material for a work of art and you could gild, enamel, or bejewel it.

Purpose needs to be declared

Unless you tell people about the purpose of your egg, the probability is that other people will see it differently to you. Leave it in someone else's care and take a holiday, and you could come back to find your egg scrambled, gold-plated, or grown into a heavyweight fighting-cock. Your business is like that egg. Until you act to assert unequivocally your purpose, you leave its definition to others. You may be happy with that or you may not.

Purpose can be engineered

In your hands, the business has potentially an infinite number of purposes. Once you decide upon a purpose, and act accordingly, all other possible purposes collapse for the present. It is now clear to anyone watching what your purpose for the business is. Perhaps it is fear of committing to the wrong purpose which prevents some people from making that decision. Instead, they sit on the fence and try to keep their balance. They let the egg remain all things to all people. They become prey to outsiders who can define a purpose for them — takeover, facilities management, wholesale redundancy. They become a source of confusion to people in the business who are chasing around trying to find some saving purpose. In the end, they topple one way or the other and it can be a messy landing.

There is a well-known saying to the effect that you cannot scramble eggs without breaking them. It is usually taken to mean that if you want something, you have either to pay for it or hurt people in the process. However, another interpretation of it is, purely and simply, that you have to make an act of commitment, and that act is irreversible. But since reversibility is not a feature of our world, why cry over broken eggs? Hatch some more.

TQM had 'a purpose' but was not purposeful

Most TQM initiatives fail through lack of purpose. We blame lack of commitment, but really that is the symptom, not the cause. No one has cracked the egg. Cracking the egg is not the same as delegating the wording of a mission statement to a supernumerary quality manager. It is not the same as pep talks to the troops or expensive training programmes. Nor is it the same as senior management team away-days. Although TQM can achieve some improvement, the problem is that 'a purpose' is bought in from outside and it remains outside. No change is seen in basic practices. Commitment to a purpose means collapsing options and restricting freedoms in everyday working practice.

Purpose is signalled by behaviour and investment

Purpose provides a visible goal underpinned by concrete investment in people, time, and money. It is to succeed, for example, in the bespoke software production market; the prepackaged software solutions market; or perhaps, software consultancy market. If you are supplying off-the-peg solutions to your purchasers, you are not creating bespoke code. This means you invest neither in tools to facilitate cutting code, nor in people who, more than anything else, live to write code. If your purpose is to provide ultra-reliable software, then you will invest in tools to improve reliability and in people who respect the hygiene of clean-room operations. If your purpose is to take software purchasers by storm with unimaginable — until you did it — software wizardry, then your investment will be in facilities and tools to support the most creative people you can buy, alongside a team of meticulous cleaners, to re-engineer and package after them. Purpose represents a long-term intent. That is not to say that your purpose becomes a dead hand. On the contrary, it is continually exercised and reviewed to ensure investment choices are correctly balanced. Too little investment and you will fail, too much and you will become immobile. Your challenge is to get the balance as right as you can.

Purpose reduces bureaucracy

The process for succeeding in your purpose is not fixed. That can be as ingenious and responsive as your purpose requires and your resources permit. It seems to me that in some organizations purpose is infinitely flexible — 'to get the work out of the door'. Yes, but which door? At the same time, their process for achieving this flexible purpose is rendered more and more immobile by rigid procedures and standards. It is as if, not sure which mountain to climb, the team keep increasing their equipment and baggage to cover all eventualities, which effectively removes their capacity for any movement at all.

Purpose provides energy

Purpose signals a real decision by senior management to climb this mountain and not that one. If your purpose is to climb that mountain, then maybe you should join that team over there. Please choose. Purpose is important because it is something which attracts people to an organization. 'Our purpose is to be the first to climb this mountain and return with all members safe and well.' It resonates with their fundamental values and provides the energy to fuel the climb. Absence of purpose is an energy sink.

As competition to earn software delivery contracts increases, I hear more and more people saying that the business is not the same as the one they joined. This is because while we have been prevaricating, the purpose of the business has been redefined by impatient stakeholders. For many years stakeholders passively watched software development groups and, from their point of view, it looked as though the purpose of software development was to perpetuate itself. The software development group, cosy in their protecting shell, were happily growing wings and bones and beak, getting bigger and more hungry for expensive technology and practices all the time. But while all this was happening, the stakeholders began to get peckish too and were ready to be lured by our competitors.

4.2 STAKING OUT THE STAKEHOLDERS

Traditional quality thinking would have us believe that there is only one customer — the person who hands over the money. In Sec. 1.5 some of the questions arising from that thinking were explored.

It is too simplistic to continue thinking in terms of a simple customer–supplier chain. Our business has multiple stakeholders, all of whom must be satisfied at any one time for us to remain a viable enterprise. Where does this lead us? It leads us to consider not just a single customer, but a number of stakeholders — the purchaser, certainly; regulatory bodies, such as the Inland Revenue; the business itself, in terms of future viability; shareholders; the public at large (although in most cases regulatory bodies set standards on their behalf, as a business you might want to implement voluntarily your own set of more stringent ethical standards). The requirements of all these stakeholders need to be taken account of when you devise your purpose (Fig. 4.1).

But does this not create an even bigger headache for us? It was bad enough having to please one customer, but if we have to please all these stakeholders, is that not going too far? The product or service would be so compromised, it would make no one happy. There would be so many captains on the bridge that we could never agree on the way ahead. These are problems. But what happens if we do not consider the stakeholders? How easy is it for us when the demands of the schedule-shrinking, penny-pinching purchaser and the demands of the business-innocent user are diametrically opposed? Do we just take the money and run?

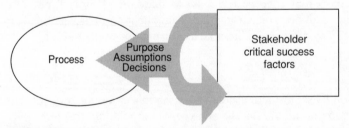

Figure 4.1 Stakeholder critical success factors provide your process with a purpose. This will form a coherent framework for making assumptions and decisions. Remember you are a stakeholder too.

Business purpose must take account of conflicting stakeholder demands

Let us work on the scenario of the different demands of client and user. You know that the users need six days' training, built-in help facilities, and special menus. The clients want the functionality at knock-down prices which will not cover all the special user interface requirements for the system to be successful. What do you do? Do you do the best you can and compromise, satisfying neither? Do you do exactly what the commissioning client asked for and put a clause in the contract detailing your charges for 'over the phone consultancy'? Do you do what the user wants, and make the miserly client pay up? Whose monkey is it? Not yours, is it?

Business purpose must assign priorities to stakeholder claims

If you have news of this sort of conflict during requirements elicitation, or at any other time during development, then that conflict represents a serious risk to the viability of your product or service and the amount of confidence which can be placed in it. As part of declaration of purpose, you need to say something about the priorities to be assigned to the different stakeholder groups. 'The Inland Revenue must be satisfied at all times by regular presentation of accounts.' You need to pull out all the potential stakeholders for your system. If your customers have stakeholders too, and they are not resolving their own conflicts, then perhaps it is in your best interest to help them, if it is likely to impact your business. This is all extra value you can add.

Identifying stakeholders with purposes irreconcilable with yours

It is also critical that you identify any stakeholders who can benefit from sabotaging the system. Stakeholders in this position have a purpose which is at a tangent to all the other stakeholders. Their purpose needs to be brought to the surface in public, so that it can be recognized and the problems accounted for, and possibly realigned with all the other stakeholders. Know who creates the most risk for your business and keep them clearly in focus. Remember when you are assessing priorities and precedence that the future of your business is also a major stakeholder.

4.3 CHARACTERS IN SEARCH OF A DIRECTOR

Have you ever been in a situation at work — a meeting or a discussion — when you suddenly felt like an alien? Think back to what exactly triggered that experience and just make a few notes here.

Purpose means everyone shares the same success story

I remember watching people read from their individual scripts, and seeing their surprise when other people made replies which were not down in the script. What happened in the next scene depended largely on the artistic temperament of the players. Anything could happen, from a gentle prompting of the 'right' lines — 'look at my lips, not your script', to open abuse, with a senior manager being called as referee. The problem was that there were no 'wrong' or 'right' lines. Each person was playing their part correctly — they were just in different plays. The best the manager could do was show a preference for one of the scripts, or one of the actors, if you look at it from their point of view.

'We can't progress this until we have sign-off.'

'Sign-off? What's that got to do with it? I can't stand down 30 staff until someone decides to sign a piece of paper.'

'Quality standards say . . .'

'Who's talking about quality standards? I'm talking about 30 idle staff. I shall carry on regardless.'

'Carry on regardless?'

'That's right. You heard me.'

'Well, I think Richard has a point there, George.'

Richard has his manager's backing in this contest, and will become a role model for the all the teams watching. This is an actor with a future.

Knowledge workers do not require scripts, of course, but they do require a play. Very rarely can that play be successfully written by themselves. It has to be provided — to give them something they can get their teeth into, and also to leave them both hands free for the work. Without a play, without a purpose, what can people believe in or aspire to? Commitment is starved without a purpose. 'Suck it and see' approaches without a defined purpose do not work. Everything is spat out by everybody.

Purpose requires leadership

Another interesting experience I once had was when I went in search of the script. The people working on the floor had no idea which play they were in, and were busy improvising lots of rhubarb. There were quite a few would-be producers and roving impresarios going round offering this script or that. But staff were concerned about who, exactly, would pay for the rehearsals, and from where, in fact, they would get the time. No, they would wait until a script had been approved by their manager. When I went to their managers for a script, a funny thing happened; I kept being passed up the ranks. All the way to the top. When I got to ask the chief for the script, I found myself being passed back down the ranks again. He thought his managers had the script.

Purpose is not more training

Fortunately, someone in human resources spotted the problem and tried to do something about it. Staff were sent on team-building courses. Back home, with terrific *esprit de corps*, they were able to act parts more convincingly, with better timing and better improvisation. The result was more energetic and assertive rhubarb. Audiences continued to dwindle — at least the crew up the road had got their act together.

What could people do? 'We just do not know whether we are heading in the right direction'. They shook their heads. So much wasted talent. So much wasted commitment. Do you know how much you have spent on team-working courses in the last five years? What benefits have you seen? What benefits have your stakeholders seen? How often do you have to relaunch team-working initiatives? See if you can find the answers.

Team-working courses are marvellous in some respects. They help people to open up and share. People learn the benefits of cooperation, but that cooperation slumps unless there is a framework in the organization to support it on a day-to-day basis. You can come back from a team-working course, fired with enthusiasm, and the other teams, who have also been on the course, are fired with enthusiasm too. But what happens when these teams are the loyal retainers of feuding knights? Do they join hands across the waste between the warring functions? Not if they value their prospects for promotion.

Objectives without a shared purpose are 'politics'

But tell me, why are the lords' knights jousting? Because they are coming from different directions. Their directions are handed down to them as company objectives. One is given instructions to hit this target, another to hit a different target. They obey, but in the process unseat each other. The software manager says there is no way the new systems can go in before April. All the other managers disagree energetically. The software manager does not know what to do. The system not only will not work, but it will also be a disaster. He takes a natural break to consider their intransigence and visits the toilet. One of the other managers follows him. While they are standing side by side, the other manager speaks to him through the corner of his mouth, 'What you are saying, buddy, is that those guys in there do not get to make their five grand bonus which is riding on having your system installed. You are going to go back in there and tell them, real nice, they can still get to make their bonus.' At last! The penny drops. The software manager realizes he is in the wrong play. Now he can go back and tell the other managers they can have the system. This is a true story.

If you parcel up an invisible purpose into separate management objectives and targets, you can place safe bets on there being evidence of massive suboptimization within the year. You will hear people say that there are communication problems or too many politics. Everyone needs to know the purpose. The work does not end at just waving the script at them. They need direction. You need to ensure that everyone practices together. Not only in annual performance reviews or monthly meetings, but also day by day, ironing out the glitches until your purpose is achieved (Fig. 4.2).

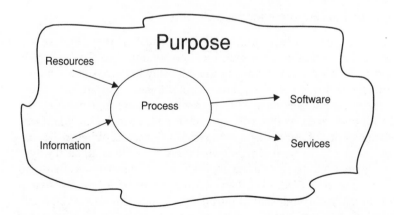

Figure 4.2 Process is the flow and transformation of resources and information to provide delivered software and services which serve a purpose.

Purpose supports decision-making

When we make decisions, we do not just choose one method instead of another. We make a choice based on an assessment of how well that particular method will help us to achieve our goals. All decision-making is goal oriented. The choice we make is only a surrogate for obtaining a goal. Those goals can be our own private goals, or they can be the goals of the organization and our customers. How much better decision-making is in organizations when the organization's purpose and goals are explicit so everyone can tune into them. One organization has a list of just nine values which sits by everyone's telephone: 'Is my decision more . . . customer-focused . . . cost-effective . . . responsive . . .?' In this way many rigid procedures to deal with all possible combinations of eventualities in making decisions can be cut.

Purpose supports empowerment

Direction seems to be almost a dirty word, but without direction, empowerment is a farce; everyone slipping on banana skins — the same banana skins, time after time. If we do not give people direction, we are denying our own worth to the organization. Our worth is in knowing the play, being able to give meaning and expression to the author's intent, and being able to coach and help other people achieve their performance ambitions.

It is too easy to fall into the trap of confusing direction with autocracy. An autocrat works with speechless, wooden marionettes. A director works with a living team to realize the play and the players.

4.4 MARKING TIME

Sport held one of the highest and most sacrosanct positions on my school curriculum, second only to morning assembly. You had to be in the last throes of pneumonia or severely injured to be excused games.

The purpose is to win, not to exert power for its own sake

Is it because of, or in spite of, the British tradition of sportsmanship, then, that in the workplace we behave as we do? Is that why we send our players out onto the field, give them a ball, and stand behind the sidelines, exhorting them to play better? Is that why we watch them running furiously, this way and that, getting injured, getting exhausted, until, bitter with disappointment, we blow the whistle? Is that why, through narrow lips, we berate them for scoring four own goals? Is that why we keep the positions of the goalposts a secret, and only take the rules out of our pockets at the end of the game? Whether we are letting people find out the hard way, as we had to, or whether, tired of the old, hard ways, we are trying to be more democratic, the confusion, bewilderment, and pain we create in our organizations are the same, and confusion, bewilderment, and pain kill. By giving people a greater sense of direction through shared purpose and goals, and by taking time to ensure that everyone is on the team and willing to play to the rules which have been agreed, we escape the tragic cycle of more controls, policing, recrimination, damaged esteem, learned incompetence, and yet more controls.

Purpose and control

If you play hockey, or football, or netball for that matter, you will know that your primary purpose is to help increase the score for your side and your secondary purpose is to prevent the opposing side from scoring. How do you prevent the opposition from scoring? By marking. This means staying on the heels of a member of the opposing side and cutting off their chances of receiving or passing the ball. How many markers does a team need? The whole side. Every single member of the team has to mark a member of the opposing team. So, each team member has to switch between two roles: an attacker–scorer role and a defender–marker role. While you are one, it is difficult to be the other. Perhaps you might like to estimate the marker to scorer ratio in your organization?

Purpose and inspection

Let us look at some real examples. I recently read in one of my professional journals about a 10-level quality metric for documents, supposedly following the strategy of the SEI capability maturity level. The levels go from 1, 'speech like', which is categorized as informal, unchecked (even by the author), and used as a substitute for phone calls, to level 10, which is 'logically consistent'. In between, five of the remaining eight levels are 'checked', 'rechecked', 'reviewed', 'externally reviewed', and 'extensively reviewed'. The authors comment: '. . . in principle, a document private to a company should be able to receive the highest status. In practice this is difficult since the variety of people available to review the document will be limited.' Any guesses of the marker ratio here?

   You are holding a review meeting for a document you want to sign off. Eighteen people turn up. You are not sure where they all come from, and why they are all there. You go through the review. An enormous list of revision items is presented to you; some of the items are totally at odds with the original requirements, but you are asked to make the revisions, never the less. You revise the document. You call another review. A slightly different bunch of people appear this time. You spot three new faces and, would you believe it, you are given another revision list. When can one person be two markers?

Purpose and approval

Even though I had a budget from the EU for a European Esprit project for which travel and production expenses had been agreed in advance, the holding organization with which I was working at the time required three signatures for each overseas travel request which had to be signed off seven days before travel or I would be left picking up the travel costs out of my own pocket. Because of the size of the organization and the unavailability of people, I could spend a day or more just walking for each authorization. If you think the marker-scorer ratio is 3:1, did you count all the EU review bodies? Did you count me?

   You are ordering off-the-peg solutions for your client. The value of your order comes to more than £10,000. Congratulations! You have just passed the threshold which requires you to have the schedule signed off by a senior manager to ensure that the kit is compatible. You leave it with the secretary — the manager is too busy to look at it right now. Ten days and much lobbying later, you manage to retrieve the signed schedule, signed by his secretary on his behalf. You have had to let other things slip while you chased it up. Now everyone is chasing you, not just the customer who is expecting the configured kit to be delivered in four days' time. One marker or two? Or more?

Control is an expensive substitute for purpose

Each of these 'one-at-a-time' sign-offs uses high ratios of markers to scorers. Even in a competitive game, this could be viewed as inefficient. But should you be competing within your own business? Is there supposed to be an internal opposition whose purpose is to stop you scoring for the team — who wants to stop you passing and receiving the ball? The argument is that one-at-a-time sign-offs are to stop rules from being broken and unchecked failures from being passed on to the customer. But what happens as consequence? People design new ways to break rules! They order kit for one customer on two schedules, each one coming to just under £10,000. They get authorization for a number of travel requests in advance, just in case — flight changes and meeting cancellations account for variation, if anyone asks. Documents are sneaked through without reviews. Everyone's purpose is survival — surviving the system and finding ways to beat it. But this means beating ourselves. Is that what we want?

Each time we have to go through a check for which there is no existing checklist, or the checklist is the private property of an individual or a group, we are inflating both schedule and costs. This applies to go/no-go checks as well as to open, review-type checks. On what basis would a travel request ever be turned down? On what basis would a senior manager turn down a technical requisition? How many different and conflicting personal checklists are in operation during reviews?

Purpose is freedom and constructive control

If the purpose is to reduce overseas travel, why not make that clear with each budget holder at planning time? A sum is agreed and reviewed once a quarter. But within budget the holder has full freedom to spend the money as effectively as possible. The budget provides control and freedom to score. If the purpose of checking purchase schedules is to reduce the risks of buying incompatible kit, then how is a busy senior manager (or secretary, for that matter) able to reduce those risks? How about a simple knowledge-based system? Then the senior manager is not pulled down to low-level tasks. Both senior manager and purchaser are freed to score.

If the purpose of a review is to ensure compliance with requirements, then one and only one checklist, which is available in advance to all, should be used in review meetings. This leaves everyone free to concentrate on the purpose.

If the purpose is to ensure accurate communication and reduce misinformation in the organization, then each communication should be semantically correct and logically consistent — even electronic notes. The rules and checks should either be implicit in the system used for communication, or be core staff competencies for which training is available, or be present as system prompts.

Of course, if the purpose is to mark time; to prevent the team from scoring by constantly intercepting and hogging the ball; to demotivate them by putting them under surveillance; to see if they are playing to rules at which they can only guess; to have them expend all their creative energy creating lots of loopholes for you to fill with ever-increasing quantities of paper and expense, then these sorts of operations are perfect. The question is: how much marking time can you afford in your organization? Would it not be cheaper and more constructive to be clear on the purpose?

4.5 STRIKE POWER

Success is relative. One person's success is another person's mediocrity. Everyone has their own mountain to climb, and each is differently featured with different terrain and challenges. So, think for a moment: what criteria constitute success in your business? How would you know how well you are doing against these criteria?

Finding a purpose

Most organizations lock their purpose on to the achievement of their success criteria. But where do those criteria come from? For some — the innovators — success criteria are linked to a hunch about something which has yet to be called into existence. (A hunch is based on information our gut has without our knowing yet.) The success of innovators depends firstly, upon their being able to detect the slightest hint of readiness in the market to change direction; and secondly, on their ability to hunt and impact just the right spot to create a controlled chain reaction. This second ability is critical. Dell hit their mark in Japan, but had problems because demand for their PCs blew up too quickly. Unable to service demand, they may lose their market before they have one. While the innovators are edging along their uncertain route it is difficult to gauge success using traditional measures: function points, MIPS, return on investment (ROI). What counts for them is the number of direct hits and the size of the explosion.

For others, success criteria have been developed in response to purchaser feedback which has often been negative, and on managers' reactions to this negative feedback. Typically criteria are very visible, such as delivering software on time, staying within budget, being more productive — often translated as producing so many more function points per person per month; providing better estimates, and so on. A much easier proposition all round, you would expect — yet who do you know who succeeds consistently in satisfying their stakeholders? There are two problems here. First, where targets seem attainable, we put up so many to shoot at that we can focus on none too well. Second, reducing your negative impact on your stakeholders does not necessarily in itself constitute success.

There are also those whose success criteria are obtained from outside their business, from other companies, from competitors, from standards bodies, from consultancies and gurus. They measure themselves by competitive benchmarking, 'Six Sigma Quality', 'Zero Defects', or quality standards conformance. An avionics software supplier assesses their performance solely against conformance to ISO 9001. We have two problems here. First, going for a target already hit by the competition is often not an inspiring mission for the troops. Second, unless your performance is enhanced in your stakeholders' perception by the adoption of these criteria, then they are not success criteria after all.

Purpose is synergy with your stakeholders

Whatever success criteria you choose, if they do not reflect accurately the key preferences of your major stakeholders, you risk locking yourself, your livelihood and your staff onto a flock of geese. When reviewing their performance against the measures they have set for themselves, many have fallen into the trap of wanting to shake themselves by the hand, while their stakeholders just want to shake them by the throat — 'We don't want extensively reviewed software! Please deliver our software soon!' So unless your purpose is for you alone, you need to lock onto and measure your strike power against the values and preferences of your stakeholders.

Total quality management initiatives did entice us out of our cosy shells and most businesses are now conducting annual customer satisfaction surveys. However, looking at examples from a number of diverse companies, many surveys are based on voting for what the supplier is either already providing, or thinks, in their infinite wisdom, should be provided. A sure way for losing touch. The organizations who first ask their stakeholders what their preferences are, and what priorities they attach to their preferences, and who then use these values as the basis for self-appraisal, succeed in getting their sights calibrated and their target into focus more easily and quickly.

Purpose is renewable for life

Once a year is probably not a sufficiently frequent interval to check out the current position of your most critical target. Spending time regularly with your stakeholders and stalking them for a few days is one of the better ways for keeping contact. You will detect issues which they themselves have yet to pick up. Test your success criteria and purpose regularly to make sure you are still on the right flightpath. Having invested time and good money in staking out their stakeholders, many companies promptly bury their intelligence reports where they can never be found by the people who need them. This intelligence is a living asset, and requires a standard operation to administer it in your experience base so it can be drawn on whenever you are formulating or reviewing your purpose. Be prepared for your stakeholder's position to change in response to their business and for their key buying preferences to shift. Do not accuse them of being flighty. It is their nature to change, and capability for response must be built into your process (Fig. 4.3).

Purpose and measurement

Test your measurement, too. Do not constrain your response by locking into rigid year-on-year measurement unless you want to prove that you are going faster and faster in the wrong direction. Intelligent missiles no longer go in straight lines: they are goal-seeking. What does this mean for you? Should you be increasing year-on-year your delivery of lines of code? Should you be decreasing delivered lines of code? How do lines of code relate to object-oriented production? Does using object-oriented techniques increase or decrease your productivity in terms of lines of code production? Would you use anything new if it made you look more unproductive in terms of your traditional performance indicators. Indicators are sensors which pick up values within a pre-set framework. The new, because it is new, needs indicators we do not yet know, and it takes time and the testing of several indicators before new and appropriate measurement can be devised.

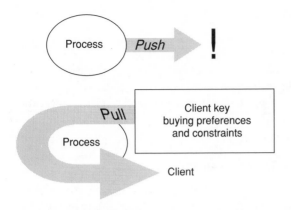

Figure 4.3 Replace the culture of software push by client pull. Work to understand customer key buying preferences as expressed by the capabilities your customers need to succeed in their business and the constraints they have to meet to survive.

If you are really keen on year-on-year indicators against which to assess your strike power, here are four. First, how much is your software costing your purchaser's business in terms of delays, failures and problems? Second, what return on investment is your purchaser obtaining from your software? (Some of you may say that your purchasers never use this indicator for themselves. This is where you need to help them, because if you do not point out the financial benefits to them of your products and services, will your competitors?) Third, what proportion of their spend available for innovation and software are they spending with you? Fourth, what ratio of total potential innovation and software spend in your designated market sector is being spent with you? The last three indicators can be normalized against your costs of product and service provision — that is delivery and support costs taken together. The first indicator cannot be normalized. Software failure is never relative, it is absolute.

4.6 RICH PICTURES

Have you thought to ask yourself how many teeth a donkey has? Would you like to make a guess? Just write down your answer below.

How did you arrive at your answer: personal knowledge of donkeys; experience with other equine animals; or a quick tally in your own mouth?

There is an apocryphal story that one day Aristotle and his students went out into the countryside and, sitting down, took for their subject of discussion the question 'How many teeth has a donkey?' They reasoned and argued for most of the morning, until one of the students spoiled all the fun by pointing to some donkeys tethered in a nearby field and suggested they go and count the teeth in a real donkey.

The meaning of purpose is not the purpose

You can spend hours in deep philosophical debate about purpose, the meaning of purpose, whether you might or might not have a purpose, and should you just happen to have a purpose, then what might that purpose reasonably be. I would be the last person to spoil your fun; so if this sort of debate works for you and helps your business, stay with it. There are many organizations who go off for two-day sessions to work on their purpose in this way.

Invite your stakeholders to purpose definition sessions

However, you may get a better return on your investment if you took some of your key stakeholders with you. Ideally, have them there with you for most of the two days. For one thing, they can experience at first hand some of the conflict and grief they may be causing you; and for another thing, it is always surprising how much people learn about each other and their needs when they are not wearing office uniform. If it is impossible to have them there all the time, then try to have them there for one of the days. This will give you a whole day to brainstorm as a group, and a whole day to put everything together. You can then present the purpose or mission back to your stakeholders later for validation.

Purpose requires a practical definition

While you have your stakeholders present, it is important that you do not get bogged down in the definition of definition. I attended one lengthy session where at least 10 managers managed to debate a two-line definition of quality for most of a day. When you debate quality, purpose or mission, debate in operational terms:

- 'Quality for me is knowing to the nearest thousand pounds how much my software will cost.'
- 'Quality for me is knowing to within two weeks when my software will arrive.'
- 'Quality for me is being able to request and get a change in two days.'
- 'Quality for me is having a clear, final sign-off.'

And so on.

Get as many of these statements out from everyone. You can either brainstorm, or have everyone write them down on cards. Then sort the cards or thoughts into issues and agree the most important six or seven to work on. Group like with like. And then, importantly, in sets which give rise to conflict. Post the cards around the room or in 'exhibition' stalls for everyone to see and to trigger their thoughts.

Purpose is not an empty umbrella statement

People can be nominated 'issue champions' to chair debates around the issues. Work through the possibilities, impossibilities, conflicts and compromises, until you have a clear picture of the process needed to bring all the issues together, and manage them successfully. This will give you an umbrella statement, if you want one. The important thing is that when it is recalled, all the source examples will be available. If you just work on an umbrella statement, or two-line definition alone, then the chances are it could be stretched to cover a multitude of sins, and there would be no reference examples against which people can test their understanding. And instead of your two-liner providing a vision of harmony and unity, it will be collapsed and used as a pointed weapon.

Purpose is made visible by Rich Pictures

Peter Checkland, in his *Soft Systems Methodology*, has introduced a useful way of developing and capturing a clear view of purpose and mission, when there are a number of competing viewpoints and when there is a need to find common ground. He calls this a Rich Picture. By drawing cartoon-like representations of what people understand and believe about the business, people can explore together their contrasting images and viewpoints, and learn to find ways forward which are relevant, feasible and systemically desirable. All the work is carried out by very careful reference to reality. This session provides an extremely useful opening for bringing out views, demonstrating that it is permissible to air conflict, and dealing with 'irrational' or vague beliefs and feelings which people find hard to put into coherent words straight away (Fig. 4.4).

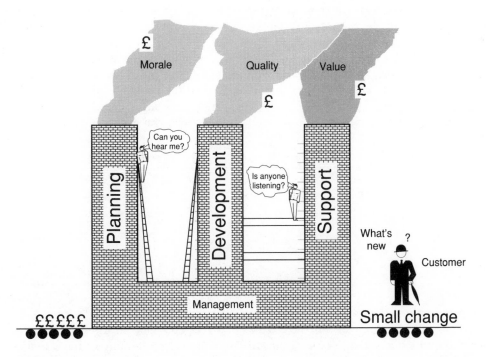

Figure 4.4 Peter Checkland's Rich Pictures are useful for visualizing the purpose and work of the organization.

Do not save talking about purpose for special events — do it all the time

The beauty of this type of session is that it does not have to be run by experts. It can be run by managers. And even better if it is. It can become a competence to be exercised in many different situations: planning meetings, team sessions, interviews, and other group events. Remembering also that meetings with stakeholders should not be just formal yearly rituals. The more often people can be encouraged to share and discuss their view of the business, the better. There are still people, even today, who think that their view of the world or the business is the only possible view which exists, and the sooner they are given the opportunity to learn that they hold just a fragment, an important fragment, nevertheless, of reality's own rich picture, so much the better for us all.

4.7 RIGHT EFFORT

What happens if, after gathering all the intelligence you can about the values and preferences of your stakeholders, you find you do not have the capability to go after them? What is going to happen if you have only a pea-shooter and a pea; how is that going to impact a Chieftain tank? How is it going to affect your business and staff? How is it going to affect your purpose and reputation?

Purpose and effort

Let us take a short break for a practice before we explore this problem some more. While you are reading these words, just let yourself become aware of your hands holding the book. Notice any tension and grip in your fingers. How far along your forearms does it extend? Perhaps you may even notice tension in your back and shoulders as you are bracing your arms to hold the book. Gradually, starting from your back and working along your shoulders to your forearms, start to release the tension. Then start to relax your hands until you have just the appropriate amount of tension and grip to support the book without letting it fall. Note any difference you experienced in the box below.

You may find it helpful to recall this practice whenever you read, brush your teeth, do the washing up, type, or pick up the telephone. By using 'right effort' you will save energy, reduce tiredness and risks of strain, freeing you to take on more of the activities you would like. 'Right effort' really means appropriate effort. It means asking what expenditure of energy and resource is appropriate to this task? Strictly speaking, there is no wrong or right effort, just appropriate, and not so appropriate, effort. Let us move on now to look at what this has to do with our capability to meet our stakeholders' preferences and values.

Matching capability and purpose

If you have a pea-shooter and a pea and you are able to use them expertly, then the question to ask is, how can you get most leverage from your capability? Look at your options. Are there any vulnerable, undefended areas you can shoot at which will have an impact? Then perhaps you can concentrate your effort in that area. Alternatively, you may decide to let your current target go, and search for other, more appropriate, targets. But do let your staff know what targets you are hunting, and how much leverage you are depending upon. Otherwise, the risk is they throw themselves and your business under a juggernaut.

If you are unhappy with your capability and you want to trade up, then you will need much more than grenades. You must not let people put grenades down pea-shooters. You will need training and safe practice for staff. You will need to change operations at a basic level. You will need new measures of success. You may need to revise your purpose.

On the other hand, you may find that you have a stockpile of sophisticated weaponry which you are not using or which you cannot afford to support. What do you do then? How do you choose which ammunition to keep and which to dispose of? Again you need to check your strike capability against your target. What is appropriate? Perhaps you have a number of targets to go for, and some weapons are right for some targets, but wrong for others. A section of your market may require small-scale and tactical approaches, another, large-scale and strategic. You need a well-defined approach for each. It is too costly to throw everything at both targets in the hope that you should strike lucky on average.

Maximizing capability to achieve purpose

Often suppliers drop products and services from their portfolio because they are too costly to deliver. Suppliers will typically carry out a Pareto analysis on the grounds that 80 per cent of their costs will be accounted for by 20 per cent of their products and services. They will then reduce their portfolio on this basis. They say their purpose is to become more focused. However, if this exercise is carried out year-on-year, with no new additions to your portfolio, you have become a business whose purpose is to devour itself. You will always have a trail of products and services which are relatively more costly to deliver than others.

Let us look at this another way: if it is too costly to apply your tools, necessary standards and methodologies to the delivery of small-scale projects, do you drop the small-scale projects to concentrate on large-scale projects only, or do you drop the tools, standards and methodologies? Is this truly an 'either-or' dilemma? Is it not the fact that things are too costly — in the current delivery system? We need to ask: in what system would they not be so costly? What would the process have to be like to produce these goods and services cost-effectively? If the tools, methodologies and standards are really necessary — by which I mean the value to all your stakeholders would be reduced if any were dropped — then you need to ask yourself under what conditions would they be appropriate to small-scale projects. And if we can imagine new processes which give us cost-effectiveness where we did not have it before, why not design and use those processes for all products, services and large-scale projects? Imagine the saving and leverage you could gain.

Regularly review your capability to match purpose

But do you know what you have buried in your munitions dump? What skills are available for you to draw on? What tools, and experience? Most organizations run annual stock-checks? Do you? How else can you judge the viability of your purpose and the efficiency of your strike power? Like stakeholder intelligence, you need to keep stock within the business and create an operation to ensure this knowledge is available for people to draw on from your experience base. It is the only way you will ever know how many pea-shooters there are up in the hills.

4.8 A LIVING HAND

Throughout this book we talk of processes: management processes and production processes. The management operation for deciding and communicating purpose to the organization and for providing policies and rules, is critical to both management and production processes. The challenge is how are you going to design this critical operation within the context of your organization? How are you to communicate your purpose to everyone and in what form? How will you create channels to feedback potential problems? How will you communciate that you have reached the top of your mountain and have to move on to the next, or equally, that you have to abandon this attempt, and try again?

Communicating purpose

Let us just consider this. We could have an annual meeting of all staff, at which the purpose is delivered by the CEO. We could issue a newsletter. We could have cascade briefing sessions. All of these are very good methods for communication. But there are problems. No matter how clearly we communicate purpose by these methods, if there are other documents or instructions which appear to conflict or override them, it will all have been a waste of time, enthusiasm, and money. So, what other instructions could possibly exist to sabotage your best-laid plans? Your budget and your order schedules.

Everyday priorities are the purpose seen by everyone

Budgets and order schedules are the realities of everyone's day-to-day existence. All else, particularly if it is seen to be contradicted by these plans, will be ignored, or at worst, be regarded as a source of dark humour. But this is not bad — we can perhaps use this to a positive advantage. Assuming that we are not going to be spending money just for the fun of it. Assuming that our spend will be linked to leveraging our capability to impact our stakeholders positively. Assuming that our order scheduling will reflect the same purpose. Assuming our budgets and schedules are properly discussed and the assumptions on which they are based are documented and that they are the subject of regular review (and by regular, I mean more frequently than yearly), then what better instruments could be available for communicating purpose? Just one more. The production process on the ground which has been designed to achieve the budgets and orders.

Use existing operations to communicate purpose

You do not necessarily have to create special add-on processes to communicate purpose which will be left wilting around the edge of the business like unwanted wallflowers. Use your existing planning cycles. But there has to be change for this to work.

First, everybody needs to be aware of, and understand, the purpose which is being supported by budgeted investments. This means everybody needs to make a contribution to the budget plan in response to an understanding of the purpose, clearly stating the assumptions which they are making. Everybody needs to know costs and how they themselves directly contribute to costs. By everybody, I mean everybody. Do not forget the secretaries, juniors, cleaners or trainees. Everyone should be involved in reviewing budgets and costs on a regular basis — say, monthly — with their peers and manager. Problems with costs and budgets need to be played back against the original assumptions, and the need for changes understood. Do not sweep problems under the carpet. The costs that are being run up are real news from the real world. Look at what needs to be changed, the map or the territory, and at what level. If you find that you are always changing the map, or always changing the territory, you have a problem. Changes to both should be a fairly regular occurrence.

Second, there has to be a map. You need to have a production or delivery process which links to the budget and schedule plans. As you continue reading this book, you will be taken through the detail of how to design and build such a process. For now, let us just work through a simplified example of how we can use existing planning cycles to communicate purpose.

An example of communicating purpose

In response to your stakeholders' key preferences for reduced lead and cycle times, and their need for reliable software, the management team formulates the business purpose: 'to provide responsive delivery of software products and services to the existing market while maintaining or improving reliability'. You may choose not to express your purpose officially in these words. In fact, you may use a metaphor or Rich Picture to symbolize your purpose.

Next, having examined a number of different routes up this mountain, you decide the reuse path is your best option for taking you to the top. You have timed your purpose formulation operation to coincide with your existing budget and resource planning cycle. The question of 'how' has next to be discussed, and the options for the organization as a whole examined. Looking at the gap between existing capability and the capability you need, you have decided to improve the existing process by creating repository operations. Notice as you work at this level, you are constrained to be mindful of the existing process, and the impacts of these new operations on the process. As a consequence, you have had to draft policies and guidelines for optimizing process performance with additional repository operations. The policies and guidelines surface extra costs in terms of development of staff competencies and new administrative procedures.You then discuss your plan with staff. For the new operations and their links to existing operations, staff listed costs and the assumptions underlying their estimates. At this stage when you are made aware of potential difficulties, some costly hot spots were identified, and the total need for training, tools, and administration were surfaced and documented. This feedback in terms of costs and assumptions was returned to you to evaluate, discuss, and challenge. (Notice the similarity between these activities, which are linked to enhancing a process, and between the activities with which you are probably more familiar — those of providing costings for enhanced products and services to your customers.) Visibility of the plan is now being sustained by frequent review, much the same as existing project management and performance review operations.

Benefits of communicating purpose through resource allocation

The benefits of this approach are clear. We are clearly focused on practical and specific process improvement which has been costed and budgeted for in advance. The emphasis is on business as usual, we have not suggested that anyone is incompetent for not having implemented a repository before. We cut bureaucracy in planning cycles by reducing the number of separate items and operations in the organization which have to be considered and balanced — although we may increase the frequency of planning operations, cycle time should be reduced overall, because information is current, in continual use, and is not being creatively massaged to match conflicting management demands. Everyone is involved and can see their and other people's parts and contribution. Confusion is reduced because there is only one set of books. People get used to change occurring, but are not perturbed, because there is a management process for change which can be anticipated and in which they themselves play a part. You should not be surprised by requests for extraordinary resource demands — these should all have been accounted for in the plan, and any changes can be handled by a standard operation. Most importantly, your plan is effective. It gets carried forward into practice. It is a living hand.

Purpose is undermined by uncoordinated improvement

Just contrast this to a typical TQM scenario where everybody is exhorted to improve. There is no common consensus on which mountain has to be climbed to satisfy stakeholders' needs. Everyone runs with their own ideas, everyone is trying to improve everything all at once and the focus is very diffused. People write problem reports which, because they are called 'problem' reports are an embarrassment to managers. There are many improvement plans doing the rounds, with everyone trying to involve and communicate with everyone else. All of this demands unscheduled resources and time. Only ad hoc budgets for time or money are available and they will have to be justified on an expensive case-by-case basis. As a consequence there are usually severe clashes between priorities. How can we carry out normal work and unscheduled improvements? How do our improvements impact the ones being carried out simultaneously by others? If there is a Quality Council, is it constituted in such a way that it can diagnose suboptimization? How do we know that it works? All in all, this looks like a process for weakening an organization, when it is probably going through a hard time already.

Purpose — the key message

In summary we can say that purpose is the thread of daily life that guides us from a secure past to an uncertain future. While our eyes are on the stars, make sure there is always a clear marking on the road under our feet for the times when the lights go out. Keep purpose visible, always matching stakeholder needs, and weave it into day-to-day procedures and practices.

5

IDENTIFYING KEY OPERATIONS

The whole object of travel is not to set foot on foreign land. It is at last to set foot on one's own country as a foreign land.

G. K. Chesterton

In this chapter we shall examine the individual management operations which provide the basic building blocks of the software delivery process. We shall take a broad management view of the following management operations: stakeholder; client; product; service; requirements and V&V; design; process; configuration; change; capability; business; cost and purchasing.

Businesses crystallize management functions around bundles of key problems, such as finance, resource management, and service delivery. Because these have developed as organizational functions, with all the associated empire-building and fortification, the necessary mesh of interrelated decision-making has been severed, and vital communication between the functions is lost or is slowed down to a deep groan by all the entailed bureaucracy. Indeed the more difficulties we experience at the interfaces, the more legislation we invoke to settle contractual disputes. Unfortunately all this legislation fuels more litigation, resulting in the organization's becoming more and more inward-facing, reducing its ability to respond to external changes and survive.

Break out of this cycle by replacing rigid organizational functions with fluid and responsive team-based operations designed by management to facilitate the delivery of products and services as they are demanded by the clients. If you are self-employed, then at any time there will be a team of only one, but you will still need to manage all the key operations I describe. If you have a large and complex organization, you will need to rethink your functional division of labour. By all means retain your experts, but pull down their walls. Design and consensus up front by all involved parties saves expensive and time-consuming ping-pong style decision-making. Section 10.3 explains some of the horrors of this common practice.

5.1 ORGANIZATIONAL DYNAMICS

I shall make the rather bald statement that the purpose of the human body is to perpetuate life. To achieve that purpose, the body requires several vital operations, such as those provided by blood-pumping, organ-cleansing, food-digesting, and balance-keeping organs. Similarly, organizations develop operations to perpetuate their own existence. Some operations are like hearts and brains, others, like tonsils or appendix.

Organization evolution and adaptation

The human body has been subjected to tens of thousands of years of evolutionary development, and we now have a very well-adapted, specialized organ for carrying out the operation of pumping blood: the heart. In more primitive organisms there is no blood to pump. But this is not to say the human body is superior to a virus, as you will know if you have had 'flu this year. All it means is that each organism has the capability of dealing with specific problems in its environment and its own internal constitution, and has developed special organs to deal with those problems. No two organizations will have the same pattern of operations. What is important is that they have the appropriate operations to succeed in their environment. Take care when you decide to re-engineer your organization on someone else's model — the fins may work fine, but where are your gills?

Organizational archaeology

Like the ancient city of Troy, with its levels of different civilisations built one on top of the other, when we look at our organization and its structure we are looking at a visible record of our mechanisms for responding to problems and changes in technology, not only in the present, but also in the past. Businesses crystallize their management functions around bundles of key problems, or 'fuzzy' situations, which demand active decision-taking. In Sec. 10.2 we shall see how business success grows not just by the repetition of past activities, but also by the proactive choice of innovative opportunity situations. If there is neither choice nor opportunity for change, decision-makers are not needed. So, if we are to set out and look for key management operations, then we need to know what sort of problems and choices are present here and now for us, as opposed to what problems existed in the past, or for other companies. Section 5.2 outlines these software delivery problem areas.

Organizational learning — position, plan, perform, package, and purge

Because organizations have the capacity for learning, problems and choices are packaged and 'digested'. This means that, when perhaps there was once a need for a specialist group to take decisions in response to a new, emerging problem, if the problem continues to be present and is fairly widespread, the business should learn and adapt, and the skills become dispersed, decentralized, and perhaps, automated. In this way, how and what the

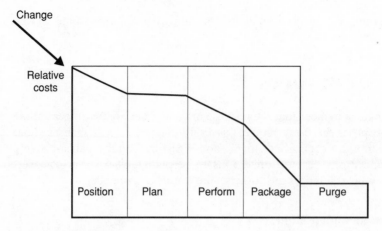

Figure 5.1 The organizational learning cycle. The business is constantly having to position itself to deal with change. It can only continue to do this effectively if there is a means in the organization of assimilating and packing change into processes. In some instances purging or out-sourcing may be required.

organization has learnt becomes visible. What were once specialist operations become competencies or systems for experts. The specialist operation can then be removed. If problems persist, it means that the competencies are somehow inappropriate to the problem, and recentralization to a specialist operation may occur. A prime example is that given by TQM theory. Initially there is focus on the quality problems. A quality manager is appointed but with a view to transferring the operation to management competencies usually within two to three years followed by disbanding the quality management function. At the extreme, certain problems will be spat out. The organization decides that the problem is a foreign body, and all associated operations and competencies are sold off or out-sourced (Fig. 5.1).

Organizational viability

We have to beware then of confusing competencies with operations — the balance will differ from organization to organization. We have to beware also of confusing operations with functional groups. Sometimes it is useful to set up groups specifically to deal with certain operations, sometimes it can be a disaster. Operations are important, but more important are the web-like decision-making relationships between operations (Fig. 5.2). Create wide divides across the business and you pour time, effort, value, and quality into the gaps.

Some organizations have recently uncoupled the software delivery process. We have moved from product or client groups to distinct functional silos — planning, development, and service or support. But the degree of coupling of information between them is far too high, and we have been made to feel the pain of the problem. We have sought to remedy it, in some cases, by making each of the functions a business entity in its own right, severing even more connections. However, as they stand, these functions cannot be viable entities. They cannot be made to be self-contained.

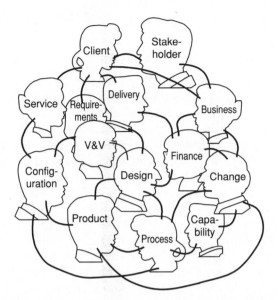

Figure 5.2 The interdependent web of key software operations. Whether they are distinct groups of people or competencies, their need to interwork defies a hierarchical organization chart.

The green field approach to re-engineering

I am assuming that the features of your organization have to some extent already been formed, and that when you look at it, it does not resemble a flat, green field. But, if you do have a green field then you may like to discover the forces that will mould your terrain. Just supposing you were commissioned to landscape a garden, what knowledge would you require to assist you in that task? The trees and plants preferred by your clients? The ideal layout of the garden? An up-to-date plan of the land? Details of climatic conditions? Anything else?

When people start to examine the opportunities for re-engineering their processes, they are keen to take a green field view of the organization. They do not want to take account of the cultural upheavals that have moulded the organizational landscape over the years. To do so would mean a certain surrender to those forces of chaos at work in the organization they are dedicated to removing. The first impulse is to withdraw behind closed doors and devise a map of the ideal territory.

People in a green field

Of course, word eventually leaks out, and very soon the whole organization knows that it is going to be rolled flat and returfed. So the seeds of anxiety and resentment are sown. What do these 'planners', or whoever they happen to be, know about the real world? Immediately, resistance starts to grow. How much better or worse will it be when you roll the turf out? Hardly a bed of roses, for sure.

Are you planning to roll out astroturf? Are you going to grow your own turf from seed, or buy in turf from specialists? Are you going to roll out all the turf at once, or just a square at a time? What will be the consequences of all these decisions in your organization?

Re-engineer management operations before production operations

Another first impulse is to start by re-engineering the production process, because this is a very tangible and interesting process. The thinking is that if we can get the production process mapped, then everything will fall into place around that. From my experience in the field I would say that most production processes are fairly well adapted — staff do what is necessary to expedite products and services. The major factors contributing to distortion and inefficiencies in the production process are management operations.

This means that if you create or buy that fresh green turf to roll out, it could be spoiled in a number of weeks by the resident moles, invasive natural flora, parched subsoil, acid rain, and all the environmental conditions that were present before. You can affect some of these conditions, but not all. I am not saying that you should not bother to do anything. But I am saying identify the conditions. Know which ones you can affect and which ones you cannot. Start work on the ones you can affect, so that the environment is better for growing grass. When you have eliminated the choking weeds and cleared away all the rubbish people have left behind, your own grass will begin to flourish, and maybe you will not need to do so much returfing after all.

Whatever you do, remember to start with the management processes first. Leave your staff in peace to get on with their jobs as you start to carry out the exercise, no matter how much you would like, for whatever nostalgic reasons of your own, to get your hands on to the production process. Both you and your staff can work on the production process later, but they cannot do anything at all about your management process, except wilt or grow wild.

5.2 KEY MANAGEMENT OPERATIONS

Our hunt for key management operations starts by looking at software management problems and mechanisms which have been applied in many organizations to solve those problems, since we can expect that there is a general set of operations relevant to the industry as a whole. The important thing to remember is that these are operations. They do not have to be constituted as separate functions, groups, or individuals. They may be competences or packages, or be wired directly into the process. In fact, it is how effectively your business organizes its operations to address problems and opportunities which affects competitive advantage.

Stakeholder management

In Secs 1.5 and 4.2 we realized the necessity for considering, weighing, and balancing the claims of not just one customer, but a number of stakeholders. In the past, when we have tried to focus on a single customer or customer representative, we have found ourselves in the middle of cross waves, with calls on our attention coming to us from several different directions. It is not surprising, then, that we have been tossed about in the wash, and sometimes ship-wrecked.

Stakeholder management is centred upon deciding who the stakeholders are and will be. For all but the most simple of businesses, there has to be a continuous proactive search for stakeholders, a proactive search for all areas of real or potential conflict, and a proactive approach to identifying and settling conflicting stakeholder demands on the business. The number and type of stakeholders to be taken into consideration will vary from organization to organization. Here are a few examples which may be important to you: the purchaser; the user of your product or services; the Inland Revenue; the laws of the land; standards bodies; carriers of products or services; your competitors; your suppliers; society at large and the environment; future purchasers; future users; and so on. The more dynamically you can read and adjust your course to stakeholder demands, the more you will be able to stave off the inevitable shock waves of sea change and save your ship and all who sail in her from capsizing.

The stakeholder management operation is at the cutting edge of the business process, and requires both far-sightedness and focus. It is not enough to see the problems between Scylla and Charybdis ahead, you have to negotiate and detail a peace between them to clear a safe passage for you and your crew. And you need to communicate the situation very clearly back to your crew so that you do not have one group hauling up the sheets and another hauling them down again.

Any decisions taken as a result of stakeholder operations will impact business and client management. Business management is affected because information netted by stakeholder management operations may signal the need to consider changes to the business direction. Similarly a change in business direction may point to new horizons for stakeholder searches. Decisions made by these operations may also have to be linked to client management to ensure the client, their values, and requirements are kept informed of current and future circumstances which could impact them and your partnership.

Client management

The need for this key operation appears so obvious that it seems superfluous to talk about it. Yet, very few of the quality assessment bodies mention concern for client management, so perhaps it may just be overlooked in the rush to acquire standards accreditation. The client is the party whose decision affects if, and how much, you are paid. Where more than one stakeholder has this power, you need to treat all the parties as your clients. Failure to do so, failure to resolve conflicts between the parties and yourself, or playing one party off against another will end in tears.

Client management is like a marriage. A marriage between your business and theirs. It is difficult to keep a marriage going if you do not spend some time living together. You need not only to understand your client's requirements, but also to understand them from your client's position. What are their business pressures? What are their stakeholder demands? It is only by walking frequently, and sometimes for long periods, in their moccasins, that you can develop empathy and insight. Insight that will help you identify more opportunities for increasing value to your customers, and for becoming a more valued supplier.

It is not just a case of harvesting annual satisfaction surveys. We need to understand the active and latent requirements of customers. What are they reading? What sort of other software do they use? What user interfaces have they? What are their opinions on what they use? We can build up a profile of these positive needs in our experience base (Sec. 2.6) either in database, spreadsheet or quality function deployment format (Sec. 6.4).

Very often a single account manager is assigned to a client to expedite their requirements and this is deemed to be client management. This is only part of the operation, an important part, but not all the operation. In practice an operation is needed which coordinates tours of duty between key staff in your business and your client's business (while remembering that your client may be several disparate parties). By key staff, I mean software engineers, testers, and help-desk staff, for example, as well as product managers. The more information and insight you can obtain from all levels of their business, the better positioned you are to create new ways of doing business together. It is also healthy for your staff to get to know each other. There is nothing wrong with setting up direct contact between clients and your staff, if your clients need or want that access. However, the relationships have to be managed and you do need an administered central clearing house for all information relevant to your clients. Staff visiting clients are briefed before they go, and staff returning are debriefed and all the information is made available to staff who need it. When the client's contact is confined to a single gate-keeper, the account manager, then there are risks that the marriage, as a business partnership, will degenerate into a folie à deux, as representatives from both sides become locked into static 'group-think'. Avoid this situation.

Client management needs to be particularly well informed of the impact of other stakeholders on the client when services and delivery expectations are being developed. On the other hand stakeholder management needs to be lobbied on a regular basis to ensure that the client's needs are not being traded off in favour of more bureaucratic business claims. If necessary, stakeholder management should lobby other stakeholders on the client's behalf. Similarly if clients are unable to balance their own stakeholder demands, between commissioning agent and end user, say, then it may be to your benefit to provide assistance to them. The decision-making links between client and change and business management have to be maintained so that provisions for creating new products or retiring old products can be planned and resourced.

Depending on how you have set up your organization, your client management operations may encompass requirements, and service management. If this is not the case then the strong decision-making links need to be recognized in practice.

I shall just single out the decision-making link between client management and service management, since links to requirements management are fairly clear. Client management is so often seen as the other end of the tail to service management. However, your process is like a Celtic serpent, it has a tail in its mouth. The intelligence gleaned by service management cannot be wasted, it needs to be recycled to inform client, change, and requirements management. Most of the feedback on the software you have provided to your client will return via service management operations. Although some of this information will be difficult to swallow, it is a valuable indicator of what is being done right and where opportunities are present for improving delivery logistics.

Product management

A project delivers a product or a service successfully. What happens next? The project team disbands, perhaps one or two members are seconded to a service group to provide on-going support, but often it is the end of the line. Once handed over to the customer, the product ceases to be an asset and becomes a growing liability. Given an anticipated lifetime of seven years, the costs to service and support that product were, in one organization where I worked, four times the delivery costs. There are organizations who are now running software which is twenty years' old, and the support costs are seven to eight times the original delivery costs, even allowing for inflation.

The traditional thinking is that software, unlike widgets, does not wear out and is infinitely malleable, therefore it can be patched and changed almost indefinitely. Software may not wear out, but its fabric becomes more and more stressed and weakened by the application of patches it was never designed to withstand, and eventually failure, particularly unpredictable failure, is inevitable. After a widget or a car has been signed off the production line for a number of months, changes are made to the design and product variants replace the original product. Eventually the car is rebuilt with all the new designs and extras built in as standard, and a new model is launched. We know that when a software product is delivered, it is likely to be in use for several years. But do we set aside any provisions for the product's lifetime? Do we have any general strategies for cost control based on preventive maintenance or proactive redesign? Generally, no. The only long-term cost controls are made reactively, long after design decisions have been implemented.

Design for the product's projected lifetime needs to be carried out as part of product specification and design. The costs to buy and the costs to use, or the costs to deliver and the costs to support, if it is a service which is being provided, require careful analysis. Strategies for carrying out preventive maintenance and periodic re-engineering have to be considered in conjunction with design management operations, so that the most cost-effective product and production process design options are chosen.

To see the delivered products and services as long-term assets, you need to see them as collections of usable components which can provide fast starts to new projects. This requires design for asset formation. What is the best way of designing this product to create a generic platform, or generic components for use by future projects? We need very simple components with the capability for being plugged into a variety of interfaces.

Service management

The problems for service management are: costing future implications of decisions taken in the present; providing assurances for delivered software; agreeing client service levels; and estimating service and support costs.

Service management is in the difficult position of having to underwrite and assume accountability for work that it has not personally produced. This has always been a stumbling block. When costs have to be cut, the first place to look for reductions is in the service management area. This is like chopping off the fingers of your left hand to avoid the pain caused when your right hand slammed them in the door. Service management is not responsible for all the entailed costs of service provision. Much of that cost depends heavily on the reliability of the software passed to it. Costs of servicing problematic software are the responsibility of the business as a whole, since those costs have been created by the collective decision-making of the business.

Because of its position at the tail of the process, service management is best placed for feeding back details of problems to requirements and design management, so that together the decisions which gave rise to the problems can be reviewed and made more effective and less costly, and better value decisions may be taken for both the customer and the business in the future. Each problem in live running has to be dealt with as it occurs, and changes made to the source operations. Feeding back information after three-, or six-month intervals is not effective. The motivation to change when the situation has cooled will be minimal. What is more, the delay usually results in the imposition of out-of-phase standards and operations.

Service management tends to be the conservative force in the organization, simply because the job is often so fraught. One might argue that if all the tests were carried out which would quiet service management, products and services would never get through the door. However, there are alternatives to client management riding roughshod over the judgement of service management, or 'risk managing' delivery, and that is to take their judgement on board, and work together as a team with design and process management to find out how the product or service can be designed cost effectively for testability, and how service management operations can be made more effective.

Requirements and V&V management

I have deliberately linked these two operations together. I see the problems of requirements management as twofold. First, to elicit and structure requirements in such a way that their feasibility in terms of benefits to the client and to the business can be assessed and optimized; and secondly, to ensure that delivered products and services meet those requirements and that appropriate customer assurances can be provided. We are embedding the 'V' model into our process.

Requirements management, together with design management, is at the front end of asset formation. How new work is quarried and sectioned impacts the future profitability and effectiveness of the business. Every request for new work affords the opportunity to fund a new generic product or service platform which could earn revenue from the same or new clients in the future. Even if you have only a single client, if you are responsible for providing on-going service and support, then no development is a one-off development. Adaptation of the product or service over its useful lifetime to meet your client's changing needs entails creating variants of your existing software. This can be done profitably, or not so profitably. It is important, then, that a decision is taken at the outset by requirements management and design management on whether to build a new product or service platform, whether to develop a variant of an existing platform, or whether patches to existing products will reduce asset value.

Customer requirements are well known for their lack of cohesiveness and organization. Working closely with design management, requirements management informs clients of current best value solutions which the business can supply to meet their needs, and, working with process management, designs better ways of capturing customer requirements, such as customer auto-definition of requirements, or better ways of designing the delivery process to cope with emerging or fuzzy requirements.

All quality management systems agree that there have to be adequate and proper verification and validation (V&V) operations. V&V has to be set up as an independently reporting body to ensure that the proper checks and balances are in place.

It is possible to build enormous organizational infrastructures to support V&V. You have only to look at the operational guides for conducting code inspections to realize that we have potentially built a factory which could be as large as, if not larger than, the development factory itself. I am not arguing for the removal of V&V operations, but rather for operations which would make the work of V&V less onerous. There is a difference between re-engineering operations and chopping them. The question I keep asking is: how can we design our process to achieve more verifiable products and services? By simplification, by suitable partitioning, by reusing components which have already had effort invested in their verification, by small incremental deliveries, and so on. We know that the chances of error and effort to test increase with complexity. Why do all compilers not provide complexity measures as standard? We know that coupling and cohesion affect design complexity — do your CASE tools have in-built coupling and cohesion indicators? When we know requirements are fuzzy and are likely to continue so, do we change our design rules for coupling and accommodate the fuzziness by isolating all the risky unknowns together in a limited number of components? Are test performance data associated with components so that vulnerable items can be identified? Much more use could be made of data which are a by-product of automated operations to provide verification data for the purposes of independent assessment and customer assurance. We are inspecting components not just to ensure that they work, but also to ensure that all critical success factors, not just safety, security, and reliability, are still being met. By linking together requirements operations and V&V operations we establish a network of assurance with direct links to the client. We ensure that requirements are stated in a testable form. If products and services pass those tests and fail to meet the customer needs, responsibility is clearly with requirements operations to improve. We also ensure that all V&V operations are requirements driven, and do not become an arcane end in themselves.

But it is only by more proactive product design for reuse that we can start to assure software more rapidly. Having a library of tested subroutines increases productivity. Having libraries of tested utilities improves productivity. Exploiting the effort already invested in well-designed product and service components will give us the next increase in productivity.

Design management

Design management operations are concerned with converting the key buying preferences, expressed by the client, into software characteristics expressed in software engineering terms. Design management has to work on deriving maximum value from available resources while meeting all the stakeholder constraints imposed upon software production. The problem is to engineer new ways of producing software which progressively reduce costs while increasing the value of products and services in the client's eyes.

Because we have been largely performance oriented and concerned with getting the software out of the door, and tested somehow, the way we have gone about designing products and services, and the delivery process also, has been ad hoc, subject to personal feelings or inclination. While still keeping our eye on performance, we need to bring into focus the considerations of conscious product and process design to establish and control the value of our products and services. Design management concentrates attention on one objective — equivalent lifetime performance for lower cost.

Design management has implications for the organization as a whole, since if the organization has not been designed to support production tasks, the business can only produce less than optimum performance or inflate costs. In which case, opportunities for competitive advantage are lost. At the level of product and process management, decisions taken on how the software is to be built, and the effectiveness of design and engineering approaches to build the software introduce or reduce costs. When there is no continuity in product or process management, costs remain inflated and suboptimum, because there is no vehicle for packaging acquired experience into the process.

Standard estimation packages show how changes to the process and its capability affect costs and schedules. Instead of accepting these extra costs and delays, it makes sense to design and engineer the delivery process. But first we have to map process and operations, and become aware of their effects on costs and competitiveness.

Process management

The difficulty with process management is that it is a double-decker set of operations. On the ground, it is concerned with the software delivery process, and, above ground, with the interaction of all the key management processes and their impact on the delivery process. Process management is the carrier that provides routeing, transport, and tracking of your client's requirements through your organization, into a functioning reality on their front doorstep. Process management decides whether it is more advantageous for the client's requirements to be dispatched in one consignment or in several, or whether there is to be a single-stream linear process, or a process composed of concurrent operations. Accountability for process management is door to door, from the customer, back to the customer. Process management is the impetus in the organization to reduce delivery lead times constantly. However, speed records are not to be achieved by steam-rollering and bringing business and production operations to a halt. Instead, process management has to explore alternative routes that are capable of providing the safest, surest, fastest delivery speed within the organization's capability. In short, the quest is to deliver products fast without blowing up the customer or the business.

Process management has a close relationship with requirements and service management operations. Requirements management ensures the process stays on the right rails by designing and providing all the necessary verification and validation instrumentation. Service management is the proxy voice of the future and provides an assessment of costs to service and support the software based upon proposed delivery options, and the capabilities demanded by any special tools, methods, and techniques which process management introduces.

Process management requires continuity. Changes have to be carefully rooted and monitored, improvements encouraged, and learning harvested and preserved. By building on the repertoire of existing delivery operations and by designing new options, process management 'composes' the delivery process from a set of components with reliable cycle times. The process is not built from scratch each time, which would create a high-risk delivery option, nor is a single rigid methodology imposed. Operations are reviewed and re-engineered to ensure that maximum capability is always achieved.

Process operations are a fundamental learning asset of the organization. People at work make mistakes, solve problems, and acquire experience. They do not want to make mistakes or to reinvent the wheel — they want to be surer of their chances of success. The only way to accomplish this is to use tried and tested operations. At the same time, staff repertoire is extended by incremental, planned programmes of process development.

Process management needs a view from the top. Whenever suboptimization affects the delivery process, a means of examining and rebalancing the key management operations has to exist. At this level, process management is more of a competence, and process-based decision-making should be a skill of all senior and middle managers.

Configuration management

It is very tempting to see configuration management as an operation within product management, however I have pulled it out for two reasons. First, configuration management is highlighted as an operation in its own right by quality management systems, and secondly, there are other business assets apart from products which need to be subject to configuration management. Tests, test packages, requirements, documentation, hardware, and data components should all be put under configuration management. Products and services are combinations of components. When the combination of components or the content of the components differs slightly from the standard or original then we have, to all intents and purposes, a new product. We would probably not call it a new product but a product variant. The role of configuration management is to enable traceability of all products and services, their variants and status, and to ensure that the correct components are delivered to clients. Major quality problems arise when we lose track of which clients are to have which components, when we combine incompatible sets of components, or when the status of all the components is not the same, for example when tested components are combined with untested components.

If we can provide this service for our clients, then we can also do ourselves a big favour by providing the same support for our own production architectures. This means, for instance, that process management has a direct link to configuration management to enable us to track which combination of operations was used by the delivery process to produce a certain product or service. What combination of tools, methods, and people was employed? This means that we can proactively track and improve process and operation components as well as future process design and engineering methods. It is not just the products and services that we build which are assets, but also the experience which goes into their production. When that information is lost we can make few reliable predictions about our process, and we are confined to the bottom of a learning curve.

Change management

If the world continued to be the same day after day then there would be little need for any change management operations. However, the winds of change forever gust new challenges which have to be survived. Our response to change can be measured on the Beaufort scale. At 0 the steam rises vertically from our coffee as we sit back, feet on desks; at 4 the dust starts to rise, and bits of paper blow round on the desk; at 6 there is a definite whistling, if not ranting, in the telephone wires; at 8 progress is impeded; and at 10 there is considerable structural damage. How we respond to change, how frequently, and at what level, has a direct impact on the efficiency and effectiveness of the business.

You can nail everything to the floor, and just hope that the wind never becomes a hurricane. You can leave everything lose and airborne and not worry about having to rebuild from the ground up after every gale. Your strategy will depend very much on your own local climatic conditions. However, you must have a strategy, and you must have practice in responding to change. Change infrequently and only in response to major threats and you may find your structure is too inflexible or slow to shift when it becomes necessary, and people are too tied down by their position and possessions to abandon them readily. Change frequently and people will come to adapt to and accommodate change, but continual turbulence may prevent you from building up any assets. Change management operations are designed to channel the power of the new. Change has to be communicated and harmonized on a regular basis so that the organization can maintain its balance and continue to perform effectively. Shifts in customer preferences and values may need to be synchronized with technical changes to hardware and software platforms, which, in turn, may need to be linked to organizational and process changes. The operations for rolling out change, exploiting all the benefits of the change, and resolving all the problems which arise (and not just sweeping them under the carpet) are essential. Too often changes are unleashed upon the organization and then left to blow around wherever the wind takes them, wreaking havoc on existing practices. 'Suck it and see' tactics demonstrate an absence of management design. Survival of the fittest is a tautology. The theory of evolution simply stated is, 'We're here because we're here.' Unless we believe in a greater intent for us, then survival is little more than accident. In business there has to be an intent to survive, to stick with the change, and to secure it completely into the fabric of the organization by designing it into the process. Change has to be negotiated, designed, and implemented to match business needs. It will be constrained by costs and human resource management.

Capability management

Although I shall discuss human resource management in detail here, I think it is important that we bring under one umbrella in our business those operations which are concerned with the management of all resources — tools and people. This is simply because a change in tools requires a change in people. I think the tendency has been to keep the two separate because we do not expect human resource personnel, or finance personnel for that matter, to appreciate the technicalities of our work. I would like to see software specialists having the opportunity to move into human resource management and training and to take their skills with them. There are many aspects to human resource management, so I shall limit myself to just those that have a direct impact on process-oriented software production such as effective staff deployment, skills management, and performance reward.

I sometimes feel that human resource management, like quality management, is seen as just another group of staff specialists, a necessary but only just tolerated burden on the organization. If it were not for the fact that no one else would particularly like to take on some of the necessary, but basically daunting, tasks of understanding employee legislation, administering staff benefits, and company car schemes, then they could easily find themselves marginalized. And like all marginalized groups intent on survival, there is a tendency to create new universes of bureaucracy to perpetuate their right to existence.

I am not sure of the benefit of everyone having five pages of job description which have to be written, checked, validated, externally reviewed, filed, and kept up to date but which never reflect the real work on the ground. Job descriptions improve no one's understanding, and lead to unnecessary entrenchment in unnecessary tasks. I am not sure about the benefit of training courses which are delivered too soon, too late, not at all, or follow training fashions rather than being linked to the process. I am not sure about the benefits of rewarding individual performance when no one truly accomplishes anything without the help of others, except by blindly forwarding their own priorities. And why do we insist that half our staff perform not as well as the other half? As the production process and operations have to change, so the shift in task orientation has to change. Why fetter our response with the administrative overhead of rewriting job descriptions? Better to map the process and operations, and to make staff accountable for the procedures entailed by the process and operations. When operations change, people's tasks change. There is just one blueprint to which everyone works. What are the skills required by the process, procedures, and tools? By the future needs of the organization? Where are the skill gaps? Coaching and training have to be designed to fit the needs of the people working on the process. Why reward people for doing more or going faster, when the effect is to throw other operations and perhaps even the whole off balance? Rewards have to be more subtle, linked to team cooperation and to the improvement and balance of the process as a whole. Human resource management is too important to be left segregated as a generalist, separate function. It needs to be reinstated as a management competence on the understanding that the driving priority is the need of the delivery process as it has been designed.

Business management

The business management operation has a number of faces. One looks to the outside world, another inward at the people, resources, and the process employed. There is also one looking backwards and intent on saving face at all costs, and sometimes another, looking forwards, ready to respond with an appropriate expression.

Looking outwards, one of the functions of the business management operation is to stand as arbitrator between stakeholder and client manager operations, to determine policies for resolving conflict, and, as a last resort, to resolve conflict. Your purpose informs and is informed by client and stakeholder management operations. Both these operations provide early warning signals of changes in the environment which are likely to affect the business mission. The earlier and clearer those signals and your readiness to listen, the longer the lead time you have to equip yourself for change and survival.

When you need to change course because of external factors, then you need to look inward and communicate change very clearly through change and cost management operations. Change management operations encompass both technical change and organizational change operations. It may be that in your organization you have separated the two to distance yourself from some of the detail. However, their decision-making practices need to be very closely synchronized to ensure that they are well balanced and operate in harmony. Changes to product or service lines, changes in the client market, changes in the balance of stakeholder claims, and changes in the organization's fortunes will all impact how you orient and equip yourself for business. Very simply then, the problem of business management operations is one of dynamic positioning. Like a Chinese dragon, you have to be able to change direction quickly and smoothly, relying on a flexible and willing corporate body to follow your steps. The steps are: position, plan, perform, and package — you must take a lead in the choreography. The measure of your success is how well you can keep the dance together, without tripping up, while always maintaining a position to face and delight your market.

Cost management

The natural relationship between cost management and software development is rather like a nanny and an irresponsible child. Nanny imposes rather strict and seemingly arbitrary rules; child creates all the dodges to wriggle free and continue more enjoyable activities. At best there is a tacit acceptance or condonation of opposing roles. At worst there are tears and frustration at the end of the day.

The role of cost management is to keep process operations focused on the current market values commanded by their services and products. If costs are allowed to increase beyond those values, then the business is heading towards loss and failure. This is a real fact of life. The budgets and resource-planning activities exist to provide not a tedious exercise, but a communication link between our sometimes remote activities and the world at large. It may seem that we are being too heavily constrained, and that our process will just not work within those limits. It is important, then, that we make this a clear statement, because what we have to do, before we leave the table, is either to change the resources available, or to change the process. It is not enough to leave thinking that we can fudge the existing process and squeeze out some more money from the purse. The question to be asked is, 'What do we have to do differently to meet our market constraints?' and not, 'What can we chop off?'

While we continue to work with fixed margins and a fixed process, the terms we can offer to our client are: pay us enough money and we will deliver your software, take it or leave it. Or at a pinch, it might be to ask how much money is available and say what we can afford to deliver for that amount. In either case the net result is the same — customer push. We are alienating our clients. Let us look at this another way. What are the client needs and constraints? What can the customer afford to pay for the capability they need? Now let us look at how we can engineer a delivery process and solution to meet those constraints. The difference we can achieve between our costs and the price the customer is

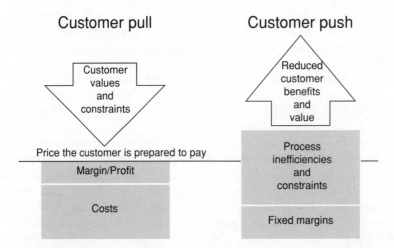

Figure 5.3 Do not expect your customer to pay for your inefficiencies. Profit made or breathing space earned is the difference betweeen your process costs and the price your customer is prepared to pay. Passing your high process charges on to your customer will drive them away.

prepared to pay is either our profit, if we are a profit centre, or breathing space, if not (Fig. 5.3). This is customer pull.

Changes in the market, expansion and contraction, changes to client bases, more commodity, and less service will be communicated to the organization via cost management operations such as financial plans and budget cycles. Proposed changes to process operations need to be tested for viability. They can only be tested within a cost structure. While change and process management operations will always want more money to launch into the future, the question to be asked is still the same, 'How can we package existing activities and automate or embed them into the process, so that we can change our performance to meet new positions for less cost?'

Having spent a number of years working on the development of software metrics and software productivity indicators, I have come to realize the importance of working very closely with cost management operations. Without that close link, performance indicators are meaningless and irrelevant to managers. By and large we have tended to operate in different languages with different sets of books. But now there is no need. Using clear activity-based costing systems, the potential for measuring and tracking product and process costs is greatly improved, and it is just this facility which allows us to start to exploit the power of software process design.

The opening up and inclusion of cost management within the delivery process provides us with the opportunity to mature and, leaving the old roles behind, enjoy a full adult life. I am looking forward to the time when cost management becomes a specialism of software engineering, and is not left in the hands of generalist accountants.

Purchasing management

Purchasing departments are another group in the organization who have a propensity for ponderously intercepting the ball in mid-flight as you throw it from base to base. They can bury you in bureaucracy, and provide piles of procedures but no guarantees of protection. While we need to obtain the best deals on volume purchases, we also need operations to assure the integrity and reliability of those products and services we buy in to package and resell to our clients in our name.

Scrutiny applies equally to subcontractors, consultants, hardware, software packages, operating systems, buy-in to development and testing platforms and tools, and telephone switchboards. Purchasing policies have to be linked to strategies and architecture, to legal requirements, and to human resource deployment. Has a central purchasing department with little specialized knowledge the capability of carrying out this operation effectively and at speed? The answer is, generally, no. But, we are told we need a central purchasing department so that we can keep a track of purchases, of purchase order numbers, and know the extent of our outstanding financial commitments at any one time. Now that we have the electronic capability to track local budgets, we also have the capability to track local purchasing. So where does that leave us? It leaves us not with a central purchasing department, but with a requirement for operations to scrutinize goods and services that will eventually be our proxy to our clients. Some of that scrutiny can be carried out by requirements management and service operations where goods are to be repackaged and assured, and by process management when the goods and services impact development operations — and this includes contractors and consultants as well as the equipment necessary for people to do their jobs. Key operations need to build up strong relationships with their suppliers, so that suppliers have the opportunity to know the work that has to be accomplished and its performance requirements.

This does not mean opening the door to chaos in the organization. All resources are negotiated as part of the standard planning cycle. People are allocated money to purchase goods and services based on proposed and accepted plans. There is no need to go through the approval cycle yet again. That is not empowerment. We should feel easy that the amount of liability at any time does not exceed the total period budget. However, executive information systems can provide the fine detail whenever it is needed to be tapped off. Purchasing can be restored to its rightful place as a management competence, with the provision of expert systems linked to an experience base to enable better purchasing decision-making. Major negotiations and contracts can be evaluated and handled by change management when major change occurs, but subsequent to the change, there is direct contact between operations and suppliers.

5.3 ESCAPE FROM FORTRESS FUNCTIONS

Many organizations wanting to re-engineer and streamline their processes are unable to do so because they work from functional decomposition maps which are the equivalent of their existing organizational hierarchy, with the difference that instead of personnel names in the boxes, it is the names of the activities that they carry out which appear.

I hope that you can see now that the main barrier to process streamlining and re-engineering is the functional fortress. The only escape is recognition that success depends upon building a client-driven process which requires the interworking of all key management operations. In the following chapters we shall move on to examine how the process can be designed to support client-critical success factors.

6

CONNECTING PROCESS TO SUCCESS

What does make design a problem in real world cases is that we are trying to make a diagram for forces whose field we do not understand.

Christopher Alexander
Notes on the Synthesis of Form

Now we have identified the management building blocks, we can start to assemble multi-competence teams to work on the software delivery process. However, first you have to design your process, and in all probability, depending on the families of products and services you deliver, you may well have more than one process. Remember that a process is an end-to-end delivery chain, it is not just a development life cycle. While we have sometimes been very good at designing products and services in great detail, we have failed consciously to design the process by which the products and services are delivered. We have relied either upon serendipity or boiler-plate life cycles, whether the costs and methods were appropriate to our clients' needs or not.

The key factor to be taken into consideration when you design your process, is your clients' perceptions of value for the target products and services. Your clients have goals and needs which they hope to satisfy by choosing your products. The whole of your delivery process must be designed and engineered to deliver requisite value. You must be doing everything that is necessary and sufficient to meet your clients' operational criteria for success. By that I mean everything to ensure that your product or service fits into the working, real-life, business world of your clients — as opposed to a hypothetical, idealized world. All this must be achieved at cost that your clients are willing pay.

In this chapter I want to show you how you can take your clients' success factors and perceptions of value and translate them into an appropriate delivery process. This process includes: marketing; product and service planning; product and service design; and product and service process design in addition to the obvious product and service delivery.

6.1 MAKING THE CONNECTION

In Chapter 5 we were reminded of the prevalent issues in software delivery which have to be addressed. These issues can be addressed by specialist functions, groups of people, individuals, or external suppliers; in some cases they can be addressed by management competences or by mechanisms embedded in the process itself. It all depends on the point you have reached on the associated learning curves.

Learning to make connections

When there is little process understanding, the tendency is that each operation is served by a separate function or group. Problems and issues arise which are dealt with on a case-by-case basis. There appear to be few generic or defined rule structures which can be made known in advance to inform the activities of other people. When this is the case, there is no reliable means of decentralizing the operation, either by automating it, or by transferring it to others as a learned management competency.

The operation also tends to be self-preoccupied. It may even demonstrate a stronger allegiance to its professional body or craft guild than to the organization which it serves. This is evidenced by the introduction into the organization of the latest professional practices, such as the latest life cycle model or CASE for instance, whether these are in balance with the particular needs of the organization or not. It could be pride in specialist expertise, or the tradition of living in specialist compartments, which has existed for too long, that causes each operation to believe it can behave justifiably as a 'black box'. There is a fundamental belief that no one can or should tell us how to do our job. We, in our field, are the fount of all knowledge, and the arbiters of 'what is good for the organization', as we see it at any rate. This was why we were employed in the first place, was it not? Were we to learn to listen to others in the organization about how they see our role, and how we can improve practices to serve them better might be seen as lacking in professionalism or even diffidence. Yet, this has to be learnt. We can only advance in professional stature by advancing the business in the direction it needs to go, and that means stepping down from the clay pedestals we and our professional bodies have built for ourselves.

Interworking

When each operation confines itself to its own black box, and behaves like a blindfolded relay runner, there are many dropped batons and wrong races run. It seems that no matter how we slice the organization, we are unable to isolate the business into discrete, independent compartments. The question to ask is, 'Why should we try to do this?'

To respond effectively to change, the organization needs to be able to form and reform itself spontaneously to meet the new demands imposed by the changed environment. Having rigid structures, even if they are changed every year, does not permit the level of fluidity and response to change which is needed on a week-by-week, day-by-day basis.

Everybody in the organization is a resource, and we cannot afford not to utilize those resources to their fullest potential. But all the time, by staying within our own close confines, we set a limit on the resources we make available and also on our own potential as adaptive and learning beings. Managers who believe they should not become involved with how their teams are doing things, even when they know there is a better way and, from the other side, the team who resents the interference of their manager or peers when suggestions for improvement are made, are denying the valuable resource available in themselves and others. It does not matter where we sit in the organization, the important thing to know is what other resources are available for us to draw on, where we can find them, and to know that we can form a collaborative unit very quickly to make a rapid response.

Making the connection is fundamental to process success and competitive advantage

There are at least thirteen key operations needed in a software delivery process, all of which are linked quite strongly to four or five other operations. If we work to a model of a simplistic internal customer and supplier chain and set up rigid communication protocols for each of those links, we shall be in the business of designing and exercising intergroup standards and procedures, and not delivering software products and services. Rather than try and pull the web apart into weakened single links, we need to use its dynamic and flexible strength to support the delivery of better designed, higher value and more reliable products. This ability to design and form work groups and processes with the appropriate competences is your competitive edge. There is no one process that will work for you, all the time. You need to understand your processes well enough to be able to engineer and maintain them yourself. But, for much of your work, you may be able to make use of existing processes, or to reuse process components from other delivery lines. For each new product or service, you will need teams for product and service planning (Sec. 6.6), and product and service design (Sec. 6.7). You also need to design an appropriate delivery process, and product and service process design (Sec. 6.8) requires a widely experienced networked team. None of these teams are homogeneous groups of specialists living together in black boxes labelled 'product design' or 'process design' but are multi-competence teams. You will also need a production or delivery team which works closely with product and process design to produce the finished goods. Most importantly, whether you have a marketing (Sec. 6.5) team or not, you cannot design effective products, services, or delivery lines, without an understanding of the fundamental values of your clients.

6.2 EVALUATING VALUE

'Value for money' is a phrase that software producers are hearing more and more frequently these days. It is a signal from our market that we are on the slide towards the commodity end of the business spectrum. As a consumer of software products and services, my expectations have been radically changed by the fact that I can now walk into my local department store and, tucked away between the hi-fi systems and the fax machines, are take-away, ready-to-run PCs. While customers have been demanding better value for money, software producers have been telling their customers they are going to receive better quality — the reaction of the customers has not been positive. This is a message that software producers should respond more to the values of their customers rather than to the sales pitch of their own suppliers. But how can there be a conflict between quality and value for money?

Success starts with customer models of value

Quality is the child of value. If we consider quality without its relationship to value, then we could be in danger of producing a heaven on earth for which there is no customer willing to pay the price. The late Kaoru Ishikawa, Japanese father of quality, stated in his book *Total Quality Control*: 'No matter how high the quality, if the product is overpriced it cannot gain customer satisfaction. One cannot define quality without considering the price.' Recently this has come home to roost at Toyota, who have had temporary troubles selling cars in America. There is more built-in quality at the moment than people value or are willing to buy. Given all their wants and desires and the wealth of options for satisfying their wants, people enter into a particular purchase because they believe it gives them the biggest total satisfaction per buck. It has the most utility for them. The product is a better combination of design, materials, and function for its price than its rivals.

Value is goal oriented

For those who think quality is subjective, I have news. Compared to value, quality appears quite concrete. Value is almost always subjective and often appears irrational. This is simply because everyone has individual goals and needs which they hope to satisfy by choosing one product instead of another. Think about it. Some needs are as tangible as minimum tog requirements to prevent hypothermia, or recommended daily calorific intake. But do we inquire about the tog value of a designer coat, or the calories in a yummy bar? The fact that a coat from our local department store might keep us twice as warm and last twice as long as the designer one, or that a salad sandwich would provide us with better nutrition totally misses the goal which we are trying to satisfy.

Our purchaser's beliefs about value have to be elicited carefully. You need to have well-designed operations to get to grips with the purchaser's preferences. Ad hoc analysis could lead you off in the wrong direction, because when people talk about value it is as though they have a sophisticated computer model implant — and the model is often quite inaccessible. We all hear people saying to each other, 'You just do not know what you want.' But not knowing what your goals are is not the isolated affliction of software purchasers. It is not a freak aberration. It is in the nature of our internal process.

Value and software

Examining the value of software presents some unusual insights. First, how do you value software? You might have a friend who has bought a similar branch banking network system to yours, and if you find out it only cost them half as much as you paid, you will feel as though you have been robbed. However, the possibility for this sort of comparison is rare.

How else can you estimate the value of software? Well, you can look upon it as an investment decision for which you would expect future returns of at least as much as you could obtain by banking the same amount of money. Most software purchasers have not been this rigorous to date, but the time has now come. What else can you do? It is possible you could compare the current costs of a software project to its first estimates. When you accept an estimate, you have played through your internal value model, and the answer has come out, 'Yes'. From that point on, it is almost as though you have spent that money. If the project comes in under budget you will be delighted. If it goes over budget or all the utilities you were expecting are not delivered, you will feel robbed. If the supplier comes to you at this stage and asks you to feel the quality, you may not give them the response they would like. Comparisons are now being made against smaller systems with which clients are becoming increasingly familiar. 'Why are you charging that much for a database? I can buy one for £500.'

Value and costs

Value is always increased by decreasing costs for the same bundle of utilities. I suppose it is human nature to ask as much from your client as you think you can get for your products and services, particularly when you know information is so scarce they can make few reliable comparisons. But even without comparisons, purchasers do have an idea of how much they are prepared to throw at certain problems. The amount is linked to business benefits and could well affect their viability as a company if costs are exceeded. But there is a wider issue. Investment in information technology is a massive overhead on a country's businesses. I am thinking about the one trillion dollars' worth of IT spend in the USA in the 1980s, and in the 1990s, the failure of Taurus, the London Stock Exchange system, and the millions of pounds of health care and local government computing paid for by the tax payer which is junked annually. We cannot remain globally competitive by creating this level of waste.

We want to deliver software within budget; the pain of not meeting budget is personally very great. So there is a tendency to pad estimates. Perhaps in this way the customer does not feel robbed, but it is unprofessional practice. We are not making ourselves accountable for our spiralling process costs, which we alone control. The customer cannot control our costs except by voting with their feet and putting us out of business. We are just taking the lazy way out and passing the costs of our runaway processes on to the customer. Let us turn this thinking on its head. Rather than saying the cost to the customer is our costs plus, we need to work overtime to design cost-effective solutions and, importantly, a cost-effective process to deliver those solutions which will provide the desired benefits for our client while yielding profit or schedule respite for ourselves. Costs are only necessary because we have not yet found a cheaper way of designing and engineering our process. When we are able to design and engineer both our process and products to meet clients' budgetary constraints, then we can say that we are delivering value for money.

6.3 CAPTURING SUCCESS FACTORS

If you were to pick one group of your customers that you know well and ask them right now what their key buying preferences were, how do you think they would respond?

Understanding critical success factors

Critical success factors are simply those features of designed capability which your clients need to have to satisfy the operational demands of their businesses, and of their own customers. Critical success factors frequently encompass the investment available, the lead time available for a competitive market strike or response, doing the job, fast staff ascent of new process learning curves, a reliable image, safety, security, fun, degree of innovation, attractiveness, desirability, and so on.

While we can see how a finished product might conform to those features, it is much more difficult to see how we can design a process to ensure that the finished product or service successfully embodies those features. But, if we are to get to grips with the software delivery process, this is exactly what we have to achieve.

Quantitative critical success factors

I spent a number of years working with colleagues across the industry who were trying to devise sets of measurements that would help software purchasers and suppliers to improve quantifiably software product and service quality. In order to do that we worked on quantifying the quality characteristics of software. These characteristics are now well defined, they are the famous 'ilities', such as maintainability, usability, reliability, portability, interoperability, security, performance, and functionality (the last three being honorary 'ilities'.) The hope was that we would be able to elicit, specify, and build software to meet these quantified characteristics.

Let me give you some examples. For reliability, we might specify a mean time to failure of so many months or years. We might also specify a mean time to recover of so many elapsed minutes or hours. Maintainability would be linked to mean time to locate the correct source code to be changed, and then mean time to effect change. All the 'ilities' apart from functionality could be represented in a scalar fashion on a relative scale of 1 to 100 say. Functionality, the capability to do the job, on the other hand, was binary, either it was there or not.

While much of the work conducted in this area took us forwards, and helped us to appreciate the problem we were up against, I did not feel very happy. First, how could we design a process or operations to build the right level of 'ility' into the software? Secondly, would the customer be happy about specifying the 'ilities' in straight 'ility' terms? And, thirdly, this 'ility'–function divide was rather like the wave–particle theory of light, and I wanted to find occasions in which functionality could be scalar, and maintainability binary.

Taguchi loss functions solve the binary–scalar paradox of product characteristics

The value of software functionality is not constant. It is time bound. Functionality value is determined by reference to prevailing market needs. Because there is so much change, what was deemed functionally useful yesterday, may be completely overturned today in the light of new social or technological advances. Every month longer you take to deliver the client's required functionality, although all functionality may be present when you do deliver, has lost one month's worth of benefits in terms of income, prestige, or foot in the door. There is a scalar falling off in value. Similarly, if any of the necessary utilities, reliability or usability say, fall below a certain level or are unavailable to support the business, then the client loses out in a decidedly binary way. These different ways in which value falls away can be charted.

Taguchi loss curves are one way of picturing fall-off of value. Let us look at how this works. Imagine catching a train. If you arrived at the advertised time, but the train had left early, then the train has no value to you, and you may also incur considerable costs, such as switching your travel arrangements, or having to spend valuable time waiting for the next train. However, if the train is late leaving, its value may only fall off slowly for every minute late it is leaving up to some threshold limit. When you start to get anxious or impatient then value begins to fall off sharply until it is time for the next scheduled train to leave for your destination, when the value to you of the train you are currently sitting on will be around zero. Figure 6.1 illustrates the idea.

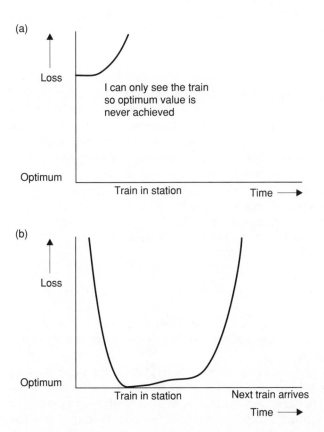

Figure 6.1 (a) Taguchi loss curve for early departing train. The train has some value while it can be seen on the platform, but the value vanishes as it leaves before I can board. (b) Taguchi loss curve for late departing train. The train has no value until it is seen approaching when we can confirm that the train does exist. Its value increases even more when we can get on board. For every minute late in departing, value falls off until the next scheduled train for my destination arrives and the value of this train vanishes.

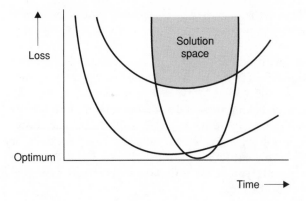

Figure 6.2 Superimposed Taguchi loss curves. One way of picturing your solution space is by overlapping loss curves for the various components. A smaller space implies more risks for production.

As you can see there are occasions when value falls off so rapidly as the situation moves away from the optimum, that to all intents and purposes value appears to be binary. It is also interesting to see how you can layer these loss curves, one on top of the other, to give you a picture of what your solution space for a particular product or service looks like (Fig. 6.2). This solution space is a picture of the constraints and their importance as they will affect your design. Think of the solution space as the size of the bull's-eye at which you have to aim. We can say that, relatively speaking, a small solution space entails more precision in product or service design and engineering, while a wider space permits more comfort and flexibility. The map can usefully convey risk. The tighter the tolerance, the more tricky it will be to design a process and product to hit the space first time, therefore the risk will be greater.

Utilities as concrete entities

Having established this pictorial relationship of value for both functionality and utilities, where does that leave us? Well, instead of having 'ilities', we can relate more directly to our clients' values in terms of tangible entities.

What do clients mean by usability? It means being able to stay on the same learning curve, or to make a painless switch from one learning curve to another. This means that demands on the end user should be within easy reach of existing cognitive repertoires. We can talk about standard user interfaces, familiar presentation of procedures, familiar layout of manuals and reports, and ergonomic keyboards or input devices. These are all 'things'.

Let us make this more difficult, now. How about reliability, dependability, and integrity? These can be expressed in terms of mean time to failure, mean time to breach of security, and so on, but as a purchaser I want, first and foremost, peace of mind. How do I get that? By assurances, reports of test coverage, warranties, guarantees, backup services, fault-tolerant mechanisms, and indemnification for losses. These, too are all 'things'.

I also want a product with in-built flexibility and growth potential. You may call it maintainability, but that is your word, not mine, the customer. I want professional service response, plug-in software upgrades, and standard architectures. Here we have things again, and also people with specific skills. By talking about usability, maintainability, and reliability, instead of looking for the words our customers use, we fall into the trap of missing our customers' goals and values. We fall into the trap, too, of expecting our customers to specify everything. Again, if I were buying a house I would not want to have to specify the shape and size of foundations. I live in a part of the world where foundations are taken for granted. One of the advantages of spending time with your clients is that you will learn to look for exactly those sorts of things which they take for granted and which would never appear in a specification.

Designing a process to produce subcomponents instead of 'ilities'

We can see that, from the customer's point of view, our 'ilities' are things and people-skills. It is much easier to design processes to produce things or product and service subcomponents than adjectives. Each subcomponent can then be described by loss curves. As we know, if the solution space is large, there are fewer risks than if the solution space is small. If the solution space looks too small we can go back to the customers and try to find ways of widening tolerances, but this is likely to reduce the value of the product or service to them. You might gather from this that competitive advantage is gained by designing to tighter and tighter solution spaces. To do this, you need to be able to build on reliable product and process platforms. If you do not bank product or process assets, you will always have to work to large tolerances, which means less value to your clients and more risk for you.

6.4 QUALITY FUNCTION DEPLOYMENT

Once we have identified critical success factors and the relative values assigned to them by our customer, one of the ways we can make things easier for ourselves is to break the product or service down into component-based utilities as far as possible. Within product operations we can set up a specialist team to work exclusively on user interfaces, who study their clients' existing machine interfaces and expectations based upon what they read or see, and who specify the background processing requirements to service those interfaces. We can set up another team to deliver encryption mechanisms, another to design telephone-based client–service interfaces, one to work on client training and mentoring, and yet another to design platforms for expandable, plug-in functions. To all this we need to add a systematic method for translating and tracking client values into engineered products and an engineered process to deliver those products. One method which has been found useful is *quality function deployment (QFD)*.

Use QFD as your process blueprint

QFD is simply a way of charting the interrelationship between factors which the business must manage. This in effect is your blueprint for process design. All that is necessary and sufficient to ensure value for the customer is translated by turns from product or service characteristics into internal operations which, when enacted, will achieve all that is necessary and sufficient to deliver the requisite value (Fig. 6.3). The charts are important because they make visible on a single design plan what is usually buried in thick documents. They focus people's attention on the key elements for success. The chart often takes the form of a matrix (Fig. 6.4). Charts can be simple and just show the relationship

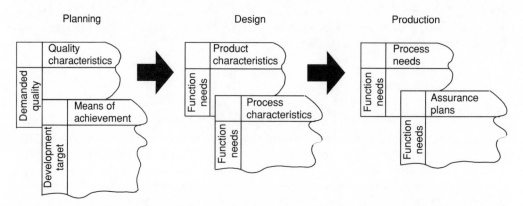

Figure 6.3 Quality function deployment charts are used to translate product and service requirements into a designed process which is appropriate to the task.

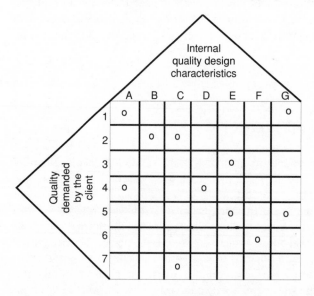

Figure 6.4 Quality function deployment charts simply translate the operationally defined qualitites required by your clients into internal quality design characteristics to ensure that all client-demanded qualities are taken into account for finished product or service delivery.

and impact of two key factors with respect to each other, or they can be substantial multi-dimensional models. There are now PC-based multi-dimensional spreadsheets available which can be used to set up QFD.

Keeping track of the parts and interfaces

The one problem we have when we start to break down into smaller manageable product or process components is that we quickly lose sight of the whole, and the important relationships between the parts. While we can concentrate on having various teams working in parallel to supply individual components and reduce risk in that way, risk is then transferred to the interfaces and the need arises to ensure that interfaces between all the components are kept compatible.

For each component identified, and remember this can either be a product or process component, a chart of interactions between components is needed which concentrates design thinking on each of the interfaces in turn and how it is to be designed and engineered for maximum dependability and robustness. Robustness means that if there is failure in one component then it will not interfere with other components. It may be that the product is to be designed so that failure in one component can be compensated for by another component. It may be that we are trying out new process operations and want to isolate any problems and delay from other contingent operations. Next, each of the components needs to be assigned a priority so that the teams engineering the components can be quite clear, not only about with whom they have to collaborate, but also in which component's favour trade-offs should be made. If graphic user interfaces represent a high value to clients, then that value must not be traded away by making compromises in favour of processing. In this way the charts reflect the relationship between client values, people, process, and products (Fig. 6.5).

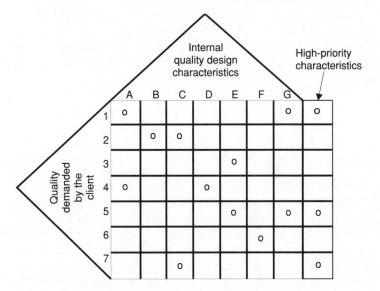

Figure 6.5 High risk, high priority and fuzzy requirements can be singled out for special design and management considerations using QFD charts.

QFD and process traceability

By mapping out the components, interfaces, priorities, and accountabilities, it is easier for the product or service process design team to see both which operations are necessary for the process in order to achieve the desired product capability, and where potential risks and bottlenecks are likely to occur. Operations to produce each of the product components are traceable back to the relevant component. In terms of control, it is easy to see what high-level reviews need to be carried out to ensure that critical success factors are met and the appropriate components are produced. Additionally, the presence of each component and interface flags the need for control points within the process. Each pre-established control point is in fact an agreement between the production, design, and V&V teams to meet production requirements and to assume accountability for confirming that they have been met as planned.

QFD as a learning design document

As a high-level product or service design capture tool, QFD charting helps us to identify all the components needed to meet the client's requirements. It is sometimes the case that we are very good at defining requirements within our existing framework of knowledge and capability. We go into great detail about the things we can do easily and about what is familiar to us, but we tend to gloss over the more difficult aspects. Every time we fall into that particular comfort trap, we introduce risk.

While we may not identify all the components at the start, if we stay with the chart we can introduce new components which are required as we find them. Then we are in a position to see how adding new requirements increases the complexity of interfaces and impacts the design as a whole. It can help us to make reasoned decisions about the viability of adding new components while helping us to trace all the design impacts, and monitor any problems. Looking back, after the product has been delivered, we can see how close to reality were our estimations of impact between the component groups. What can we learn to manage better next time?

QFD and tracking changing client values

Once we have captured the client's values and priorities on a QFD chart, it becomes a reusable asset, and we put it under configuration control along with design documentation and the finished products or services. Easier to read and keep up to date than long verbal reports, the chart can be used to maintain an up-to-date picture of changing client values. It can be made available on-line as a component of the experience base (Sec. 2.6). It can be used as the basis for client satisfaction surveys, or for gathering data during staff debriefings when they return from client sites. Next time work is undertaken for that particular client, having an existing snapshot of their values ready to be validated helps us to a quicker start.

6.5 MARKETING

Not all software suppliers have a marketing team and the majority, in my experience, tend to use client operations in a quasi-marketing capacity. Marketing departments were children of post-war plenty and buoyant demand. In many people's minds, marketing is associated very closely with the product push approach — make the product and then decide how we are going to sell it. Now, things are very much changed, and the whole concept of TQM reflects the change of emphasis to product pull. For marketing, this means listening very closely to customers and understanding the changing environment in which the customers live and work. So the two important roles of the marketing team are first, collecting information about clients and the factors which influence client needs from all available sources, and that could be from client interfaces within the business, and secondly, feeding that information back into product and process planning teams.

Early capture of client values

Use QFD charts early on while you are prospecting and begin to capture customer values. What factors do those values depend upon, and how sensitive to change are they? It is useful to identify ways in which your competitors or collaborators influence client values, so that you can design client awareness programmes which capitalize on synergy with your collaborators and competitors, and maybe also neutralize the influence of competitors, if no synergy is possible. It is important to chart not only the current values, but also predictions about emerging values which can be validated as they appear, so that you can be early to market with the future products and services that your client will need and value. You will also capitalize on this information by using it as the basis to design and engineer your future process and, working with change management, to create incremental plans for process and operation changes.

Keep marketing in touch with the organization as well as with the outside world

The problem with most marketing departments is that they have a different language and culture to the rest of the organization. It is important to keep strong links between product and process design teams and marketing to ensure a common approach. Product and service operations together with V&V and requirements operations need to be represented on the marketing team. And, just to say it again, because it is critical, marketing needs to be talking all the time to its own service and support teams to capture as much feedback as possible about positive and negative perceptions of delivered software and services (Fig. 6.6).

6.6 PRODUCT AND SERVICE PLANNING

Product and service planning (which includes first-cut product and service analysis) can add an enormous overhead to cycle time if it is done on the critical path. Product and service planning needs to be on the back burner all the time, so that when decisions have to be made, it is just a question of feeding in very recent developments before swiftly progressing. There are three key factors to be considered: first, the functions or capability

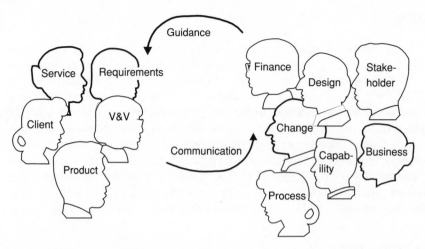

Figure 6.6 The marketing team is composed of product, service, and V&V aware personnel. In order to limit production risk, it is important that the marketing team maintains close links with other operations.

which will provide clients with the biggest benefits; secondly, the expected lifetime of the functions or capability needed; thirdly, the level of investment available. Again use QFD charts to get a picture of where you need to target the main thrust of your resources to obtain maximum positive impact on your client.

Developing client benefit profiles

It is important that we fix on client benefits and the profile of those benefits over time. So much of what is produced is just a short-term quick-fix reaction. That in itself is not the problem, since competitive response is important, the problem is evaluating the benefits of one competitive response over another, and perhaps constructing a portfolio of responses which not only set off the fireworks, but also keep the sky lit for a long time. If the new product or service represents a major competitive thrust, then putting all the effort into one shot may give you the temporary edge, but if the competition brings up their artillery while you are reloading, you have only created the means of your own destruction. For every major product or service, plans should be made either for an incremental salvo, or for rapid follow through, designing the product as a working but disposable prototype.

Planning for product life spans

The projected life span of a product or service is not always taken into consideration and used to leverage opportunities. There are some systems that we know will have a long life span, banking, insurance, and so on, and while some of the smaller functions will change shape as the environment in which they are used changes shape, the core functions, such as tracking creditors and debtors, will persist over many years. The life of the product is determined by the life of its main function, and we need to make plans early on about how the product and service is to be maintained, and under what conditions re-engineered. Will there be dedicated staff available to make enhancements when they are needed? On what basis will enhancements be made — as they are required, or in quarterly packets? Will enhancements be designed as separate plug-in modules to the basic product platform, or will the platform itself be allowed to evolve? Will there be scheduled maintenance and re-engineering on say, a three yearly basis, or will you wait until there is a significant technological change before re-engineering? Other products and services are at the mercy of annual legislation changes. The challenge there, knowing that change is a state of nature rather than something irritating the universe seems to throw at you every year or so, is to keep a rapid response slot available for planning and turning out new product variants, rather than risking throwing the whole of your plans and process off balance on a regular basis. In this case planning itself must be simple. It should never take longer than the life span of the solution.

Planning for available investment

There are many important factors which influence investment decisions and not all of them are linked to financial gain. As we have said before, the value attributed to product or service availability is goal driven. Some people may want to make an expensive statement because they place a higher value on the prestige it may bring than on anything else they could purchase at present. With respect to product planning, the important financial considerations are lifetime costs of functions: the costs to buy and the costs to use, and the relationship between the benefits and cost life cycles. It is usually the case that as benefits start to fall, costs of maintenance are ready to take off, which creates pressures and problems for supplier and client alike. The better the benefits and costs life cycles can be projected and planned to follow each other, the more value you can deliver, and the smoother your planning process will be. Portfolio planning can be smoothed when we are not confronted at every turn by the need to make sudden major re-engineering commitment.

The product and service planning team and QFD

You can expand on marketing QFD charts by assigning functions and costs to customer benefits and making a simple time-series to show how you expect change over time. As you can see from Fig. 6.7 the team involved in product planning needs to be widely drawn from across the organization. It is not a task to be carried out by a single specialist function.

6.7 PRODUCT AND SERVICE DESIGN

Product and service design includes detailed analysis, design, and detailed design activities. To the product and service design team, client values, time-based benefits, and investment availability should be no shock. They must not be in the position of saying to another group, 'You promised them what? For how much?' This is where the traditional handovers between planning and development or analysis and design functions fall down. Product and service design teams will have been party to discussions of the new product at the early planning stages when outline strategies, tactics and analysis were prepared (Fig. 6.8).

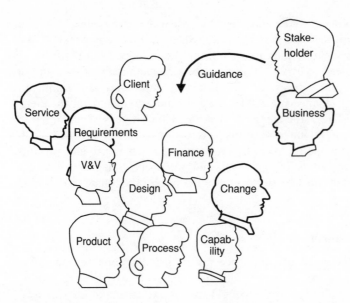

Figure 6.7 The new product or service planning team. The key software operations which are stakeholders in new product or service development are supported and guided by business and stakeholder operations.

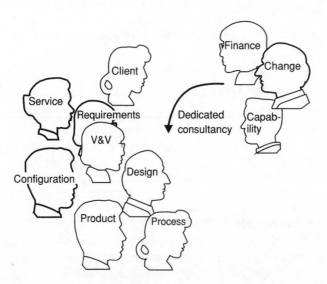

Figure 6.8 The new product or service design team. When a new service or product is being designed, capability, change, and finance are available to serve and guide the team on relevant decisions.

Cost-friendly design

Design is where the most important and often expensive product decisions are made. Look at the chair you are sitting on, or if you are not sitting on a chair, look at some manufactured item near to you. Whatever it is that you are looking at, it did not come together of its own accord. It was designed, and the design is a sum of decisions which have been taken with regard to cost, function, ease of manufacture, reliability, and so on. The chair you are sitting on is a set of decisions. Some decisions were probably well made, others you may find, could have been improved upon.

We must learn to design to cost, that not only includes costs of effort, materials and tools, but costs of the production or service environment in which they are to be made, costs of testing, lifetime costs to use, and so on. The first question to ask is, 'How could we design this solution for next to nothing?' What would have to be different for this to be done as cheaply as possible? We talked about solution spaces in Sec. 6.3. The wider your solution space is, the cheaper it is likely to be because you will have a considerable amount of design leeway. Use this as a starting point.

Time-friendly design

In traditional projects, by the time you had completed this design phase, you would have consumed over half the amount of elapsed time needed by the project, and time can never be reclaimed. The problem is that up until now, project burn rate will have been quite low in terms of staffing costs. Only after the product passes the design phase are significant production costs incurred, so it is often the case that it appears cheaper to stay in this phase, than to commit and move on. The consequences of this are the tremendous and injurious loading of time pressures on all downstream activities.

To some extent we are victims of our past. Products and services have been very expensive to produce in the past, so the reasoning goes that, if it is going to cost that much and take that long, then we must be absolutely sure that we have taken account of everything. Time goes by. Because it is going to be so expensive, we must make sure it is perfect, we must ensure there are tighter procedures controls in place. Time goes by. The products become proportionately even more expensive. And we do it all again, only more so. It is a runaway situation.

Evolutionary design approaches

If you have captured on a QFD chart key client benefits and function life spans, then you can take some of that destructive time-pressure off. Break it down. Design and produce increments. There are so many benefits to be had from incremental and evolutionary delivery, and many leading software production practitioners and coaches have been strongly advocating this approach for a number of years now. Let us just look at a few of them.

If you break the work down into chunks, you can have early news of environmental problems, people problems, and process problems which can be corrected and improved to save time in the next increments. When you break it down, you can work in a number of parallel and overlapping streams to reduce product cycle times. You can control to a better extent the complexity of interfaces, each increment as it goes out will have frozen and stabilized interfaces against which new functional interfaces can be designed and made. You can limit some of those costly overkill controls, knowing that if there are problems they will be limited to a single increment.

Complexity

Complexity is expensive and time-consuming. The more requirements, the more interfaces, the more complexity and the tighter your solution space will be. Again use a QFD chart to expand requirements to minimize interfaces when you are breaking down for product design. Highlight those requirements which are likely to persist in a fuzzy state and segregate them as much as possible into well-isolated components. Identify areas of inescapable complexity, treat them as high risk and manage them closely. Establish early-warning complexity indicators to be used in production which will trigger a return to the drawing-board if complexity of components or interfaces goes above a certain threshold. You can make a judgement of complexity based on the number and orderliness of decisions which have to be taken by the component, or equally, if you are not that far down the design path, the number and orderliness of the decisions you are making about the functionality required by the component.

Identify learning needs early on

Learning on the critical path can lead to disaster. Design your process to learn as much off-line and early. The sooner you can say that new or unfamiliar technology, tools, or methods are going to be needed, the sooner they can be brought in and training and familiarization begun. Product and service design works hand in hand with product and service process design, so that a fast response to learning needs can be made. Wherever it is possible, see if chunks requiring new learning can be delayed to later increments.

Product design and reuse

Consider early on whether you are going to be able to use existing components as platforms for your product or service, and to what extent there is the opportunity to lay down new component assets for the future. Again, because this is not a blind hands-off process, product design should be very much aware of new products in the planning pipeline, and should be able to refer to the future needs of clients gathered by marketing teams to help in this decision-making.

6.8 PRODUCT AND SERVICE PROCESS DESIGN

We are very good at designing products and services in great detail, but we have not been very good at designing the process to build the products and services. We have relied on boiler-plate life cycles which had to be followed by all projects, whether the costs and the methods of the process were appropriate or not. Large-scale phased planning was brought in for the massive aerospace projects conducted by NASA, where phase containment and the many checkpoints were necessary for managing high levels of risk. This process may not be useful to us. What is?

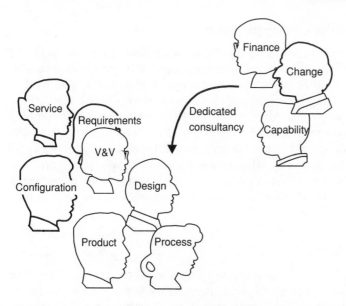

Figure 6.9 The new product or service process design team. This operation is similar to product or service design except that the client's interests are represented by requirements and V&V operations.

Designing processes that are appropriate to cost and risk

Process design has to be carried out consciously and in parallel to product design. You need planned processes with the appropriate controls and not skunk works. The process is designed with very close reference to the QFD charts you have developed. You intend to make sure that all your activity is focused on producing exactly what is required by your client. You are not interested in process for process's sake. This means that I cannot give you a boiler-plate process to take away and work on. You must work together as a team and take the time to think very carefully for yourselves exactly what production and management support operations you require to achieve everything that is necessary and sufficient for your target product or service (Fig. 6.9). I assure you that you can do this without help from outside.

If it is adaptable and rapid response processes that you need, then you design them. If the product allows parallel and overlapping operations, then you design a process to exploit that time advantage. Again, if product design allows or demands incremental or evolutionary delivery, prototyping, or joint application design, then a process is designed specifically to match the product's needs. Processes can be constructed from existing operations components, rather like threading pearls, or they can be designed specifically to fit the product. The one important process that must always exist in parallel to other processes is the one for pulling out the plug. This is a frequently executed option, but no one ever designs this process. Maybe it has something to do with the thinking that if you are going to get married, it seems a bit callous to be designing the settlement in case of divorce. While we are confidently telling the client that we are the partner for them, will they not think it a little odd that we have a quick cut-off plan? My answer would be that it shows prudence and concern for the client.

Designing the working conditions and environment

Yes, we can proactively design the working conditions and environment to meet the product needs. Why take it that teams are split over five sites? Why take it as read that your clients are not very computer literate? You can do something about it. You need to design the optimum working conditions to support delivery of the new product or service. Take nothing as fixed. Bring people together in small teams within conversational distance. Insist that a dedicated team is available. Demonstrate by reference to process and operation charts the reduction in cycle times, delays, and bottlenecks you are going to achieve as a consequence. Because it is delay and bottlenecks which will cripple the product. With no visible process, you cannot hope to spot them. With no designed process, you cannot hope to eliminate them. In Chapter 8 you will find the tools to help you.

Process monitoring during delivery

The job of process design does not finish with the handover of the product designs to production, it continues throughout production and is available, together with product or service design, to re-engineer the process or product if bottlenecks occur. All data on bottlenecks and delays are collected as they occur and are fed back into the experience base to support improving process design for future products.

6.9 PRODUCTION AND DELIVERY

As we have seen, the QFD is the single blueprint against which you design your process. There are no other special, whizz-bang techniques. Process design is all about understanding exactly what you need to produce and what decisions you need to make

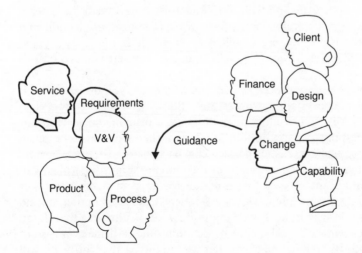

Figure 6.10 The service or production team is now considerably slimmer, but there is a real continuing dialogue with finance, capability, change, design, and client operations.

to deliver the necessary value to your clients: no more, and certainly no less. We shall talk more in Chapters 8–10 about how to ensure that your process and operations are as efficient as possible. All of the work you have carried out so far in capturing critical success factors, process and product planning, and design is to ensure production is efficient, smooth, and balanced. The job of delivery is carried out by the production team in collaboration with the product and process design teams. It is important to stress again that none of these teams is separate, one from the other, rather they constitute an overlapping group working towards the same common objective. It is a fluid, dynamic, but dedicated team, skilled in product and service knowledge, process awareness, and all the technical skills they need to carry out a successful delivery (Fig. 6.10).

Production checkpoints, such as component and critical success factor reviews, are detailed on product and process QFD charts. Any delays are immediately signalled. Any bottlenecks are immediately signalled. Any problems are immediately signalled. No fudging, instead, professional redesign, and capturing and keeping that experience for future benefit.

7

A PROCESS MANAGEMENT FRAMEWORK

Une réflexion prématurée de l'esprit sur lui-même le decouragera d'avancer, alors qu'en avançant purement et simplement il se fût rapproché du but et se fût aperçu, par surcroôt, que les obstacles signalés étaient pour la plupart de effets des mirage.

Je ne vois qu'un moyen de savoir jusqu'où l'on peut aller: c'est de se mettre en route de marcher.

Henri Bergson
La conscience et la vie

(Too much early thinking discourages you from venturing forth when, by simply moving forward you would have reached your destination and found out from experience that all the expected hurdles were for the most part mirages.

I know of only one means of finding out where you can go: that is by striding out.)

We have seen now how QFD charting can be used to express your clients' values in terms of your internal process requirements, so that you have a blueprint for the process and operations necessary and sufficient to deliver requisite value to your clients. But we must not forget that you already have a process, or a number of processes, which may be working for you already. There is no need to bulldoze away years of good practice. Why not discover some of the process assets you already have, compare them against your needs, and use them to greater effect? Your existing internal operations can be validated against QFD charts as you start to build up your collection.

Let us focus now on creating a framework on which you can grow your process management experience, train that experience into your day-to-day business, and continually improve on it. This is a framework you can build incrementally. It requires no major shifts of effort. You can set your own pace. It is a four-phase approach, and when you have completed three of the phases you will be in a position to gain standards accreditation, if that is what you are seeking.

7.1 GETTING A GRIP ON THE PROCESS

One of the biggest problems confronting software managers is to decide where, exactly, we can get a grip on the process to improve it. The software development process is like one of those mythical Celtic serpents which weaves a complex pattern and ends up eating its own tail. If you start at the end and work to understand the causes of defects and problems, people say they do not want to be told after the event that they have got things wrong. If you start at the beginning and prescribe preventive measures such as inspections or reviews, so that the chances of people doing things wrong are reduced, you also run into trouble. Few seem to believe sufficiently in the efficacy of the remedy to invest their time in following the course of medication. I can sympathize with both of these points of view. It is not a problem of detail, but of the whole management framework.

The problems of trying to improve everything all at once

Many software producers are now attempting standards accreditation of some sort, this may be TickIT, ISO 9001, military or defence standards, or a rating against the Software Engineering Institute's *capability maturity model* (Sec. 7.2). Each of these accreditation programmes requires a vast amount of investment in time and money to create and document organizational procedures and standards. Some people get lost trying to do everything at once, without properly understanding the process or the business demands. I wonder sometimes at the usefulness of drafting procedures for hooking up the patient to life-support machines and procedures for administering intravenous feeding. Should we assume that this is the normal state of the patient? I would rather see health as a norm and focus on helping the patient to health while providing a staged support process to maintain and improve the patient's fitness.

The problems of measuring and diagnosing without knowledge of the process

Some people get lost at the beginning. They dash in, gathering data, to make a diagnosis. Gathering data is not a problem for most of us. We can usually provide data such as how many problems occur in live running, how many function points are produced per person-month, and so on. But we have to be clear that these data are only symptoms. What we need to know first is, 'What is happening to result in so many errors or so many function points, and most importantly, is that a problem?' We do not want to be like the doctor who has the equipment for taking blood pressure and a thermometer, but who does not yet know about hearts, systolic pressure, or systems for regulating body temperature, nor even what a reasonable blood pressure count or temperature is for this particular patient. Measurement and diagnosis lead us into problems when we do not understand the process.

Fitness is not an abstract ideal, it is relative to the environment

It is also difficult to improve a process without some idea of 'fitness' or 'wellness'. Some people might define fitness as the capacity to respond and play a constructive role in their environment. You need to develop your own picture of fitness. Whatever it is, it must be related to your market or environment, and it must be one you can share with your organization. Then you can conduct a health check. There is no point rearranging or removing internal organs or administering medicine unless you know what your present state of health is. And it will certainly be dangerous to undertake remedial action if you have no knowledge of anatomy — the process.

7.2 THE CAPABILITY MATURITY MODEL

I, along with many of my peers, felt that the biggest breakthrough, in terms of getting a grip on the software process, came with the Software Engineering Institute (SEI) capability maturity model (CMM). A group working in the SEI at Carnegie-Mellon University in the United States put forward a five-stage model of software process maturity which has been documented by Watts Humphrey in his book *Managing the Software Process*. This model helped us to break down from an immense and defeating problem to something much more manageable.

The five-stage CMM approach

The CMM maps out five progressively more 'healthy' states of the software development process. They are called: initial; repeatable; defined; managed, and optimizing. Each level has its own characteristics. At the initial level, operations are ad hoc and chaotic; the repeatable stage is reached when there is responsible project management, configuration management, and product testing. In order to reach the defined stage, standards, reviews, correct training and tools, and a software engineering group have to be present. At the managed stage, there is change management, measurement, and prototyping. Finally, the fifth stage, the optimizing stage, is characterized by the ability to plan and replace obsolete technology and to make the software process error-proof. We can picture this model more clearly by looking at a *state transition diagram* (see Sec. 8.6). Each line or state is a CMM

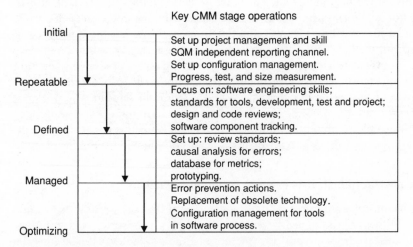

Figure 7.1 State transition diagram: the capability maturity model showing the key operations which are introduced into the software process to move from one state to another.

level, and the spaces between the levels can be expanded to show or reference the operations which are needed to make the transition from one state to another (Fig. 7.1).

Using the CMM to assess your process and improve

The model is underpinned by a fitness assessment which is available to provide a read-out of your health. At each level, the assessment examines vital characteristics in a number of areas: organization; human resource management and training; technical management; standards and procedures; process metrics; data management and analysis; and process control. The importance of this assessment is not just to say, 'I'm at level three', but rather to say, 'If I can manage to project code and test errors, then I could be running at level four.' So the real importance of the model is that it provides a diagnostic for managers which enables them to target areas selectively and effectively for improvement. It supports an incremental approach to improvement; we no longer need to arm-wrestle the ocean. However, the model does have some weaknesses.

The CMM does not take account of the business or its clients

Having used the model to map out improvement plans, as opposed to simply using it for assessment, the first deficiency I had to compensate for was the absence of any links in the model to the business, or to clients. We do not produce software in a vacuum. We produce software to enable other people to become more profitable or expert in their transactions within their environment. The amount of money they have available to pay for our delivered systems is finite, and we must value-engineer our work. There is nothing in the CMM to require us to check out our procedures to see if they are appropriate and relevant to our customers and business. We cannot afford to add costs without adding value.

The problem of repeatability before process definition

I was also asked how we could reach a repeatable process before having a defined process. If we could deliver software repeatably, what need was there to do much else? This made me look once more at the progression of the levels from a state transition angle. Perhaps 'repeatable' had not been the best choice of word. But, when I changed the order of the 'repeatable' state and placed it after the 'managed' state, the model became more easy to communicate. Now we were talking about going from a state of ignorance or chaos, to having an awareness and understanding of what we have and what we need to accomplish. From there, active management intervention, process design, and redesign took us to a repeatable stage (Fig. 7.2). Then, once we had that degree of control which would enable us to replicate, predictably, software delivery success, we could begin to optimize the process.

The lack of clear process behind the CMM

Again, working with state transitions, the CMM seems very uneven. Sometimes the CMM requires quite high-level operations, such as a mechanism for managing and supporting new technologies. In other instances, there is very detailed prescription. For example, it specifically requires software engineers on the systems design team (but no mention of clients or testers). I found myself trying to piece together all these requirements to get a picture of what process problems they were aiming to solve, and what goals they were

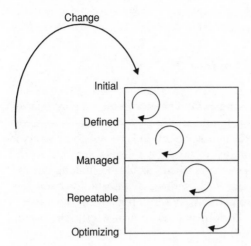

Figure 7.2 State transition diagram: a process management framework. The process is defined and made visible before it can become repeatable.

trying to achieve. For the main part, all I could see was a ranking and distribution of known tools and techniques across five levels. The CMM is uneven and it misses out on helping us to understand the systemic relationships between the parts.

The CMM cannot be used for 'growing' a better software process, because it is not, in itself, process oriented. But that does not mean that we cannot take the good ideas from the CMM and make them process based. The CMM is not business or market focused, but that does not mean that we cannot build these requirements into our model. The CMM might just be assuming a sick person as the norm. We can bear that in mind, but not blinker ourselves to other possibilities.

7.3 PHASED TRANSITION

The benefits of taking a staged approach to improvement or accreditation are very important. First, the pressure and strain on the business can be distributed to minimize disruption to existing work schedules. Secondly, we can plan and resource the work more effectively, because it is is clearly targeted. Thirdly, people can see the progression from one stage to another and mentally tick them off. And fourthly, instead of there being one big bang, pass, or fail conclusion to the accreditation exercise, we can feel more comfortable as we pass intermediate stages one by one. If resits are necessary, then it will be only for the stage we have just completed, and not for the exercise as a whole.

A learning framework for process management

When I speak about the CMM to clients, their usual question is, 'What happens when we reach stage five?' Is it Nirvana? Have we reached the twelfth dan? They speculate that it is like going up a down escalator and that when you reach the magical fifth level, more levels will become apparent. These questions and speculation occur because the model is finite in its content and linear. But life is not quite like that. There is always something new over the horizon. There is an endless learning and internalizing spiral in human activity systems. For any task, what once was difficult and unclear, we make clear, we fit it into a routine, we make a habit of it, then we do it unconsciously. Then we move on to learn and incorporate new skills in our repertoire. Sometimes we also need to unlearn skills, in order to replace learned habits which are no longer effective, by more appropriate ones. Learning happens over a period of time and tends to be cyclical. We need to take account of these facts in our staged approach.

A business-oriented framework for process management

We also have to remember that our goal is to evolve a balanced, synchronized process which delivers effective value to our clients. Adding to operations without reference to the whole process creates problems and adds costs. We can make progress by removing and restructuring operations. Instead of being keen to solve problems by adding a compensating activity, perhaps the answer is to 'cease to do evil'. When we 'ensure compliance to standards', are we sure those costly standards are not just compensating for costly uneducated practice? When we have ten levels of document reviews, is the next stage of maturity to add an eleventh? Or, instead, should we identify the problems which give rise to the need for all the reviews, peel off all the costly band-aids, and invest instead in making the process error-proof? Everything we put in place to support the process has a cost. The question to ask is, 'What is the cost we are trying to remove by adding more costs — can we subtract the original costs at source?'

A process framework for breakthrough

As we progress, is it not important that as we free ourselves from problems and bureaucracy, we make important breakthroughs? That we escape the linear progression of things and do something that is radically different to enhance the value and services we provide, and the viability of the organization as a whole? It is a case of getting the right balance: too much emphasis on controls and efficiency and we have hard-boiled eggs; uncontrolled creativity and we have scrambled eggs. We need both.

Just to summarize then, our framework needs to be incremental, it must be able to accommodate the new and unforeseen, to enable learning, to result in change that is advantageous to business stakeholders, and to allow breakthrough.

The process framework

Let us work with the state transition of Fig. 7.3. Instead of each transition being a one-off step, we are going to make each transition an operation which is cyclical. It is repeated on a regular basis to test for effectiveness. Even when you have reached the fourth and final phase, you will still be carrying out first phase operations, because they will be helping you to recognize, assess, and develop new policies to manage and exploit changes in technology, clients, and business needs. The framework stops you getting stuck in the tar pit of perfection. It stops you doing things and investing in things which were useful

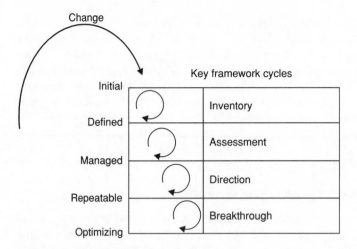

Figure 7.3 State transition diagram: links to the process management framework. A process-oriented maturity framework showing how change is constantly assimilated and built in to the process.

yesterday, just because they were useful yesterday. It makes you look at what is happening today, and what is likely to be happening tomorrow.

You move from one level of maturity to the next when you have embedded the corresponding operation into your everyday business practices. It is rather like learning to spin plates on sticks. At the first level you have only one plate to spin. When that is properly balanced you can pick up the next plate, and so on; you may even be able to automate some of the operations. It is up to you to determine the pace at which you go. It will depend to some extent on your current state and the size of your organization. As it is a staged approach, you will be able to plan, monitor, and flex your plans as you go along. We can check that the requirements of each stage have been met by sampling organizational information and practices. If information is inaccurate, or if practices are not established or appropriate, then we know that there is a problem with the stage and it needs to be revisited.

Inventory phase

To make the first transition, from initial to defined, we need an operation which allows us to know what our assets and liabilities are at any time. What is our product portfolio? What work is in the pipeline? Who are the stakeholders, clients, suppliers, and staff? What are their skills? What tools do they have to work with? And so on. This is called the *inventory phase* (Sec. 7.4) and it is there to provide you with a baseline, not only in terms of supporting the phases which are to follow, but also in monitoring how you have managed your assets to be more effective and your liabilities to be potentially less damaging year on year.

Assessment phase

In the second transition, from defined to managed, you build an operation which gives you information on how well your process and operations are engineered to meet your stakeholder needs. This is the *assessment phase* (Sec. 7.5). It provides you with radar (Sec. 11.4) to assess your current position relative to your goals and your market. To what extent are you meeting client and stakeholder needs? How well does your capability match the capability needed by your market? Where are the brakes in the organization? This is the assessment phase — another baseline operation to support the ones that follow, and to give you a snapshot of how well you are hunting your target which can be compared with the snapshots you have taken on previous occasions.

Direction phase

The third transition, from managed to repeatable, occurs when there is a standard operation to provide appropriate, prioritized instructions and resources to the organization to act to close any gaps which may have been detected. This is the *direction phase* (Sec. 7.6). The direction is synchronized and balanced across the organization as a whole. You can then monitor the results of your direction. Did the directions have the desired effect? What happened unexpectedly? What can be learnt? When you have attained this level, you are ready to seek accreditation. As time goes on this becomes a tuning operation which will free up more and more resources for breakthrough.

Breakthrough phase

The final, fourth, transition is the breakthrough phase (8.7). This means that you are able to engineer your process and learning curve. You are generally a responsible, responsive, and innovative supplier. You have your costs under control, you can value-engineer your process, and you deliver value for money. But if you had only breakthrough phase operations, without the preceding phase operations, you could be in a mess. You would have no mechanisms in place to package and track the effectiveness of your products and operations. You would be perpetually reinventing the wheel.

Putting the process framework together

At first sight, this framework may seem a little odd. It is not making prescriptions that you set up your organization in a specific way, that you have brand X inspections or reviews, that you have standards for this particular activity or that. It is inevitable that you will have an organizational and reporting structure, it is inevitable that you will have standards and work procedures. But because you have a framework which ensures you know where you are and where you need to be, you, yourself, can determine the most appropriate mechanisms to put in place to support your software production process needs. When you are engaged in actively seeking out what your particular business needs are, and what your particular problems are, you are spared the pain of working through someone else's medicine cabinet in the hope there is something in there to make you feel better.

We are really looking at building competencies and Table 7.1 shows you what these are.

7.4 INVENTORY PHASE

Whenever there is talk of change the old adage, 'know where you are, decide where you want to be' trips tritely off the tongue. Everybody goes into workshops to thrash out future direction. For some reason we take it for granted that we know where we are,

Table 7.1 Process management competencies

Key operation	→ Defined Inventory	→ Managed Assessment	→ Repeatable Direction	→ Optimized Breakthrough
Stakeholder	Constraint mapping	Assessment prioritization	Conflict resolution	Proactive collaboration
Client	Awareness	Assess values	Stratify client families	Proactive collaboration
Business	Market awareness	Assess influence	Segment market Define strategy	Educate market
Delivery	Map processes	Assess processes	Define delivery pipelines	Compete with better logistics
Change	Awareness	Assessment	Management	Engineer
Capability	Capability database	Process-linked assessment	Process/operation descriptions	Capability engineering
Requirements	Methods awareness	Problem definition	Policy strategies	Requirements engineering
Service	Client interfaces	Assess potential	Re-engineer policy	Value-engineer services
Product	Portfolio awareness	Gap analysis	Platform policy reuse	Design for ease of production and reuse
Process	Mapping	Assessment	Measurement	Engineering
Configuration	Identify configuration items	Assess needs	Support product reuse	Automate
V&V	Detection operations	Causal analysis	Error prevention	Error proofing
Purchasing	Identify	Assess	Partnerships	Joint products
Cost	Tracking	Process links	Indicators	Cost engineering

because, well, we are where we are, are we not? But do you know who your clients and stakeholders are, their values and constraints? What products and services your business supports?

If you do not know this information immediately, can you get it quickly? Is it accurate? Is it understandable? You may be in the fortunate minority, since many organizations, although they may know who their clients are, do not know their stakeholders, what their product portfolio is, what projects they have in hand, nor what proposals there are in the pipeline. It is always worth while to work through this phase. It is surprising what you find out.

Creating an operation to take you from chaos to a defined state

The purpose of this first phase is to take you from an initial state to a defined state. It is a very simple phase designed to help you know yourself and to raise the business awareness of the organization. It is largely a raw data gathering exercise and you should be able to complete it fairly swiftly. However, the duration of the phase will vary depending upon the size and complexity of your organization, what existing inventory operations you already have in place, and, to some extent, staff availability for collecting the information. Like all the other phases, it is not a one-off exercise. Create and map an operation which provides you with access to this information in a readily communicable form, on a routine basis. The map needs to show the sources of information, how the information is stored and kept current, how and when it is communicated, who is responsible for the overall operation and change management, and who are responsible for all the component activities.

The need for inventory

All of the answers to the checklist associated with this phase represent assets and liabilities of some sort. When you have the lists you will have an idea of how big an elephant you are working on, what areas of duplication there are, what potential for reuse may be available, and so on. This will provide you with a base from which you can determine any potential shortfalls or excess during the assessment phase. If you do not have an up-to-date inventory then you could be spending money on tools and methods, skills and supplies which you already have. Equally, you could be in the position of not having the capability to support some clients and products.

Table 7.2 is an outline checklist of the minimum information you need to gather.

Table 7.2 Outline checklist

Key operation	Inventory items	Collected?
Stakeholder	Who are your stakeholders? (Legal, government, staff, community, business, shareholders, etc.)	
Client	Who are your clients?	
Business	What is your market?	
Delivery	What work is there in the pipeline?	
Change	What work is there on the order books?	
	What proposals are out?	
Capability	What people, skills, and tools are available?	
Requirements	What means of requirements capture exist?	
Service	What SLAs are in operation?	
	Who owns them?	
Product	What products and services exist?	
	Who owns them?	
	How many gigabytes capacity?	
Process	Map the high level delivery lines.	
	What process/operations maps exists?	
	What tools, techniques, methods, etc. exist?	
	What standards exist?	
Configuration	What is under configuration control?	
V & V	What failures and faults are known?	
	What failure capture mechanisms exist?	
Purchasing	Who are the suppliers?	
	What contracts exist?	
Cost	What spend is available?	
	How is that apportioned?	
	What cost monitoring/control systems exist?	

7.5 ASSESSMENT PHASE

Once you have an inventory, and have created the operations to provide the information on a regular basis, you may start to feel quite happy. 'Just look at all the products and services we supply! No one can accuse us of being overstaffed now!' The good thing is that you now have a clearer picture of the organization. But, you do need to take a critical look at your inventory and assess what liabilities you have stored up there.

Creating an operation to take you to a managed state

The purpose of this next phase is to provide you with the operations you need to assess the gap between where you are and the direction you need to be pointing in to satisfy your market needs. You may not find this phase as gratifying as the first, and, in fact, it may be quite painful, if you have not sought this information in the past. Do not worry, it will provide you with information about how you can quickly start to make improvements. This phase is there to help you recognize the key policies, process, and standards you need to run the business. If you are seeking accreditation, this phase will prevent you from proliferating standards.

Some of the questions require you to go outside the organization, so it is probable that this phase will take longer than the first. Again, map the operation you create: how you capture the information, how you go about conducting gap analyses and assessments, what tools and techniques you used, how and to whom the assessment results are communicated, who is responsible for the various activities, and who is responsible for the assessment operation overall.

The need for assessment

It is so easy to become complacent about the organization. We accept its ups and downs as inevitable, and often assume the causes are 'out there', beyond our control. It is also too easy to become blinkered and isolated, and think we have all the answers to our client's problems in our own heads. The assessment operation makes sure we keep referencing our environment on a regular basis for feedback and information.

Once you have all the information detailed in the Table 7.3 checklist, carry out a *gap analysis*. Where are your weaknesses? Where are you going to obtain the greatest leverage to help you close the gap? People working in all the various operations will need to collaborate closely to obtain this information.

7.6 DIRECTION PHASE

It is all very well finding that we have drifted off course but what do we do then? When you have a nasty shock standing on the bathroom scales, after the initial seizure remember how logical you become? Only half a stone overweight. Seven pounds. If I eat a little less, I should be able to lose that in seven weeks. No hardship. You weigh yourself again after a month. You have put on three more pounds! What is going on? Usually the answer is that we made pious resolutions but no specific plan. We have not systematically re-engineered our eating habits. If we want to lose a pound a week we have to reduce our daily energy intake by 500 kilocalories. We need a day-by-day plan to help us. We also need to maintain our new behaviour, otherwise, soon after we reach our target weight, we find that

Table 7.3 'Gap' analysis

Key operation	Assessment items	Collected?
Stakeholder	To what extent are their key constraints met?	
	What difficulties are there?	
	What are the common areas of conflict?	
Client	What are their key buying preferences?	
	To what extent are they met?	
Business	What factors govern your market?	
	To what extent can you influence them?	
Delivery	What is the delivery performance record?	
Change	What capability is needed to meet orders?	
Capability	What capability does the business need?	
Requirements	What major problems exist?	
Service	What is the service performance record?	
Product	How old and fragile are products and services?	
	What is the status of products and services?	
	What capability is needed to support them?	
Process	Request operations maps from all of these key operations and assess.	
Configuration	What problems are there?	
V & V	What are the major problem areas?	
Purchasing	What are the supplier performance records?	
	What contractual problems exist?	
Cost	What are the three highest costs?	
	What are the three lowest costs?	
	What are the major causes of cost overruns?	

we are saddled with more pounds. But hopefully, that day-by-day plan will have helped us to develop more appropriate eating habits.

Creating an operation to take you to a repeatable state

This third phase builds on the previous two. Having taken stock and found out your position relative to your market, you now need to take coordinated action to re-establish your course and realign your processes and operations. You need to re-establish purpose and direction. You need to plan, set priorities, and allocate resources. Just like your standard planning cycle. In fact all the three operations are designed to complement your standard planning cycle. You might even like to consider streamlining this operation. Annual planning means good ideas and important change have to be kept waiting a whole year.

The need for direction

Most organizations just hand out the results of assessments and tell staff to reduce defects by 50 per cent, or to reduce costs by 20 per cent. But success is limited for three reasons. First, unless you know the process and have a measured plan for change, then all striving towards targets is random, wasted effort. Secondly, there is no coordination between contingent operations; suboptimization breaks out. Thirdly, the resources are not there to support change, just quick fixes. This is why the whole organization needs to develop direction based upon purpose, goals, and gap analyses. Policies and standards must be complementary. They must be linked to a visible process which can be re-engineered to produce the required ends. Finally, priorities have to be agreed. There is not the capability in any organization to remake itself over night. Change has to be targeted at areas where there is maximum leverage, secured by budget and resource allocation and different decision-making habits. Table 7.4 provides you with a checklist.

Table 7.4 A checklist of priorities

Key operation	Direction items	Completed?
Stakeholder	Policy for managing stakeholders and conflicts. Stakeholder driven standards.	
Client	Clients grouped according to client values. Client service improvement plan.	
Business	Rationalization and segmentation of market along client and stakeholder lines. Purpose, goals, and performance indicators.	
Delivery	Re-engineered delivery pipelines and fastpaths.	
Change	Capacity plan.	
Capability	Recruitment, training, and resource plans.	
Requirements	Re-engineered requirements capture operations.	
Service	Client service improvement plan.	
Product	Product maintenance and re-engineering policy. Component database or repository.	
Process	Re-engineer process and operations. Rationalize tools, methods, and standards. Link standards to process and operations. Establish cycle-times for operations.	
Configuration	Establish policy. Remove major problems.	
V & V	Establish V & V plans. Remove major problems.	
Purchasing	Establish supplier policy. Remove major problems.	
Cost	Integrate costing into the process — (ABC), etc. Re-plan resource allocation.	

7.7 BREAKTHROUGH PHASE

When inventory, assessment, and direction operations have been incorporated within the standard planning cycle, when there are clear policies and guidelines for key operations, and when there is a visible process which has work standards embedded in it, then you are in a position to seek standards accreditation (Sec. 7.9). Now you can go for breakthrough.

Enter into joint partnerships with stakeholders and clients

You can become more proactively involved in your clients' and stakeholders' policy and decision-making. Being with them while they work on their future will put you in a better position to understand their ambitions and values and to respond to their needs. When you are very familiar with client values, you can begin to anticipate new needs and educate them to accept new directions or offerings. Work to obtain a better understanding of the market and to extend your influence and recognition there.

Develop logistically different delivery processes

You can analyse the different logistical needs of your clients and value-engineer different delivery processes to serve their needs even better. You do not need to tie all your clients into the same bulk delivery pipeline. Who are the clients that want to be actively involved in prototyping and joint application design? Who are the sophisticated clients that can produce their own designs ready for you to build and test? How much customization does each of your client groups require? How are their service requirements different? How can you become more involved with your suppliers to ensure they understand your ambitions and values more clearly? How can you help them overcome their difficulties?

Invest time in product and process maintenance and reuse

Now is the time to start to develop strategies for design for product reuse. What changes to operations need to be made? What skills do your staff need? What policies do you need to formulate? How can you work on the liabilities in your product portfolio? It is often said that software does not corrode or deteriorate. That is not my experience. As new releases are produced to provide enhancement or fix errors, the software definitely 'ages'. Each time software modules are patched they become more prone to failure. Why not schedule preventive maintenance and product re-engineering into your plans?

Consider designing for ease of production, ease of enhancement, and ease of testing

In the same way as you improve your product asset base, you can improve your process base. You do not have to wait until it becomes an important re-engineering task. What can be tried? What can be tuned? If your estimation cycle time is 20 days, ask how it can be engineered down to 2 days (and not how it can be cut down to two days.) How can you reduce operation cycle times and still maintain process balance?

Automate tedious operations, and push decisions out to staff

What can you start to automate in the process? How can you get rid of necessary but tedious tasks to free you up to take on more breakthrough work? What do your staff dislike doing most? If they dislike a particular job, the chances are that it will be a job that is not completed as well as it should be. Perhaps you can do away with the task completely? It is always useful, too, to review the pattern of decision-making in the organization. Can you get rid of some of that cycle time gobbling decision-making by having more open policies and guidelines, or by coaching and empowering staff to take their own decisions?

   The list in Table 7.5 summarizes these opportunities. This is not a fixed list, you will have lots of thoughts of your own to add to it.

Table 7.5 Breakthrough phase

Key operation	Breakthrough items	Achieved?
Stakeholder	Get involved in stakeholder policy and decisions.	
Client	Understand the factors influencing client values.	
	Get involved in client policy and decisions.	
Business	Understand, influence, and educate the market.	
Delivery	Delivery pipelines for different client needs.	
Change	Capacity optimization.	
Capability	Using learning curves for competitive advantage.	
Requirements	Provide clients with tools to prototype.	
Service	Value-engineered services.	
Product	Platform and component reuse.	
	Preventive maintenance.	
	Product re-engineering.	
	Design for ease of production and resilience.	
Process	Process re-engineering.	
	Process value engineering.	
	Improve dependability of cycle times for operations.	
Configuration	Automate and error-proof.	
V & V	Automate and error-proof.	
	Design for testability.	
Purchasing	Re-engineer your supplier processes to meet your stakeholders' needs.	
Cost	Value engineer.	
	Work to reduce overheads burdened on staff.	

7.8 BUILDING THE EXPERIENCE BASE

One of your most important assets is your experience base. It does not sound like a tangible asset, but it can provide you with powerful competitive advantage. The experience base is a means of capturing the intelligence in your organization using whatever tools you have. I recommend the use of object-oriented tools, but relational databases are fine, too.

Competing with your learning curve

When you tap the potential of your experience base you are competing with your learning curve. The more advanced you are on learning curves, the better your estimations and analysis, and the lower your costs become. That is why it is important to spend time defining a clear purpose and making strategic decisions about which learning curve you will climb. The longer you stay with a specific market, the longer you use certain tools and practices, the more learning and advantage you can bank. If you are constantly throwing out technology and making radical switches, the longer you will find yourself at the bottom of learning curves, and losing the edge. This fast becomes a nosedive. The more you find yourself losing edge, the more frenzied your switching to new learning curves becomes.

Sticking to a learning curve does not mean that you are set to become another candidate for Jurassic Park. You can plan to take on new learning curves. The emphasis here is on 'plan'. Planning learning curves is like planning new products. You examine your position on each learning curve. Being able to exploit a high position on a learning curve is like having a 'cash cow'. If you seem stuck on a learning curve which has become a sink for effort and money, then you have a 'dog' which needs urgent review. Similarly, you need to anticipate and invest in the learning curves which will become your new 'rising stars'.

The experience base brings organizational learning together

The experience base captures the products of the inventory, assessment, and direction phases. People in the organization need to know who the customers are, what their values and key buying preferences are, and how well you are meeting them. If staff are to become more business oriented then they need to know stakeholders' demands. They need to know the status and reliability of product platforms and components. Complete, tested, available for reuse, about to be renewed? The experience base is also there to provide you with performance indicators. How much better are you getting at satisfying client needs? How do operation cycle times compare with last year, or the year before? Where are the brakes on the process?

7.9 STANDARDS ACCREDITATION

If you are seeking standards accreditation you may be concerned that this approach leaves you stranded. Let us just look at what we are doing in a little more detail so that you can have a clear picture of how you can achieve accreditation using this approach. The first thing is that the standards body you are seeking to satisfy is one of your named stakeholders. You have to assess yourself against their requirements.

Next, you will achieve a more robust process with less conflict than if you were just seeking to satisfy the standards body alone. This is because you are taking into consideration the needs of your clients, your shareholders, and the business as a whole. There is nothing in the standards to ensure that the work you undertake is economically viable for your business. No matter how sound the quality is, if your business collapses mid-project because of poor financial practices, your clients will suffer. Your auditors would highlight any potential illegal practices, but again, there is nothing in the standards to discourage you from such acts such as falsifying test documentation.

The other advantage is that you are considering the whole of your process as a quality system. Quality is not a subset or an add-on to your process. Everyone is engaged in 'quality' activities. This is the way it should be. Quality is not something done to product and services by a specialist group acting on special instructions. Your process is designed to deliver products and services in such a way and at such a cost that your customers' needs are totally satisfied.

Does this not increase your documentation? On the contrary, you can use the information you really need to run the business to satisfy standards documentation needs. You do not have to document and review a separate quality system. Your process is the quality system. Figure 7.4 shows what the standards structure for your organization could look like.

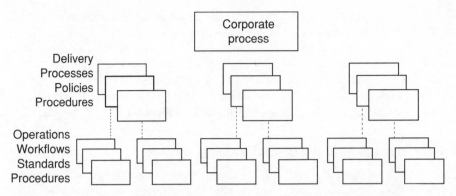

Figure 7.4 Standards structure: a process management framework. This makes use of process and operations maps which relate directly to work on the ground. Because they are built in to staff job descriptions, what you see is what you get.

There is a high-level schema of the corporate process, beneath that are the workflow diagrams of operations, procedures, and policies attached to each process. No lengthy volumes, just clear maps which are the current work instructions. Your experience base will record product, training, and customer documentation among other information.

We have looked at how the framework maps on to the CMM. Table 7.6 shows you how the framework maps on to the 13 elements listed in the TickIT accreditation guide.

Table 7.6 How TickIT/ISO 9001 standards requirements are met by the framework

TickIT element	Provided by:
1 Implementing and maintaining a quality system	Business purpose, goals, and client performance indicators. Process maps.
2 Maintaining the organization and its interfaces	Process maps and synchronized direction production.
3 Reviewing	V&V policy. Process and operation maps.
4 Documenting projects and products	Process and operation maps. Experience base.
5 Recruitment, training and staff development	Capability management plans.
6 Configuration mangement	Configuration management policy.
7 Security	Product policy. Process and operation maps.
8 Quality system reviews/audits	Regular process inventory and assessment.
9 Procurement	Purchasing policy.
10 Progress	Product and capability management plans.
11 Non-conforming material	V&V policy. Process and operation maps.
12 Corrective action	As above.
13 Quality information	V&V policy. Experience base.

MAKING THE PROCESS VISIBLE

Trurl takes the appeal, and without reading it at all, orders it returned to sender and writes diagonally across it: 'Unacceptable — Proper Forms Not Attached.' And he signs his name illegibly.

Stanislaw Lem
The Cyberiad (The Fifth Sally)

There are a number of complementary tools available to help you carry out process mapping and modelling in the inventory and assessment phases. The tools which we use for process mapping should enable us to see clearly what is happening in our processes and operations, to help us make diagnoses, and to identify where improvements can be made. In this non-technical chapter I want you to see how you can customize tools to meet your specific needs.

I have used a very simple, end-to-end process, that of serving food to a hungry customer, as an example to illustrate the strengths and weaknesses of each tool, and to explain how the tools can be used together to give you the most insight. It would be difficult in the space I have here to work through the delivery of a software product. And, if I had the space, the chances are that you would have to say, 'This is not how we do it!' 'The principle of strategy is having one thing, to know ten thousand things.' However, as we expand our understanding from this small example of the forces at work which lead to ineffective and inefficient processes through Chapters 8, 9, and 10 which follow, I shall introduce management and technical operations which are common in software production environments.

Having said that, I would like you to remember that even if you have not consciously designed and implemented a process, a process exists. The problem for you is that it may not be the most appropriate or effective process. If you allow these invisible processes to run their own sweet way, the chances are that you are leaking value. The amount of value you can earn is linked directly to your process. At the beginning of the Industrial Revolution in Britain, it was not new technology that brought about the initial increases in productivity; in the first instance it was the reorganization of work when people were brought together to work in factories. The technology followed on from those new forms of organization.

8.1 GOING FISHING

Because the aim of process mapping is not simply to mount beautiful diagrams under glass on our office wall for the admiration of peers, managers, and standards auditors, we need a process mapping tool which will help us in the inventory phase (Sec. 7.4) and assessment phase (Sec. 7.5) to identify, quickly and accurately, effective targets for improvement.

Choosing the net

The tools we choose for process mapping should enable us to see clearly what is happening in our processes and operations, to help us make diagnoses, and to identify where improvements can be made. If this support is not available we risk going round and round in circles and getting lost at sea, or worse, making changes which just take us from one tar pit to another.

How our net is constructed determines what sort of fish we catch. While we may not know what our problem fish look like, we do know that they have a common characteristic — they feed off value. That means they consume time and effort needlessly. When you start, you will use the biggest mesh nets, *block diagram* (Sec. 8.5) and *state transition diagram* (Sec. 8.6), because if you use a small mesh you will catch more fish than your boat can carry without capsizing. When you no longer catch big fish, then is the time to go fishing for smaller fry with a *deployment flow chart* (Sec. 8.7) and possibly a *Petri net* (Sec. 8.8).

Catching rework

We know that rework operations consume valuable time and effort, but how can we quickly identify rework as distinct from work as usual? One person's view of rework is often another person's creative activity. How will you be able to tell the difference? Most process mapping methods are quite clear on this. Rework is identified by work flowing backwards in the process. It is like watching the clock being turned backwards, except we can never turn the clock backwards, we can only take up more time or add to cycle time without making progress. In any operation or process the potential cost of rework varies geometrically with the amount of elapsed time between error introduction and detection. Barry Boehm draws our attention to this phenomenon in his book *Software Engineering Economics*. For this reason, we need to spot long delays between associated production and inspection activities.

Spotting bottlenecks and interrupts

Delays and bottlenecks are enormous value-guzzlers. How can you spot these? We need a convention which will flag delays and bottlenecks to us, as well as their magnitude. To do this we need to introduce time and the magnitude of elapsed time into the process maps.

Interrupts can be terrible value-destroyers. Planned or synchronous interrupts can be managed to some extent, although time is lost because someone, somewhere has had to switch from one task to another with all the cost of changeover and preparation time that is needed to make that switch. Unplanned or asynchronous interrupts, on the other hand, wreak havoc because they introduce indeterminateness into our process, and our ability to measure or estimate cycle time starts to breaks down. So, we need a means of marking operations which are subject to interrupts, and also those operations which create interrupts and whether the interrupts they generate are synchronous or asynchronous.

Trawling for cycle times

Knowing the cycle time of an operation and its magnitude of cost gives us the opportunity to identify significant leverage for improvement. While we may not be interested, or are unable to measure, precise cycle times or costs, a means of capturing and exhibiting ranges for both often provides benefit. Even knowing there is a wide range of fluctuation is useful information for management and costing purposes.

We have talked about cycle time from the production point of view. But how about cycle time as it is experienced by the customer? Sequences of operations, when queuing or bussing is involved, can be rearranged to reduce cycle time or wait time for the customer without changing the internal cycle time of each operation. Until recently, in many supermarkets, customers had to queue twice if they were buying fresh vegetables: once to have the vegetables weighed, and then later at the checkouts to pay for their purchases. Thankfully, these operations have now been collapsed into a single weigh and pay operation at the checkouts. Cycle time from the customer's experience has been reduced by the amount of wait time in the weighing queue. Again, a means of identifying differences in this respect can provide opportunities for immediate improvement.

Separating value-adding from value-eating activities

In one organization where I worked, it was estimated that 30 per cent of time was spent in meetings. A target was then set to reduce the number of meetings. This made life very frustrating when you knew you had to communicate vital facts. Suddenly, no-one was willing to be involved in meetings of any kind.

Much of our work in the software production business involves the transfer of information from person to person or from group to group. How can you identify necessary communication and unnecessary communication? Like error production and detection, the potential cost of communication failure depends on how far away from the communication source the receiver of the information is. Information does not travel well and a means of associating operations which reprocess and transcribe the same set of information helps to flag where unnecessary delays, costs, or risks may be involved. Sign-offs are a prime example involving delay, cost, and risk which could be reduced by a single managed event. Again, how do you signal criticality of information? How do you signal information gate-keeping, where information is being funnelled unnecessarily through a translator?

Finally, and most importantly, how do you identify which operations are effectively creating stakeholder value? It is important to ask how does this operation add value for the customer, but it is equally important not to recommend operations for the axe which at first sight seem to add nothing to customer value but are an intrinsic part of the delivery infrastructure. We need a means of linking some operations to stakeholder requirements.

8.2 LUNCH IS SERVED

I have become an inveterate 'process watcher' and 'process mapper'. My handbag rapidly fills up with corners of paper serviettes, shopping lists, and till receipts all covered with spidery diagrams and notes, totally incomprehensible at this stage, I am ashamed to admit, to anyone except myself. A word of warning: in time, you may find yourself doing the same.There are two benefits to be had from this rather addictive activity. First, you will become practised in the art of benchmarking — everything. And all the while you will be adding to your process experience. By working on and improving other people's processes, you are exercising your skills and developing an insight into how your own processes could stand improvement. Secondly, process mapping is a great stress reliever. Whenever you begin to feel your temperature rise in a queue or a delay, or because of poor service, remember you are a victim of a process that could stand improvement. By examining the process, you can detach your emotions from your immediate situation and put yourself in a better position to offer constructive criticism.

Just think back over the last week or so, to times when you have been a victim of a process. What were the occasions? How could you equip yourself to do some process mapping when the next occasion arises?

Process experience from a handbag

I want to give you one example from the top of my handbag, because I think it provides us with a fairly simple model which, at the same time, brings up issues that are relevant to software delivery. It all began when I went into a café with my husband to order lunch. Service was from the counter. There was a lone assistant at the counter filling orders. In the kitchen behind were two more assistants who were preparing sandwiches, making salads, and baking cakes that could be used by the counter assistant to replenish stocks. Customers arrived in bunches. There was rarely an even flow of orders. Soon after we reached the counter with our empty trays, two other families joined the queue. Instead of filling our order and taking our money there and then, the assistant, seeing a growing queue, changed the process. She just took the orders of the waiting customers, one by one, and promised to bring the snacks over to our table. We all sat down to wait. And wait. And wait some more. Finally we were delivered parts of our lunch, but not the parts that would enable us to eat together or even make a start. My husband's coffee had arrived, but my tea came with no milk, so we could not start to drink. I had my vegetable soup, but my husband did not have his salad, and so on. In fact, instead of our lunch we had been delivered a number of problems which we had not ordered. How long would it be before the soup and tea had passed their enjoyable temperature peak? Should we wait until the milk and salad came? And when would they come? Should I have my soup before my tea? Our welcome break had become an anxiety trap. We decided gently to press our case. As did everyone else. At the same time as another bunch of customers arrived. At the same time as the bunch of customers who managed to eat before us wanted to pay their bills. At the same time as children, having had a chance to read the menu for themselves, began to demand changes to their orders. Another bottleneck was created. It swallowed up and lost more of our wants while delivering yet more problems. Fortunately there was no shortage of paper serviettes.

An innocent change to the process creates chaos

I was interested to see an example of a decision which, taken in all good faith to save the customers' time and feet, had resulted in the customers having to wait even longer, and though feet were saved, tempers unfortunately were not. The (by now) thoroughly confused and dispirited assistant was having to mop up as much anger as spilt milk. Sadly, although the assistant was the only person there accountable, she too, like us, was a victim of the process she had unwittingly created. Intuitively it seemed the best process. But the solution needed was counterintuitive, and as a result, was difficult to discover, unless you had process awareness skills.

The problems of the uncoupled process

In her best efforts to reduce customer wait times, the assistant had sought to improve efficiency by division of labour — her labour. She had 'uncoupled' her process. That is, although she was taking down the orders 'on-line', she had taken the order-processing 'off-line'. However, there was nowhere off-line she could take the order processing to, unless she chose to close down her order-taking and bill-settling operations, which would have frustrated her original goal of saving customers' time. I see many managers who take their work processing off-line in this way. During the day, they are order-takers, or trouble-shooters, and the actual order-processing has to be done either at home, or behind closed doors while staff who require help are kept waiting and other jobs are delayed.

Changing the process to increase cycle time

In fact, instead of reducing cycle time and customer wait times, the assistant had probably doubled them. Let us look at her original process for serving a customer. This involved order-taking, say one minute; order-filling, around three minutes; and money-taking, say another minute, making a total cycle time of five minutes. After uncoupling the process, she introduced two additional operations: delivering orders to the table, two minutes; and sorting out mistakes, another three minutes. Process cycle time was now up to ten minutes.

Queuing, delays, and interrupts reduce process predictability

This is just the simple picture. When we look further, we see that it is not only additional process cycle time which has been introduced, customer queuing times have also been increased. The customer is not only queuing to have orders taken, but also to pay the bill on the way out. The process is wide open to unpredictable interrupts now. These interrupts will not only increase cycle time, but also introduce an element of indeterminateness into the system, that is, making it more unpredictable and difficult to manage.

Problems when you extend the interval between error insertion and error detection

Information and correction loops have become extended. Instead of immediate correction of order errors at the counter, errors are not detected until some time later when they are delivered to the table. All in all, the process has become, when modelled, more complex, chaotic, lengthy, and costly, that is, it can only deliver less value to the customers — the reverse of what was intended. But how would you go about spotting this and putting it to rights?

Alternative process options

What would have happened if the assistant had delegated the uncoupled operations to the other assistants? How would this have improved the situation? Would customers have had to wait longer until an economical number of sandwiches had been ordered before an assistant was released full time to prepare them? How many customer change requests have to be made before you can justify a new release? How do you bundle the request for changes? In a way that enables you to maximize your efficiency, or in a way that enables your customer to synchronize immediately the delivered changes with their mix of work? Would cakes have to be taken off the menu because customers were unwilling to wait an hour for the baking? Do we lose projects because delivery infrastructure is missing, or because the costs of building that infrastructure are loaded onto a single customer, making the project uneconomical from that client's point of view?

What would have happened if the assistant had continued processing one order at a time and allowed the queue to form. Could a visible queue be understood as a message to the process? When the queue is three, assistant number two reports to the counter to process orders. When the queue is six, assistant number three reports for duty. What is the message when the queue grows to nine or more?

The purpose of making the process visible

The only way you can start to understand what is happening and whether it is for the best is by mapping the process and seeking more advantageous alternatives. It goes without saying that process mapping is only a means to an end. Unless something is changed as a result, either our processes or our understanding, we shall fail in our objective to deliver more value to our customers. Menus in themselves are an unreliable source of nutrition.

8.3 EARNED VALUE

I do not want to get too deeply involved in measurement and costing here, because the subject has a chapter all to itself (Chapter 11). But what I would like to do is to raise your awareness of how your process affects not only performance, but, more importantly, I believe, your ability to make performance predictions and create earned value with any degree of confidence.

Performance is the ratio of costs to earned value

How you perform is judged by the ratio of your costs to earned value. It may be that you are in a position to vary your costs, in which case the process you choose will affect your costs and, as a consequence, performance. However, let us make it harder, and consider a situation which is closer to real life. Let us look at the café scenario again from Sec. 8.2. You will only ever have one assistant, you do not have the seating capacity to justify two, and it is ridiculous to talk in terms of half an assistant since you need someone there all day. Then, at the end of the day, the costs for each process are identical: the effort and wages for one assistant for one day. So what is all the fuss about? There is no point in changing the process. It will just upset the assistant.

Well, you might be interested to know whether you can afford to stay in business. This is linked not only to your costs, but also to the amount of earned value you can generate. Given your capital investment in premises and equipment which support the seating capacity you have available, are you obtaining a suitable return on this investment? Any return? Or is it a temporary negative return, until things pick up? I am assuming that even if you do not want to make a profit, as some people quite validly do not, that you might like to know the break-even point at which you would start to earn a profit, or you might like to know the amount of subsidy you will need to keep running. I am not assuming that you want to maximize profits, make a quick killing, or find yourself running a soulless fast-food business when this was never part of your dream. The question is, can you continue to get by, doing what you enjoy doing, and providing a service which people value and which increases well-being without creating unnecessary waste?

Process and earned value

Let us look at this some more. The potential earnings from your investment are fixed by the value earned per chair per hour. The number of chairs you have available is a variable. You can have as few chairs as you want; you can take out the chairs altogether and have people stand round counter islands, up to a maximum capacity determined by safety and comfort. The number of hours you operate is variable, too. Given that you only have, and only want to have, one assistant then the hours you can operate each day will be determined by legislation. But there are two more important variables to be considered. First, how long do people stay in their chairs? And secondly, how many people are wanting to sit in one of your chairs in the first place? The number of hours your chairs can earn value in your lifetime, say, depends on the number of people willing to come through your door and keep on coming through your door to buy the service and products you are delivering. A percentage of your customers will be passing trade, a percentage repeat customers. Lose your repeat customers, and that means loss. That loss is not only revenue, but also loss in terms of client knowledge and the predictability of your job security. When you have repeat customers you can start to provide for known tastes; develop a relationship so that you keep in touch with their changing tastes; and make some assessment of your security based upon that knowledge. When you find yourself having to provide for passing trade, then it is very much a lottery of whether you will have hit on the right combination to match their key buying preferences.

Earned value is fixed by your process

Although it seems as though we have come a long way from our original point about estimating performance, we have made this journey in order to appreciate that, although costs may be fixed and must stay fixed, it is not useful to believe these are grounds for leaving the process to follow its own sweet path. The point is that the amount of value you can deliver and earn is not fixed by your costs. The amount of value you can earn and the degree to which you can predict that earned value is fixed by your process

Some processes allow you to predict and engineer earned value better than others

In the two processes in Sec. 8.2, it is difficult to estimate the value earned by the the second process which has been revised to take order-filling off-line and deliver orders to table. Two sorts of indeterminateness have crept in: the length of time people sit in their chairs, and the probability of repeat custom. The length of time people sit in their chairs is governed by the nature and length of the push-down stack approach which has been created to cope with the growing queue at the counter. Customers now have to wait until all subsequent arrivals at the counter have been serviced before their order is filled and delivered. This is a first-in, last-out approach. Although you can make estimates based on known lengths of queues (a first-in, first-out approach), you cannot base estimates on the length of a queue which may or may not form following a customer's arrival. As a consequence, the service becomes more complex and more work is involved which was not present before, such as delivering to the tables. This means that the customer will certainly experience longer delays and, in all probability, increased problems. This could impact their decisions to come back and fill chairs in the future. The consequences are that the capacity for earning value is reduced because seats are occupied longer for no proportionate increase in earnings and seats which might have been filled remain empty in the future. The net result is that the earned value per unit cost, or performance, decreases.

Cost reduction and earned value improvement demand process re-engineering

When senior management examines performance, that is, costs to earnings ratios, and does not feel happy with the numbers, the pressure is on either to reduce costs, or to improve productivity. If the process is not visible, then the choices might be to cut the costs and quality of food inputs or to replace a skilled assistant by a less skilled assistant, in which case costs go down at the risk that customer value goes down even more sharply, creating a cycle of decline. If the pressure is to improve productivity and earnings, the assistant will say she is overworked, which she certainly is, given the increase in the workload she has created for herself, and will ask for more staff. In which case costs could be increased faster than value is earned. The problem does not go away. The process is the real culprit and will survive, at least as long as the business, to gobble value and inflate costs unless it is made visible and re-engineered.

8.4 STRUCTURED ANALYSIS AND DESIGN TECHNIQUES

Structured analysis and design techniques (SADT) are now widely used for analysing customer systems and the software production system itself. A number of tools exist to support the automated production of charts and associated documentation. The conventions are well known by most analysts, and although there are a number of different brands, they are sufficiently standard not to present too many problems to someone looking at a new brand who is familiar with the technique. Developed to provide a common means of communication between customer and supplier, the diagramming technique has enjoyed some success, although problems still remain. Some customers, even after training, find the technique difficult to interpret. Whether this is due to the diagramming technique, or to the newness of thinking about work in a systematic way, it is difficult to say. However, it should not be taken as read that charts using this diagramming technique are self-evident. Just to remind you of the conventions: the bubbles represent operations; arrowed lines represent the flow of information, goods, and services; parallel lines represent information stores; and square boxes represent terminations with the outside world. Full written definitions and descriptions of the operations, flows, data stores, and terminators would normally be present to provide support documentation to the diagrams. I am not including them here, as I trust we have enough information now to understand the mapping of the processes described in Sec. 8.2.

Using SADT

The problems of using SADT for process assessment (Fig. 8.1) presents us with an overall picture for both processes. What I would like to know, looking at Figs 8.2 and 8.3, is which one shows the more effective and efficient set of operations for serving my customers. Can I tell, just by looking at the maps?

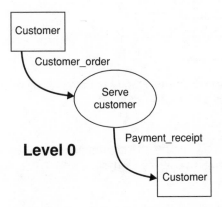

Figure 8.1 SADT: serving the customer scenarios 1 and 2. The level 0 diagrams for both processes are identical.

SADT and error mapping

How would I know how much rework is entailed by the system, and the distance that separates error production from detection? There is nothing explicit here, only flows which indicate wrong or changed orders. There is no way of knowing the size of the problem. We might deduce that the more operations present, the more possibility there is for error. Similarly, data stores might highlight for us the possibility or risk of transcription errors. Other than that a search on names for 'wrong' or 'incomplete' may provide us with further

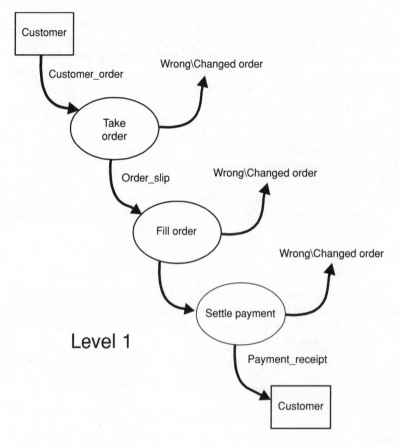

Figure 8.2 SADT: serving the customer. In the first scenario the customer waits in the queue, places an order, waits to have the order filled, and then pays before sitting down to eat.

clues of possible problems. However, there is nothing certain in this respect, since the naming of parts is often very much a personal prerogative of the analyst.

SADT and bottleneck mapping

How about spotting delays and bottlenecks then? There is nothing explicit here to help. Data stores could represent a bottleneck, or they could represent a very efficient method of handling asynchronous communication between a number of people. We really cannot say which from the diagram. Interrupts are not shown at any point. Fill order in Fig. 8.3 could be expanded to show that it could include a recursive operation to Take order for a new customer. But it is interesting to think how exactly the diagram could deal with requests for order changes and notification of wrong orders, say. Imagine what would happen to change requests which interrupt the flow in the danger zone of Fig. 8.3.

Cost and cycle time mapping

Costs and cycle times are not shown. The diagram does not have a time dimension. But there is no reason why cycle times and costs cannot be included in the process descriptions,

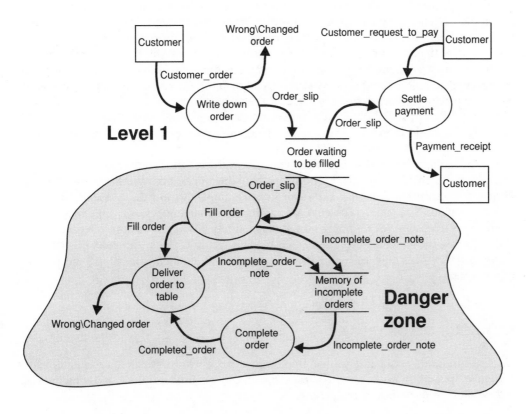

Figure 8.3 SADT: serving the customer. In the second scenario it is obvious that complexity increases when the order filling is taken off-line, but is the customer better off? It would depend on how many people were available to serve the customer.

or why standard wait times cannot be specified for customer interactions. Customer cycle time is not indicated for the same reasons. One might be tempted to assume that because the customer has two interactions in the map of Fig. 8.3 and only one in Fig. 8.2, customer cycle time has been increased. But there is no sound information on which to make this assumption. However, there is nothing to stop this information being provided.

SADT and communication mapping

Communication is centred on flows between operations not between actors. Critical information, and its sources, is the only information mapped. We cannot see how much redundant information had to be processed to obtain the critical information.

Disadvantages and benefits of using SADT for process mapping

In terms of effectiveness, if we consider the final output — payment_for_order_receipt — we might say that both processes are equally effective, we have been paid for our services. Again, that might be a misleading conclusion. The customer might just be paying up as a means to escape the chaos. I am particularly concerned about the settlement process in Fig. 8.3 since the customer has to trigger the request to pay. While normally most people are honest, it just might be the case that some customers do leave without paying, for whatever reason. One could also say that depending upon the resourcing and what exactly has to be produced, both systems are just as effective. If your market could bear the costs of having different staff taking orders, filling orders, delivering orders, and settling bills, then Fig. 8.3 could represent a very efficient and effective service. But we know nothing about resource deployment.

The advantages of SADT are that you can quickly see the overall picture — the constituent operations and the relationships between operations. We have said that the difficulties with cycle time and costs can be surmounted within the conventions of the existing system. The main problems are to do with flagging rework, bottlenecks, and interrupts. It is useful for mapping how things may ideally work without rework, delays, and out-of-sequence change requests, but SADT seems to have difficulty in mapping reality as it happens, and as such I think it provides little diagnostic help to aid process improvements.

8.5 BLOCK DIAGRAM

Block diagramming is an easy way of representing processes. Although it is very simplistic, I include it because with some customizing, it can be used to show, at a high level, important characteristics of the process.

An annotated block diagram for getting the big picture

Normally block diagrams are just hierarchical maps of operations. What is striking about them is the isolation of operations in their tree-structured compartments. Here I have used a few symbols from the deployment flow chart (see Sec. 8.7), to show communications between the operations, and to flag cycle times and delays (Figs. 8.4, 8.5).

Using block diagrams to assess the overall process

Sources of error production and detection are not mapped at this level.

Block diagrams and delays

Delays are shown by the hexagon. Sometimes the hexagonal delay symbol has a clock attached which shows that the wait is for a determined period. Delay symbols by themselves indicate that the length of wait cannot be determined or has not been measured. Comparing the two maps we can see that the customer has only one queue in the first process (Fig. 8.4), but appears in several queues in the second (Fig. 8.5). While the customer is standing in a queue only on two occasions, there are three occasions when the customer is seated and waiting — effectively in a queue. Since there is no clock attached to

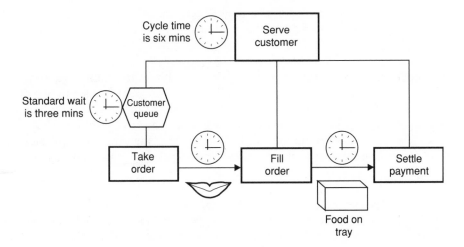

Figure 8.4 Annotated block diagram. This high-level diagram shows the flow of work for serving the customer in scenario one. The stages are linked by synchronous process 'messages': word of mouth and the customer's food itself. A simple, predictable process which could be maintained under statistical process control.

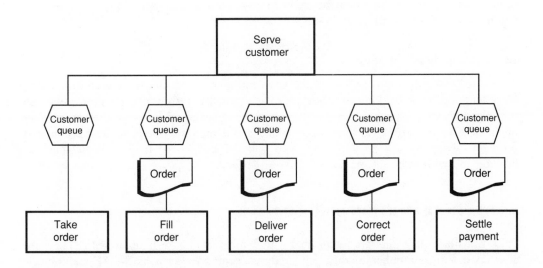

Figure 8.5 Annotated block diagram. In scenario two we can see the destruction of the balanced and synchronized horizontal flow which we saw in Fig. 8.4. All the operations are uncoupled and are contingent upon asynchronous customer interrupts. This means that the process cannot be deterministic or subject to process control. Also note that a written order is now required to maintain communication between the uncoupled operations. The voice of the process has been lost.

those queues to indicate the length of wait, we might be concerned, given that we are a fast-food café. If we were a restaurant, then that pattern would not seem unreasonable.

Block diagrams, cycle times, and costs

Bottlenecks and interrupts are not explicitly shown. We could infer from any cycle times given that if they appeared inflated there might be a bottleneck or delay hidden in one of the operations. In that way we could turn our focus on to that operation for a closer look.

Cycle times are given where they are known. The difference between Figs 8.4 and 8.5 is that the second map has no clock notation at all. It looks as though there is a problem there; I would want to investigate why no statement about cycle times has been made.

Block diagrams and communication

It is interesting to compare communication between the two maps. In the first, word of mouth is the means of communication between Take order and Fill order, while the food on the tray is the communication between Fill order and Settle order. There is no paperwork involved, no translations, no transcriptions. On the other hand, in Fig. 8.5 we have a written order which is the means of communication between all the operations. It is the same piece of paper, so there is no transcribing, but maybe some translating, depending on how many people have to work with the order. Again the pattern resembles more that of a restaurant than a fast-food café. But the most striking difference is the uncoupled nature of the second process. Process flow has been segmented. There are no links between the operations. When process flow is segmented in this way, the process requires well-synchronized choreography to ensure that the customer perceives a seamless service. This is where you would be likely to start your assessment of Fig 8.5 in greater depth, at the five-customer interfaces.

Benefits and disadvantages

Annotated block diagrams provide a simple overall picture which can be used to home in on potential process weaknesses. They are easy to construct, store and reference. Because they are high-level maps they do not show you the detail of mistakes, or interrupts. You might be able to spot the existence of problems at the high level because there are named problem-solving operations. However, you will definitely need a second-level map to provide you with more information for investigation.

8.6 STATE TRANSITION DIAGRAM

State transition diagrams are again charts that most of us are familiar with. They are associated with a number of different analysis techniques such as SADT and object-oriented techniques. They are simple charts to follow and can be used to provide us with a bird's eye view of our process, only this time as experienced by our client. If other interests have a stake in the process, we shall need to create a transition diagram for them, too.

Let us look at how this works. Figures 8.6 and 8.7 are the two processes from Sec. 8.2 set out in state transition diagrams. Each bar in the diagrams represents a state which could be experienced by a customer coming into contact with our process. The arrows represent transition steps between states. In other words, if our customer is hungry, from that state

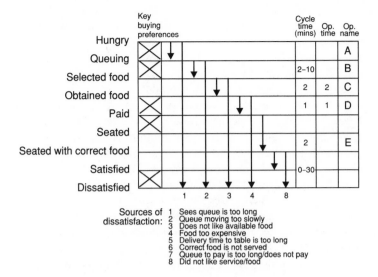

Figure 8.6 State transition diagram. In scenario one we can see the states the customer passes through in our process. The customer may not want to be in some of these states, such as queuing, sitting without food, and paying. We need to remove unwanted states, but since the business is also a stakeholder, then paying should stay! The operations to support the transition from one state to another are cross-referenced on the chart.

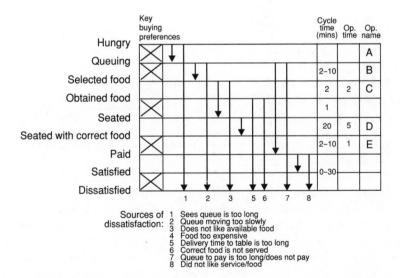

Figure 8.7 State transition diagram. In scenario two despite a dislike of queuing, the customer is queuing twice now, once for food and again to pay. There are more sources of dissatisfaction and the cycle time has been considerably increased. The customer will not like it!

they could move to a queuing state, or a state of dissatisfaction. They cannot move directly from their state of hunger to being seated with correct food. The gap between states will be used later to cross-reference to the operation on a deployment flow chart (Sec. 8.7) which has been designed to take the customer from one state to the next.

Working from your process, draw out all the possible states your customer could go through. It is important to identify all the states when they could be waiting or queuing. This provides you with the words to go down the left-hand side of the diagram. I always include the states 'satisfied' and 'dissatisfied' because these are of prime importance, I hope, to us. Moving over now to the far right, there are three columns to link the states to the internal operations that we have just mentioned, to the cycle time of the operation, that is, the wait experienced by the customer, and operation time, the time it actually takes to carry out the operation shorn of all delays, etc. The column on the left needs some explanation. I have used this to indicate which states the customer, when asked, would prefer not to be in. It does not represent one of their key buying preferences. The customer does not want to be hungry, the customer does not want to queue, the customer would, understandably, prefer not to pay! Here I have worked with a simple prefer/do not prefer marking. You could refine this to indicate shades of preference as you begin to learn more about your customer's profile.

Assessing the process from a state transition diagram

What can we tell then, from looking at these maps? At first sight there seems to be nothing particularly striking about either. I can tell nothing about rework or interrupts.

Spotting clashes with key buying preferences

I can spot that the customer is involved in queuing states in both processes which rank zero against their key buying preferences. That is obviously a delay worth working on. I can see that the second process in Fig. 8.7 has two separate queuing states for the customer which I would be keen to cut out. If this were a restaurant, then the customer might actually prefer to have a wait before giving their order, and we would rank this state against some desirable range of wait times. (But they may not like a wait without a menu.)

Identifying and resolving stakeholder conflicts

If we saw that the customer was in any state which did not correspond to a key buying preference, we would give that our first attention. However, it is important not to rush in and just remove those states. If we removed the Paid state, we would have a delighted customer, but problems for our business. We need to examine the needs of other stakeholders and ask if the state is a requirement of any of them. If not, then we are free to work on removing the state. If it is a requirement, then we need to spend time understanding just how that state is important to someone other than the customer. What would be the consequences to them of removing the state? Can constraints be re-engineered so that they do not conflict with customer values? Would removal undermine the other states which are important to the customer, such as security and safety? For many financial institutions there is the client as individual, and the client as a corporate investor. While the individual may be delighted with a windfall from an automatic telling machine, with a corporate hat on they may not want to belong to a bank which does not have secure money-dispensing systems and for which they are subjected to an extra charge.

All these conflicts need to be resolved before you remove a state. But, for every conflict you can resolve in the client's favour, there is potential for major breakthrough.

Assessing cycle times

We have included cycle time and operation time on the diagram. How does this help? It tells us how long, and possibly how much, if you wanted to include costs, it takes to change the state of your customer. We can add up all the cycle times and work out how long it takes to create a satisfied customer for the process in Fig. 8.6 and how long for the process in Fig. 8.7. Just doing some quick arithmetic I can see that it takes 40–50 minutes to reach a satisfied customer state in the first process, and between 100 and 120 minutes in the second. We might question that from two points of view. Does the customer want to take so long to reach a state of satisfaction? Can the business afford to spend so long having the customer reach a state of satisfaction when we could be making one more satisfied customer (if there were a hungry customer waiting)?

Tracing customer dissatisfaction

Communication is not covered by this chart. What we can see on this chart, though, which is not so easy to represent on other charts, are all the occasions we have provided to make our customer into a dissatisfied customer. In the second process, we have created three more ways to make a dissatisfied customer. That is something we can act on. State transition diagrams provide a useful overview or complement to block diagrams, but, by themselves, they can be used as a first stage, wide net, to help you see where some of your problems with client interfaces may lie.

8.7 DEPLOYMENT FLOW CHART

Workflow analysis and modelling techniques have been used in industry worldwide in one form or another since the Second World War and are a competency within the discipline of operations management. There are a number of standards, but the Japanese have proved how this technique can be simplified to meet special needs of individual organizations.

In Fig. 8.8, I have deliberately blended my own cocktail to demonstrate the types of information that can be captured in these maps. I have included special symbols to enable later diagnosis and streamlining. These will be discussed in much more detail in Chapters 9 and 10.

I have included symbols for capturing delays, service-level agreements, cycle times and operation times. Cycle time is the elapsed time between the start and end of the operation. It may coincide with operation time, or it may be longer depending on whether there are any internal delays or bottlenecks in the operation. Cycle time is simply the customer's view of operation time. Deployment entails attributing accountability for actions to the cast of stakeholders involved in the operation. When a customer acts, an entry appears in the column under Customer; when the assistant acts, an entry appears in the column under Assistant, and if there were more characters, then more columns would be required. Stakeholders do not have to be individually named people, they can be groups of people. Now what are the benefits from using this technique? Let us look at the two processes from Sec. 8.2 (Figs 8.9, 8.10).

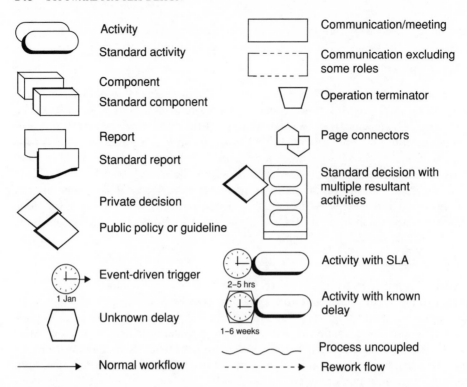

Figure 8.8 The basic symbol set for deployment flow charting. All standard symbols represent public, reusable, and named product and process components. Time ranges can be annotated beneath clock and delay symbols.

Using the deployment flow chart

Our immediate experience is that of being drawn down to a level of detail we might not have seen before. It is not obvious at first glance, what, exactly is being examined. That is why I would always advocate that you start with a block diagram (Sec. 8.5) first and have it on hand as you create the deployment flow chart. The symbols on the far left of the diagram have been added to show links to the corresponding state transition diagrams, Figs 8.6 and 8.7.

The acid test is can we tell by looking at the maps whether the process of Fig. 8.9 is better than that of Fig. 8.10? Can we see the problems inherent in Fig. 8.9, in fact?

Highlighting rework loops

Because there is a backward-flowing, dashed rework loop, I can see exactly where in the processes rework is incurred, and the extent of how much backtracking and possible rework could be involved. The rework loop points to the links between error production and error detection. Assessing the cost of rework is helped by having operation and cycle times annotated on the map.

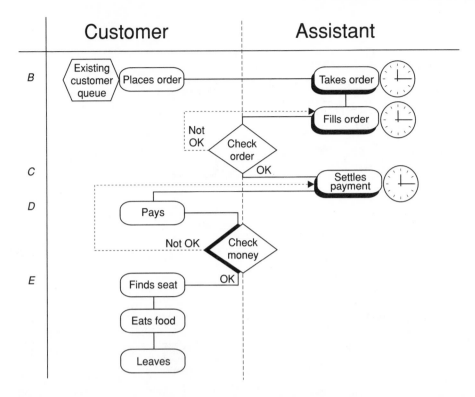

Figure 8.9 Deployment flow chart. The first scenario has three standard operations: Takes order, Fills order, and Settles payment. Each has a predictable cycle time shown by the clock. Standard checking procedures for food and money ensure that any problems are quickly resolved. Letters on the left link into the state transition diagram.

Signalling delays and interrupts

Delays and waits are also clearly marked by the hexagonal wait symbol. I can see by comparing the two maps that the customer is involved in more waiting time in Fig. 8.10 than Fig. 8.9 and this could be bad news for my customer satisfaction ratings.

It is very interesting to see the process uncoupling in Fig. 8.10. We can see that the uncoupled process is subjected to interrupts from incoming customers. We can guess that these are likely to be asynchronous, that is, they cannot be planned for, and the process becomes indeterminate at this point. We would obviously have to check that this was in fact happening before leaping in to engineer any change.

Assessing cycle times

Cycle time and operation times are shown, and we can work with those numbers to identify potential hot spots. I have deliberately not included costs in this example, but there is no reason why costs cannot be added if that is something to be worked on. We can see that the process of Fig. 8.9 has more annotated times than that of Fig. 8.10. This may be because the second process has yet to be measured or is indeterminate. But we have

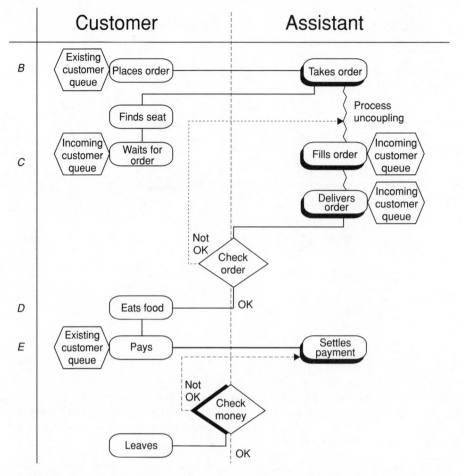

Figure 8.10 Deployment flow chart. Where before the customer was subject to only one delay, in this second scenario there are now three. Two of the delays are indeterminate since they depend on an unknown number of customers arriving who will create interrupts to the filling and delivering of orders. This is caused by the process uncoupling, which has occurred between Takes order and Fills order.

been nudged that some more work is required on the second process. If it is indeterminate, then it will become a priority target for re-engineering.

Advantages of deployment flow charts

We can also say, I believe, that the process in Fig. 8.9 provides a more efficient and effective fast-food service than that of Fig. 8.10 on a number of counts, the most important being that the customer has the food quicker and is not involved in as many waiting situations. We could also go on to look into the problem interrupts in more detail. But this is just to give you a flavour.

So the advantages of this technique are that, once we are happy to be working with the detail, we can obtain very useful diagnostic information from our chart. It is also a very flexible tool, we can design the map to suit our own purposes. The customer is an active participant, so there is less danger that we go off on our own, designing grand activities for ourselves which have little, or no, positive impact on our customers. It does need a big picture to stop us getting lost in the detail. We constantly need to be asking, 'What is the purpose of this operation?' It is so easy to be drawn into the fascinating self-justifying logic of the operation, that we forget to ask if it is necessary. That is why a link to a state transition diagram is useful. It helps us to see how the operation is making progress for the client, or not, as the case may be.

There are now a number of flow-charting tools available for a PC, and some of these are mentioned in Appendix A. To start with I just created my own icon set within my existing graphics package. I am sure you could swiftly tailor something for yourself.

8.8 PETRI NET

Petri nets do look and can be very complex. A recently developed technique by Carl Petri in the 1960s, Petri nets can be used to model a wide range of scenarios, the best known of which are concurrent systems. Because of their abstract appearance, they appeal to some people and not to others. People with systems and programming backgrounds in my experience have no problem with them. For those without that background, the best method I have found for introducing people to Petri nets is to play my own version of tiddly-winks. I am including Petri nets, because even if the method is arcane, the charts themselves make very distinctive patterns, and just comparing charts which show two versions of the same process can be instructive and can prompt useful questions. Just look at the two charts of Figs 8.11 and 8.12. Which do you think is likely to present most problems?

I hope you have recognized our good old processes from Sec. 8.2. Let me first give you enough information about how to play through these charts so that you can follow them with me. Each circle represents a place, each horizontal line, a transition. Each transition corresponds to a real activity which can be carried out only if the place before it has a token (or tiddly-wink) sitting on it. The token starts at the top of the graph and every cycle it moves along to the next free place, firing the activity in between.

Easy so far — but life is not quite that straightforward. Token-passing is subject to a few rules so that we can match reality in all its variety. When the token reaches a junction, tokens are passed to all the following places. When a number of places converge onto a single place, then all converging places must have a token before the token can be passed to the following place. There are two important Petri net patterns for us to recognize, the conflict pattern (Fig. 8.13) and the deadlock (Fig. 8.14).

Assessing the process using a Petri net

In Fig. 8.11 we can see that the token will just flow through. For some interest I have included three feedback loops which allow the customer to check or change the order as it is made and as the items are put on the tray, and also to allow for correcting any problems with the payment transaction. One would expect there not to be too many problems, since detection and correction are so close to the originating operation.

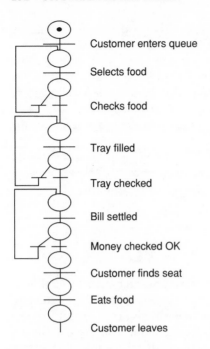

Customer enters queue

Selects food

Checks food

Tray filled

Tray checked

Bill settled

Money checked OK

Customer finds seat

Eats food

Customer leaves

Figure 8.11 Petri net. In the first scenario when the customer is served at the counter the process is simple. Food and money can be checked and corrected with no long feedback loops. The time taken for the customer to obtain food will be determined by the length of the existing queue.

A useful tool for highlighting process conflicts

What happens in Fig. 8.12? We have a different kettle of fish in this net. We can spot a conflict situation immediately. We can either fill orders which are waiting to be filled, or take orders from customers waiting to be served, but not both. The same situation exists for delivering orders too. If the order is not right when it is delivered it has to be returned, and progress cannot be made on the order until the counter is quiet again. When the customer has finished eating, they have to rejoin the queue at the counter to pay.

Spotting process complexity

So how much do the charts tell us about the process? We can see immediately how complex and how recursive Fig. 8.12 is compared to Fig. 8.11, particularly before the customer gets any food at all. Depending on the flow of customers coming through the door, the seated customer could spend a very long time waiting for food. We can see the length of the rework loops and how much work has to be backtracked before progress can be resumed. We can also anticipate the bottleneck and delay, and knowing the conditions which have to prevail before the order can be changed, we might want to work out a simulation to estimate the expected waiting time for our poor hungry customer.

Cycle times, operation times, and costs are not annotated on the chart. But there is no reason why these could not be added. Again, working with a big picture diagram, we can get an immediate overall picture and pattern of processes which complements our other maps by showing obvious process design problems and bottlenecks.

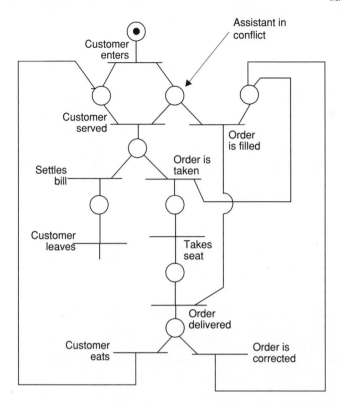

Figure 8.12 Petri net. In the second scenario it is now clear that the process has become more complex. There are more dependent operations, feedback loops are extended, and the critical operation Order filled is dependent upon there being no subsequent customer interruptions. When will that state occur? If this does not convince you that your process design makes all the difference, then maybe nothing will.

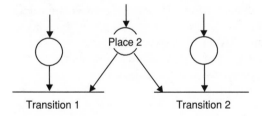

Figure 8.13 Petri net: conflict situation. The token from place 2 can trigger only either transition 1 or transition 2. The result is conflict.

8.9 THE PROCESS MAPPING TOOL BOX

Here we have looked at five quite different tools for mapping processes and operations. All have benefits, all have their drawbacks.

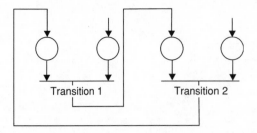

Figure 8.14 Petri net: deadlock situation. Transition 2 is dependent on the completion of transition 1, but transition 1 cannot complete before transition 2 has completed. The result is deadlock.

- Structured analysis and design techniques are widely used in most software production organizations for analysing customer systems, however, in its present form it does not capture enough information to allow you to diagnose the system.
- Block diagrams are useful to get that top level view before you drill down into the detail. Remember to capture the interfaces between the blocks to help you with your diagnostics.
- State transition diagrams link into object-oriented techniques and are a very powerful means of displaying the impact of your process and operations on your customers and stakeholders. Link these to deployment flow charts to give you full traceability of operations.
- Deployment flow charting is a tried and tested technique for mapping operations in detail and has been in use since the end of the Second World War. This tool is extremely versatile and can be customized to give you the diagnostics you need.
- Petri nets, although perceived to be complex, create very distinctive patterns which, more than any tool, show up the effects of complexity, conflict, and deadlock.

I leave it up to you to choose the ones to give you the most leverage. This will very much depend upon whether you are doing top-down strategic mapping, or bottom-up operations mapping, whether your culture uses SADT as a second language, or whether the culture of your organization can assimilate Petri nets. You alone know the purpose to which you need to put the tools, and the cultural base from which you have to work.

9

DIAGNOSING THE PROCESS

One day, through the primeval wood,
A calf walked home as good calves should;
But made a trail all bent askew,
A crooked trail as all calves do.

Since then two hundred years have fled,
And, I infer, the calf is dead.
But still he left behind his trail,
And thereby hangs my moral tale.

The trail was taken up next day
By a lone dog that passed that way;
And then a bell-wether sheep
Pursued the trail o'er vale and steep,
And drew the flock behind him too
As good bell-wethers always do.

And from that day, o'er hill and glade,
Through those old woods a path was made.
And thus, before men were aware,
A city's crowded thoroughfare.
And soon the central street was this,
Of a renowned metropolis.

And men two centuries and a half
Trod in the footsteps of that calf.
Each day a hundred thousand route
Followed this calf about.
And on his crooked journey went
The traffic of a continent.

A hundred thousand men were led
By a calf near three centuries dead.
They followed still his crooked way
And lost one hundred years each day.

For thus such reverence is lent
To well established precedent.

Samuel Foss 1858–1911
excerpt from *Path of the Calf*

For those managers who are not in a position to wrestle with the entire organization overnight, this chapter focuses on bottom-up process mapping, diagnosis, and improvement. You can use these methods right away to start to improve the effectiveness of your operations and teams. Let us make a start by understanding how it is that sensible human beings tend to make a nonsense of apparently straightforward operations, then we will move on to look at what, exactly, constitutes effective work, so that you can have a standard against which to judge the effectiveness and productivity of your operations. The final part of the chapter will take each major hurdle to effectiveness and productivity in turn, explaining how you can recognize it, make it visible, and then, most importantly, clear it out of the way of your team and keep the track clear in the future.

9.1 THE WAYWARD PATH

We are not unintelligent beings, you and I, we run businesses, families, homes, we have had a long apprenticeship in looking at things systematically, and yet, for all our knowledge, experience, and good intentions, we do not always operate in the most effective way. How can this be so? Just think back to the last time you were under pressure. Did you maintain a systematic approach? Did you maintain communication? Did you reuse assets, and make best possible use of existing resources to give you a step up? Did you consciously engineer a fast-track process?

The cycle of waywardness

When we work under pressure, we do the best we can with what we have at that time. It is almost as though we switch on to automatic and leave our bodies or our 'native wit' to find the most well-trodden way out of the situation — and that is precisely where some of our problems lie. Because we are under pressure and most likely experiencing discomfort, we do whatever we can to regain comfort in the here and now. That short-term comfort of relying on old, familiar patterns can suck us into a vicious cycle. The more discomfort we feel, the more we narrow our focus and limit our capability for future action. At the extreme we are just postponing pain from one second to another and doing nothing else. While we are so focused on short time intervals, we lose mastery of our future and become even more prey to external events, so increasing our discomfort. All the time we are seeking a way out, rather than a way in. It is this counterintuitive act of 'getting into' the pressure and discomfort, seeking a new route, which can provide us with the only way to manage the problems. Who wants to be first? Of course you do not want to be first. It is like asking you to jump into the swimming pool and not to hold your nose, and to keep your eyes open. The water hurts your nose and makes your eyes sting, but maybe you just keep your eyes open a glimpse. Maybe, while you are under the water, you just try taking a quick peek, and find it does not feel as bad as you thought, so you open your eyes some more. Now you can see where you are. Suddenly it is interesting. You do not have to be first, you do not have to dispense with your comfort all at once. Just try working with a bit of discomfort, be interested to find out where it is really coming from. Do not try escaping from it. Get to know its dimensions. Work with it. Work into it. Discover what you have learnt, what you can see that you did not see before, and how much you have increased your skills in a very short period of time.

We lead the process off track

Just as we learn to avoid and compensate for problems in our day-to-day life by expending more energy and anxiety than we need, so in our work in the organization we also build in an avoidance of problems. We go on getting three sign-offs on expenditure claims because it is easier doing that than trying to take on the system. We claim a customer high priority, even when it is not, as an excuse for rushing a software release, because it is easier than taking on the whole issue of cumbersome and unworkable release procedures (which you have proved by the success of your 'rushes' are not that necessary after all). We make up little cadenzas in our reports, hoping they will not be seen for the rhubarb they are, because we could not take going back to customer X again to ask for clarification of this point for us. And so it all continues.

Human origins of waywardness

We make things more and more complex for ourselves because our bodies remember the pain of past experiences and past encounters, and by reacting to that remembered pain, we never learn a different way. By never taking the risk that it might be different this time, we never give ourselves the opportunity to break the pattern of learned incompetence — because learned incompetence is what it is. It is a kind of dying. Our present and our future have been cut off, surrounded, and choked by our past. All that is left is the robotic following of the well-trodden path. Which leads to where?

Be aware, now, when you are diagnosing the process, of how that process came into being. It came into being through fear, panic, a dash for safety, not knowing your critical path, and just not knowing any better at the time. Think about all the times you have felt similar fear and impending embarrassment. Will this affect your approach to diagnosing the process? We are part of the problem. Once we understand that, then perhaps, as we work to untangle the process, we can learn to understand where all the fear and panic came from and to remove their causes from the work place for good. Now we are managing!

9.2 WORKING WITH YOUR TEAM

Operations

Operations spring up like antibodies in reaction to a troublesome stimulus. Some operations are consciously introduced by management and staff in response to external market demands. Some are put into place by staff working on their own initiative in response to a management deficiency. Others spring to combat existing internal operations. Yet others are parasites enjoying a free meal while masquerading as antibodies. How could operations be set up by your team without your knowledge, and for what purpose?

If you were able to take some systemic medicine which would eradicate all those operations you had not sanctioned, the chances are that, while clearing your system of some parasitic operations, you might completely undermine your organization's immune system. Some of those operations, whether you have approved them or not, are probably serving vital, positive roles by coping with problems no one has told you about.

Now how would you go about discovering, in a non-invasive way, what operations exist, and for what purpose. I say 'non-invasive', because it often happens that when we are seen to be looking, all but approved operations suddenly vanish. The reason for this is that some operations have been set up to defend staff against you! How are you going to make your staff comfortable enough to talk to you about these?

How accurately do job descriptions reflect operations?

One easy way is to voice your belief that job descriptions no longer reflect the amount of work carried out by staff. People are not being recognized for all the work they are doing. As part of next year's performance appraisal cycle, or, if you do not have appraisals, at the beginning of next quarter, ask your staff to write their own, simple job descriptions. Instead of working from any existing job descriptions, they are to work from their own knowledge of what has to be done. Make it clear you do not want wording like 'to develop, monitor, and control quality systems in line with organizational objectives, so that staff can achieve error-free working practices'. This tells you nothing. At best it indicates that they do not have a clue what they should be doing, but you asked for it, so they put it down.

Be product and service oriented

Ask people to write down the current products and services they are delivering. This could be 'providing in-house inspection seminars' or 'analysis of client requirements'. Very simple, but complete and accurate statements are all that are needed. When you have those statements, the next stage is to go through them. Set aside time to do this. You can do it during the time you would normally set aside for staff reviews. You will need to obtain more information on five points and the pro forma (Fig. 9.1) will help you in this task. Fill it in side by side with each member of your staff so that they can learn to use it for themselves. Make it clear that the objective is not a time-and-motion study of their work. You just want to be clear about the pattern of demands on them. Start with yourself so you are absolutely clear and can resolve any problems before working with your team.

Name of Team Member . . . . *Date* . . . .

Product/ service	Trigger	Frequency ad hoc? plannable?	Effort cycle-time	What next? Checks? Returns?	Satisfaction/ conflicts

Figure 9.1

Understanding what is going on

1. What exactly triggers production of that product or service? Does the member of staff initiate it themselves? Does it coincide with a certain time or date? Is it triggered by a receipt of a document or message? Is it requested by someone? Does the member of staff know what causes the trigger? Are they aware of a chain of procedures, of which their product or service is part? Note the details.
2. On average, how frequently does the trigger occur? Does it occur on a regular basis, or an infrequent basis, can it be planned into a work schedule, or does it have to be accommodated in an ad hoc fashion. If it is ad hoc, what are the maximum and the minimum amounts of notice given for the work to be done. Note the details.
3. How much effort goes into producing the product or service? What are the minimum and maximum cycle times or duration in elapsed half-days for producing the product or service? What resources and information are needed? What are the minimum and maximum delays experienced in obtaining resources and information? Are there reasons for delay? Note the details.
4. What happens next? Who receives the product or service? Is the work a trigger for someone else? What is the average delay on turnaround, if it is a request for someone else's action? Are staff aware of what decisions are taken on the basis of the product or service produced? Is any checking carried out by the producer, or the receiver, or someone else? Does the producer, if they do not do the checking themselves, know what checks will be carried out? How frequently is work returned? Is it possible for the work to be returned more than once? What are the minimum and maximum turnaround times, if work is checked? Note the details.
5. How happy is the member of staff with that work? Is there any conflict, any grievance? Note both positive and negative aspects.

Towards process-oriented job descriptions

Now you have some pieces of the jigsaw, but you will not have all of them, because some will be external to your team. Using a block diagram (Sec. 8.5) and a deployment flow chart (Sec. 8.7) construct with your team, using the information from the pro forma, as much of the associated operations as you can. Use this opportunity to coach them in using the tools. For now just note the source and flow direction of the operation as they go outside the scope of the team. Let each person have a copy of their operations maps and ask them to keep this list up to date for the next review. You now have job descriptions which will meet the requirements of BS 5750 or ISO 9001. What is more, you now know what people's real workloads are, rather than what they think you think they should be doing. You now have information which will provide a much sounder and fairer basis for carrying out performance appraisals and target-setting in the future.

Validating operations

Coming back to our original purpose of validating operations, using your own judgement look at the products and services being produced by your team. What is new to you? Is the purpose clear? Find out why new operations have come into being. Do not try and get rid of them until you have discovered their positive contribution. How does your staff's idea of purpose map onto yours? What are the differences? What have you learnt? Perhaps it is time for you all to be clear on your purpose. The information you have gathered will provide you with useful input for a team exercise in process-oriented effort management (see Sec. 12.4).

9.3 EFFECTIVE WORK

As human beings, we like to be active, on the go, busy, occupied. This generous expenditure of energy is an expression of our vitality, of our being alive. There is nothing wrong with activity, but there is a problem if activity is confused with effective work. Activity may not always be effective, and effective work may sometimes be characterized by inactivity — thought, reflection, learning, listening, or purposeful suspension of activity when a problem has occurred.

Effective work is purposeful and informed work

Effective work is purposeful work. We are seeking to transform some resources, such as time, computer memory, or paper, into some other resource, such as transferred knowledge and skills, application software, or communication channels. To be effective means that we accomplish this transformation with preferably no, or minimum, waste of resources, loss of process equilibrium, and no damage to ourselves and our environment. In order to do this, we need to know first, what resource is required from us, to what purposes it will be put, in what environment used, and how we can test that we have, in fact, met the service or product requirements. Secondly, we need to know what resources are available to us, to work on and work with. Thirdly, we need to know the context or environment in which the transformation is to be carried out. When we have this knowledge we can design an effective process.

Effective work in a context of uncertainty

I realize that in the real world not everything is knowable, and sometimes we have to work with a good deal of uncertainty. If there is genuine uncertainty about what we are to produce, what materials we are to use, and the environment in which we carry out our work, we can design our operation to be effective within the context of that uncertainty. We can design to wider tolerances and to more general parameters. To discover whether there is genuine uncertainty, the question which can be asked is, 'If your life depended on getting this information, could it be obtained?' If the answer is no, there is genuine uncertainty. Otherwise, there is an information block which it is possible to remove. Every effort should be made to remove it.

Assessing effectiveness

To assess effectiveness, we need to know if our process is designed to make the best use of all resources, including the environment in which it has to operate, and if it minimizes waste and delays, while meeting the operational needs of our clients. There are four parts to the assessment:

1. Operational descriptions of inputs to our process. What are we receiving? Is it in a form that is acceptable to the work we have to do? If not, can we go back to the source and provide a better definition of our needs? What are the constraints on our source? Can they match our needs if their lives depended on it, or do we have to change our process to take account of their limitations? Seek to improve your inputs before adapting your process.
2. We gather the same information for all our out-going products and services, except this time, we are the source. Check that the operational needs of the people who have to work with the outgoing products and services are met. Seek to change your process before compromising the operational needs of the people who need your work.
3. What is the environment in which the process has to function? Is it conducive to your process? Can it be engineered to be more conducive, or does the process have to be designed to take account of a poor or hostile environment? Seek to change the environment before the process.
4. What waste and delays are products of the process? Seek to tune out the waste and delays from the process while maintaining products and services constant.

9.4 CYCLE TIMES

When we undertake work on behalf of someone else, we take on a responsibility to fulfil the promises we make, explicitly or implicitly. Whether a contract exists or not, to maintain credibility with others and with ourselves, we need to keep promises. While one might plead the mitigating effects of unprecedented disaster, it is expected that promises are made on the basis of knowledge that they can be delivered; confidence that the environment upon which the promises depend can be managed; and known availability of indemnification or bonding to cover delivery failure in extreme situations.

Confidence is based upon known cycle times

When we make a promise to deliver, or create a service-level agreement, this should be a positive expression of confidence, based upon experience and our capacity to manage our delivery environment. In order to manage the delivery of the final product or service, we need to manage the delivery of all interim components. If we are unable to determine operation times or cycle times for the components, then we can only guess, not predict, and certainly not promise delivery to schedules and service levels. If we have operations which have not been designed to remove bottlenecks and sources of indeterminateness, and which are prone to interrupts and delays, then we cannot predict operation times or cycle times. We can only enforce them, and by enforcing them, we risk unbalancing and crippling the process as a whole.

A managed process is designed to enable prediction of cycle times The first sign of a managed process is that operations are defined, and are being actively assessed with the purpose of reducing all the above sources of unpredictability. When the process is repeatable, the sources of unpredictability have been removed, and operation times, cycle times and service levels exist. We need to be able to predict that we can get the elephant through the hoop comfortably, rather than relying on grease, our brute force, or the goodwill of the elephant.

Use deployment flow charts to assess cycle times

For each operation which results in a software component, then, we need to know if there is a cycle time. Is there a reliable range for cycle times? What components reduce the predictability of cycle time? For this sort of work, the detail of a deployment flow chart is needed. Indicate known cycle time values by attaching a clock to document production, checks and inspections, standard meetings, and known turnaround delays. It may well be that there are no known cycle times. If that is the case, do not force people to come up with magic numbers. It is just as important to know that there is no cycle time available, as to know precise cycle times. The absence of cycle times shows that the operation is, as yet, unpredictable and repeatable only with difficulty. Very likely, it will need conscious design effort to make the operation predictable.

9.5 REINVENTING THE RIVET

Proliferation of components creates confusion

In many manufacturing industries, where once they gloried in a proliferation of components which were bespoke for every product, every product model, and often every yearly change to product models, the numbers of components are now being drastically reduced. To take a liberty in translating Occam's razor — widgets should not be proliferated without necessity. What is the purpose of producing 100 different types of one-inch rivets? What is the cost of storing them, of their inventory control, of maintaining the machine instructions for making them? And how frustrating when production grinds to a halt because type 22 rivet is out of stock, but there are thousands of all the other one-inch rivets about.

How many of the components which we produce during software delivery are bespoke for this particular product, or this particular project? How many documents are there which people have had to learn specially how to create, that will be confusingly similar, but never the same as other documents they will be asked to create in the future? How many documents for which there will be no test of effectiveness? How many which have to be maintained and housed? And it is not just documents or tangible products which are components, events and services are also components. When you walk into a review, will it be type 22 or type 122? How will you know what to expect, what the rules are, how you are expected to contribute?

Reduction and standardization of components saves time and money

As you move towards a more repeatable process, standardization within your own organization of product and process components to reduce the number in use, and to save staff from reinventing the rivets, will save you time and money. Taking one good example of each component and designing your products and operations to use that component will give you an overall advantage, not only for production and maintenance, but also for communication. People will know what to expect, what form it will be in, how to handle it, how to know when there are problems, and so on. They will not have to learn so much about inessential differences and will be free to concentrate more on essentials. They will not be wasted developing what has already been adequately developed, but freed to look further for opportunities to innovate. But standard parts need to be effective; if they are ineffective or used just because they are there, they will quickly become cost drivers instead of cost reducers. The standard must serve your process and your stakeholders, and not the other way around.

Use state transition diagrams and deployment flow charts to map components

At a process level, use a state transition diagram to show how product and process components support the change of the final product or service from one stage to another. At an operations level, use deployment flow charting to uncover components. For each product, review, or meeting, check to see if a standard format is used. If a standard format is used name the product. Again, be careful not to force the issue. Your objective is not to force the creation of one-off standards for this exercise. Knowing component variety exists is important process information.

9.6 SECRET GOALPOSTS

If people know the success criteria for their particular piece of work, and how it will be judged, then, provided they have the necessary skills, they will achieve those objectives.

Visible goalposts help the organization succeed

Managers, in their role as staff coach, make as much visible as possible to ensure that their staff and, by association, they themselves succeed. Perhaps some people mistake the coaching relationship for the teacher–pupil relationship, in which pupils are being continually put on the spot and tested. We should not run tests in day-to-day operations to see if people pass or fail. But sometimes people do. How many times are reports submitted for your approval which you are tempted to rewrite? How many times do people have to submit their work to a cycle of reviews for which there are no agreed up-front success criteria (Fig. 9.2)? How many times do you say of staff, 'We just don't seem to get quality people anymore'?

Invisible goalposts create unnecessary work and costs

Every time we go through a check or an inspection of work for which there are no success criteria, we can guarantee that there will be a high percentage of unnecessary rework activity. In fact all work which is carried out with no well-defined test cases is at best a hit-and-miss job. How long after the event do we make our pronouncement that Sam needs to play it one more time from the top? How long do people have to wait after the event before we are available to run a check? When goalposts are secret, checking and review of work appears to be an overhead which is too expensive to bear.

At each level in the organization, in the project, in the delivery process, there must be goal posts and these must be visible. When the goalposts are not visible, let us assume that no one knows what is going on. Perhaps we genuinely do not know where the goalposts are yet, in which case there is no harm in making that fact known. At least decisions can be risk-assessed on the basis of that information. So, the business itself must have clear success criteria which are the operational definitions of organizational purpose. Products and interim components need clear success criteria incorporated into design and related directly to checks and inspections.

Mapping the goalposts

A state transition diagram is used to spotlight the existence of success criteria. The success criteria should detail what exactly has to be achieved for the product to move from one state to another. At the operational level, using a deployment flow chart, you will look to

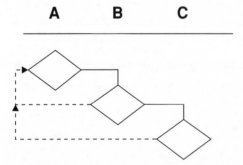

Figure 9.2 Look for referred decisions. This pattern of referred standard decisions shows lack of empowerment.

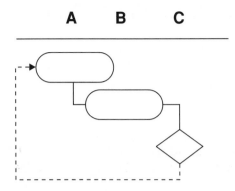

Figure 9.3 Look for unnecessarily long feedback loops. Is the check as close as possible in time to the activity whose results are being evaluated? Long delays in feedback could mean wasted activity or no opportunities for process improvement.

see whether product exit criteria exist in the form of clear, operational standards or checklists which are available prior to product design and build, and how long after production the checks take place. The longer the delay between product completion and test, the more costly the checking and rework operations will be (Fig. 9.3).

9.7 COMPLEXITY

Complexity is entanglement. A dish of knotted spaghetti. A mess. Complexity is its own fuel. Complex processes grow like fractals. Complexity never becomes spontaneously simpler. Why is this? Basically, because whenever we have a problem, we always think of things to do to remedy the problem. Our solution is almost always additive. I have yet to meet people who are happy to create solutions which mean taking things away from or out of the initial situation.

Complexity is additive

Creativity is additive. If something is worthy, it remains for posterity. So we prefer to add our bit, given a choice, and every time we add something new, even if it remedies the initial problem, it doubtless entails problems of its own. It is rather like the grit that gets into an oyster, and the irritation it causes produces layer upon layer of secretion that in time builds up into a pearl. We are not, however, building a pearl of great price when this occurs in the business, we are building a pearl of great cost.

Complexity always inflates costs

Complexity always inflates costs and schedules. It may increase value up to a point, but it will decrease value beyond that point. What is important to you is that you are able to make some assessment of the level of complexity built into your process against the value that is being created as a result. How can you tell? This is why you have to make the process visible.

Complexity is the mother of risk

When operations grow unwieldy, it is natural for them to be bypassed. People just will not go along with having to sort out three signatures for a requisition, seven forms to gain access to a slice of code for modification, or a committee vote for an authority to proceed. All these hurdles which have been put in place to safeguard the organization are totally useless when they grow in complexity beyond a certain threshold. The result is that the safeguards, which have grown and grown to deal with all possible hazards, expose the organization to massive risk.

State transition diagrams give you an overview of complexity

As a first step, the state transition diagram will give you a general overview of complexity and its costs. Work through all the operations you carry out, and see them in terms of, first, the changed state of the customer as a consequence, and next, the changed state of the product or service. How many of these states could you do without? Ask yourself and your customers what each particular state accomplishes and whether it adds value for them, or for other stakeholders. If you can reduce the number of strands there is less to get tangled. However, the state transition diagram does not show how much tangle exists.

Petri nets show you the degree of process interdependence

Once you have sorted and taken out redundant strands, use a Petri net or a deployment flow chart to work on the interdependencies. How many instances are there of multiple operations which need to arrive together before progress to the next operation can be made? How many upstream returns are made? How long are they in terms of operations to be recycled? How many points are there for indeterminancy to creep in? How many push-down stack situations occur? At how many points can interrupts be made? These are all indicators of complexity.

9.8 CHINESE WHISPERS

Perhaps someone will tell me how Chinese whispers got their name. Was it a Chinese colonel wanting to go to a dance? I shall never know because no one told me the context. Chinese whispers are messages or products without a context.

The single most important feature of Chinese whispers as far as we are concerned is that the context is never transmitted with the message. Let us not just confine ourselves to verbal messages, but also consider the progressive building and delivery of a product or service as a sort of message in its own right. Without context, we cannot construe the intended sense or significance of information given to us.

In the absence of context one will be created — the wrong one

This is not to say that we do not make sense of the information. The problem is that we do not rest until we do make sense of it, no matter how much noise has crept in or how cryptic the message first appears. We project our own context if one is missing. 'Somebody said something about the colonel wanting something.' 'Old Charleston Charlie?' 'Yes, that's right. By Jove, that's it, Freddie! He wants to go dancing!'

It is a waste of time and money to respond to the wrong message correctly

So we sent three and fourpence instead of reinforcements, and we all know that it was a total waste of time and money under the circumstances. On how many occasions is information transferred during one of your projects? This number signals the relative degree of risk for you of wasting time and money. How many interim documents or components do you produce? How are these taken and transformed from one person or group to the next? How many times is information abstracted, interpreted, and passed on?

State transition diagrams give you an overall view of how knowledge is transferred

You can start by using state transition diagramming to show how the knowledge of the product or service is transformed by each of the interim documents or components. You can link each state to a document or component as well as to the operation involved to produce it. What sort of picture do you get? Does it make sense? How representative is this of the total information which is passed around the organization?

Deployment flow charting highlights the risks of increased communication noise

When you have used the state transition diagram to get a feel for the overall use of messaging, then you can move down to a further level of detail. Create deployment flow charts to track the life cycle of each major document or component produced. Look for evidence of information being transferred as a sort of baton in a relay race. Why can it not be transferred directly? Why are all the middle-men needed? Information may also be passed back and forth between just two groups, in which case it will have a pattern of dislocated vertebrae. In this case the group or person in the middle is acting as a gate-keeper or translator. Is that necessary? Can the information be designed better so that translation services are not required? See Figs 9.4 and 9.5.

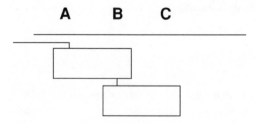

Figure 9.4 Look for unnecessary buffers in communication. This is a case of 'send three and fourpence'. Either get everyone together at once or dispense with the middle-man.

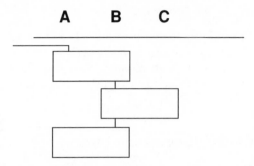

Figure 9.5 Look for unnecessary translators. Get everyone together or cut out the middle-man.

9.9 INTERRUPTS

Interrupts are the punches the universe throws at us which stop us throwing punches at the universe. We could wax very philosophical about whether or not we should be allowed to have our way with the universe without restriction, but now is probably not the best time. However, it is worth pausing to consider how much more we could achieve if the doorbell stopped buzzing; the telephone stopped ringing; and people did not wake us while we dreamt.

Interrupts create disproportionate disturbances

What happens to us when an interrupt occurs? On a personal level we have to surface from our self-absorbed state in one world and readjust to problems or demands coming at us from a new world. It is this shift from one world view to another which is exceptionally onerous, as remarked by Tom DeMarco and Timothy Lister in their book *Peopleware*. While the total interrupt itself may not account for more than five or ten minutes, it could result in an hour's lost time. When we are delivering software, the network of interdependencies is so thick that the interrupt is felt as a disturbance across the network like a ripple across water. Now think about the pattern of ripples on water when it is raining, hard. Interrupts cause unforeseen delays to scheduled work. Work in hand is either queued or put onto a push-down stack. Because interrupts are difficult to map, it is often only by seeing the effects that we realize that an interrupt has taken place. This is discussed more in Secs 9.10 and 9.11.

Synchronous and asynchronous interrupts

Interrupts can be either synchronous or asynchronous. A synchronous interrupt is a planned interrupt. You know it is going to happen and you can schedule it to fit into your plans with least disruption. Asynchronous interruption cannot be planned and is usually associated with crises or fire-fighting. If you have a help desk, then their total day is probably spent handling synchronous interrupts. They are geared up to deal with it. They are probably not geared up to deal with asynchronous interrupts such as being evacuated in response to a fire alarm.

Use deployment flow charts or Petri nets to map main sources of interrupts

At process level there are four main sources of interrupt: fault detection, change requests, sign-offs, and staff changes owing to sickness or reorganization. For each major operation create a deployment flow chart or Petri net and trace through the impact on your scheduled work of: faulty work being handed back to you; requests for a change; waiting for approval to continue and obtaining that approval; and staff changes — what would happen if you lost three key members of staff next week? Do you have a standard operation to handle each of these events? If you have not, now is your time to design them.

9.10 DELAYS

I remember asking a testing team to log the delays they experienced with work being handed over, and work being returned for testing after correction. The response was not what I had expected. 'We are never waiting for work. We always have something to do!' This is true of everyone in our business, there is always more work for us to be doing. We are never idle. There is an unwritten rule that we must always be seen to be busy.

Having work to do is not the same as moving forward on the critical path

The question I would ask, then, is that work on the critical path? Is it taking you forward, or is it push-down stack work? It is not the moral issue of people being gainfully occupied or not that we are wanting to address, it is the issue of keeping work flowing along the critical path. If everybody is busy looking busy, how can we tell when there is a delay on the critical path? Who is ever rewarded for saying, 'We are waiting'? This person would be ranked either as an arch pain or severely lacking in initiative by their manager or supervisor at performance review time. Yet, if we allow the process to be the message, then what clearer message of problems to be resolved do we have than when, instead of bustle and activity, there is quiet and stillness?

Masking delays masks underlying problems and creates waste

When we usually wait six weeks for requirements to be signed off, do we stand down the project team, or get on with the work in the meantime? Arguably, the work is on the critical path so it makes good sense to continue. The risks are that the requirements are not signed off and the project is changed or abandoned. In the first case, work is scrapped or has to be reworked. In the second case, people say that they would have been paying the staff anyway, so it does not matter that their work was scrapped. However, we may be covering up a generic problem with the operation for capturing, documenting, and signing off requirements which needs to be addressed. If the six weeks is a deliberate cooling off period to consider whether the system is really required or not, then other work can be planned for that period, for example, documentation and preventive maintenance.

I strongly believe that no one should ever be put in a position where their work could be potentially scrap. This shows a total lack of respect for people and their efforts.

Capturing delays on state transition diagrams and deployment flow charts

Not only do we need to highlight and encourage information about delays, but we also need to map them. At a high level, on a product state transition diagram, you can ask what the expected delays are when the product passes from one state to the next. Your answers might be: waiting for sign-offs; waiting for project review boards; waiting for the next release cycle together with the delay, expressed, perhaps as a range of elapsed time. At the operation level, using a deployment flow chart, you can attach a clock to each component produced, each meeting, and each inspection to indicate the average delays experienced before this activity can be completed.

9.11 JACK-IN-THE-BOX

Creating the push-down stack

Whenever you take material out of your in-tray and put it on a 'to do' pile, you are creating a push-down stack. Whenever an item comes up in a meeting and you decide to tackle the issue off-line after the meeting, you are creating a push-down stack. Whenever you hastily sketch in a few paragraphs in your report, or pencil some guessed figures in your budget statement you are creating a push-down stack. Whenever you feel like the juggler trying to keep lots of plates spinning on sticks, you are a victim of push-down stacks (your own).

Push-down stacks give the illusion that work has been achieved

Push-down stack approaches can be useful for prioritizing work. However, beware, you may always have work coming in of a higher priority, and that might be because the low priority work you buried has become critical. A push-down stack is an effective way of camouflaging a queue. This is where all the problems come from. Because there is no visible queue, it looks from the outside as though the work has been completed and capacity for processing the work is adequate. In fact, the work has only been displaced. It is still waiting to be finished, but now it is hidden. As any project manager knows, it is the 90 per cent finished modules, not the modules still to be assigned, which are the greatest headaches.

Push-down stacks and crisis management

Like a jack-in-the-box, work on push-down stacks tends to jump up and whack you unexpectedly when you least want it to. It gains kinetic energy with time, and the longer it is pushed down, the more force it has when it springs up again. Often caused by an interrupt, it is the cause of larger interrupts, and can lead into a crisis management nosedive. Work on a push-down stack will generally take longer and cost more to finish than if the work had been tackled when it was first taken off the queue.

Spotting push-down stacks on Petri nets

Let us think about how you can spot process push-down stacks. On a Petri net it is a conflict. I can do either this or this, right now, but not both. The issue is resolved by using the push-down stack. We can only take things off again when we are not busy. In Sec. 8.2 we can fill and deliver orders only when there are no more customers waiting to place orders. I can handle the 'to do' stack only when there are no other demands on my time. I can type the final figures in my budget when demands on my time thin out so I can get the information I need to complete the work. I can finish coding this module when I have a long enough break to clarify the interface detail.

At a process level, spot the operations which are pushed into the background, those with the lowest priority such as documentation and preventative maintenance. If this work were put back into a queue, how would capacity requirements be affected? Is that a problem for you?

9.12 BOTTLENECKS

Bottlenecks are caused by a lack of capacity in part of the process. It may be that there are just not the physical resources required to complete an operation, or that the resources are not of the right kind. In either situation the result is the same — unforeseen delay.

Bottlenecks occur because the right resources are not available

Bottlenecks are usually caused because the right number of staff are not available at the right time to start work on a project. If staff are drafted in from elsewhere, so the project can start as planned, we are probably just moving the bottleneck from one project to another. Bottlenecks occur when target hardware is delivered behind schedule, or when the customers are not able to release staff to carry out acceptance testing. We also get bottlenecks occurring where staff are stuck for information they need to get on with their jobs, or when they do not understand the standards or procedures for their work.

Bottleneck engineering

In some industries, what has come to be called 'bottleneck engineering' has become a discipline in its own right. Bottleneck engineering is to trouble-shooting, what thermometers are to elbows in babies' baths. Having assessed the risks of where bottlenecks may occur, the process is re-engineered either to eliminate them, or to be as tolerant as possible of problems over which there is a lesser degree of control.

Bottlenecks occur when we are unsure of cycle times and also when the process is susceptible to a high proportion of asynchronous interrupts. Both these problems make resource planning a very hit-and-miss affair. Work on the cycle times and interrupts first when they occur with the bottleneck problems. When these problems have been cleared away you will have a clearer picture of the nature and extent of the bottleneck, if it still remains.

The critical question to ask next is whether the organization, product, or project success criteria can be met with current capabilities in terms of technology, resources, and skills. If the answer is no, then there is a bottleneck. The size of the bottleneck depends on the capability gap.

You have four choices when dealing with the bottleneck. Change your inputs, change your outputs, change the environment, or change the process. When you identify a bottleneck, it is a good time to reassess all the process needs and check the assumptions on which they are based. Are you overengineering? Can you change outputs and still meet customers' operational needs, and so reduce your capability gap? Can you act on your environment to make it more conducive to increased process effectiveness? Can anything in the process be automated or re-engineered to give you greater leverage? Do you need to change the volume or nature of your input resources?

Finding bottlenecks

Bottlenecks are signalled by an unscheduled delay. If it is not permissible in your organization to admit delay, you will never really discover and get rid of your bottlenecks. Where delays are shown on state transition diagrams and on deployment flow charts, the question to ask is, 'what would have to be in place for there not to be this delay?' Another way of uncovering bottlenecks is based on the premise that what people can do easily will be done, and what is troublesome will, by and large, be left undone or half-done. Look at the work outstanding on push-down stacks.

9.13 BECOMING A HERO

Now that you understand how processes go for a wander and what the causes of ineffectiveness are, you are in a position to help your team off to a flying start. From now on not only will you be able to diagnose and eliminate sources of pain and frustration, but you will also be able to design operations and processes from scratch, free from all potential hurdles. You are becoming a process engineer, but to your staff, you are becoming a hero. Congratulations.

10

STREAMLINING AND SIMPLIFICATION

So, returning to boiled linseed oil, I told my companions at table that in a prescription book published about 1942 I had found the advice to introduce into the oil, toward the end of the boiling, two slices of onion, without any comment on the purpose of the curious additive. . . . Signor Giacomasso Olindo, my predecessor and teacher, . . . smiling benevolently behind his thick white moustache, had explained to me that in actual fact, when he was young and boiled the oil personally, thermometers had not yet come into use: . . . one judged the temperature of the batch by . . . immersing a slice of onion in the oil on the point of a skewer; when the onion began to fry, the boiling was finished. Evidently, with the passing of the years, what had been a crude measuring operation had lost its significance and was transformed into a mysterious and magical practice.

Primo Levi
The Periodic Table (Chromium)

When you are in a position to look at patterns of operation across the organization, this chapter will help you to focus on five key strands for process improvement. Each strand is provided with a five-stage assessment to guide you on your way. The five stages are the revised stages of the capability maturity model proposed in Chapter 7. They are: level 1, initial; level 2, defined; level 3, managed; level 4, repeatable; and level 5, optimizing.

The first of the five strands is *client focus*. We hear this term so often that we have probably gone a bit deaf to it. What do we really mean when we use that phrase? Organizations are discovering that it is impossible to satisfy all their clients, all the time, with a single 'do-it-all' bulk process. Tremendous opportunity for improved effectiveness occurs when we are able to segment client groups and provide logistically different processes to satisfy their needs. The second strand is *decision-making*. If you ever want an indicator of organizational complexity and bureaucracy, you can obtain it just by mapping the patterns of decision-making in your organization. Third, there is *information criticality*. The entire process of software delivery depends upon information logistics — the right information being in the right place at the right time. So far all we have done is 'push' information. Now we need to concentrate our attention on information 'pull'. The next strand is *balance and synchronization*, and the fifth is *standardization and automation*, both of which speak for themselves.

But to start, I shall return to one of the central, nagging themes of this book, the need for purpose.

10.1 A PURPOSEFUL UNITY

Without a unified purpose there can be no streamlining, and no simplification. Without a purpose, complexity prevails, because everyone's individual interpretation of purpose tugs the organization in different directions simultaneously. When you tug a large ship in many different ways at the same time, all the movement cancels out. For all the energy expended, there is no progress. It is all very well talking about a unified purpose, but what does this mean? What use is it? How exactly does it help us to streamline and simplify activities in the organization?

Purpose addresses all stakeholders

All stakeholders in the organization must be able to recognize themselves and their role in the declared purpose. What is more, purpose must address explicitly the conflicts which arise between stakeholders, and set clear priorities and stick to them until there is an explicit change of purpose. If staff are really the most important stakeholders in this organization then should we be making so many redundant when our share price takes a tumble?

Perhaps it would be simpler and more honest to declare that the first priority is to the people who have staked their money in the company. In that way staff would know that their security depended upon creating stakeholder value by creating more earned value through satisfying and growing the client base. Shareholders recognize that their fortune depends upon an expanding, satisfied client base, through either investment or acquisition. Clients expect the whole organization to be focused on their satisfaction. This is just a simplistic example for you to work on.

Purpose and client policy

While our purpose defines stakeholders and their priorities, we need to be clear on which customers we intend to serve, and how we expect to serve them. Is it on a no-expenses-spared basis? Customer satisfaction at any cost? Customer satisfaction only when there is a visible return to the business? Are we prepared to go in with loss leaders? Does every project have to recover its own costs? Again let us be clear about this, otherwise we tangle ourselves in endless debates, discussion, mind-reading, and second-guessing.

Purposeful decision-making

The point of having a clear purpose with respect to stakeholders and clients is that it makes decision-making so much simpler and less bureaucratic in the organization. With clear priorities and understanding, decision-making can be pushed out to where the situation demands a decision. All customer and stakeholder interfaces need that degree of empowerment to support rapid response to needs. If decision-making has to travel all the way from the client interface to the core of the business and back again, then value melts away rapidly; value to the client in terms of delay (and, maybe, anxiety) and value to the business in terms of interrupts, lost meaning and yet more complexity.

Purposeful information flows

Even though we have the wizardry of electronic mail, office automation, and perhaps the luxury of a personal assistant, there is still too much untargeted information consuming people's energy and time. Much of this information is concerned with lobbying, or keeping people informed so we have covered ourselves in case of problems. All this occurs when there is no clear purpose. It does not mean that we should stop networking, or forming alliances, but the networks and alliances are in support of the business purpose rather than a defence against its arbitrariness.

Purposeful process

Without purpose, investment is ad hoc and short term. In order to serve the stakeholders, strategic investment decisions have to be made, and perhaps the most important investment decision is in the production process. In software production, as in any other knowledge-intensive industry, there is very little in the way of a visible 'hard' process line. But nonetheless, processes are needed to support the effective delivery of products and services to different client families and to meet the different demands of stakeholders. In the absence of clear process investment decisions, time and money will be spent on ad hoc plumbing. It will be impossible to get the delivery pipelines across the organization to meet up, and there will be very expensive and complex interfaces, and considerable value leakage.

Purposeful utilization of resources

When there is a clear purpose, underpinned by targeted investment, we can streamline and simplify by reusing process and product platforms. Instead of constantly reinventing new variants of the same old products, we can focus, instead, on responding rapidly to the market by recycling and customizing existing assets in our product and service portfolio. Every new product we create requires its own set of documentation, version control procedures, test harnesses, and so on. The less there is to manage, store, and track, the simpler and less error-prone our processes can be.

10.2 CLIENT FOCUS

Organizations are discovering that it is impossible to satisfy all their clients, all the time, with a single 'do-it-all' bulk process. (Remember that stakeholders includes all those groups of people with a vested interest in the process. They may be clients, internal groups, regulatory bodies, shareholders, and so on.) There are two tendencies. One is to divest yourself, if you can, of those clients whose needs are too expensive to satisfy, given the existing process. The other is to establish specific processes customized logistically to meet the different needs of well-defined groups of clients.

Segmenting clients

The constraints of security, costs, product lifetimes, standards requirements, and product uncertainty, taken together, create conflicts which are difficult to resolve and which impose a considerable cost burden on delivered software services and products. However, if you look carefully at your product and service portfolio, and map out the client requirements for each, then it may be that your products can be segmented into discrete families along client lines. You are likely to have some products which require stringent security; others, less. There may be products which require long analysis phases, because the customers or products are unfamiliar. Other products may have been built from customer prototypes. Some products may have had long lead times; others might have been fast responses to changing government legislation.

Creating processes to meet the requirements of specific clients

Different pipelines can be built to suit the requirements of different client segments. In this way you can remove extraneous constraints which serve to confuse people on the process. 'This customer says they do not want code inspections, but we have been told to carry out code inspections on everything.' 'Even if the customer has written their own specification, the standards manual says we must have an analysis phase.'

When you produce goods, only those clients who have a vested interest in that product or service need to be involved in discussions. There are fewer interfaces to manage, and this means, too, that the amount of communication and documentation can be reduced and decision-making is considerably simplified.

Once you have created separate pipelines, you can then set to work streamlining them to ensure that all effort is being targeted to produce value for that group of clients alone.

Assessing the maturity of client segmentation

- At the initial stage, clients are not segemented. Relationships among stakeholders have not been identified and conflict exists between stakeholder interests. This is interpreted by members of the organization as irrationality.
- At the defined stage, clients and stakeholders are clearly identified. However, the relationship between them and the precise nature of their demands is still unclear. There is no clear link between stakeholder demands and specific products or services in the business portfolio.
- At the next stage, identification of client and stakeholder demands and links to products and services is proactively undertaken, but bulk process lines still exist and conflict is still present.
- At the repeatable stage, profiles of client and stakeholder demands and the relationships to products and services have been identified and an attempt is being made to stratify products and process lines against the demands of more coherent

client groups. Because patterns are not clear-cut there are a number of fuzzy groups, with some overlap. Only two or three subgroups are identified.

- Finally, there is evidence that processes are being actively designed to meet the needs of discrete families of clients and stakeholders. These processes provide a striking contrast to the previous lugubrious bulk process. Work continues to streamline and refine the processes even more. For example, where cost is an important client constraint, you might find that the process is a string of lean sequential operations which are being made progressively leaner and more efficient. Where time is critical, highly resourced concurrent operations are being worked on to ensure quicker response and reduced costs.

10.3 PATTERNS OF DECISION-MAKING

If you ever want to compile an indicator of organizational complexity and bureaucracy you can obtain it easily by looking at the patterns of decision-making in your organization. How far away from the level of the action is the decision taken? How long after the choice situation is the decision taken? How long before the the decision is implemented? How many decisions are simple go/no-go referrals, inspections or reviews? How much rework is required when a no-go decision is made? What is the ratio of case-by-case decision-making to decision-making where a well-defined policy exists? What is the ratio of problem to opportunity-driven decision-making? How much decision-making is built into the process and automated?

Decision-making life cycles

There is a decision-making life cycle. Let us recognize that decision-making needs to be undertaken proactively. By deliberately engineering choice situations we can constantly expand our business influence and opportunities. At first, the new types of situations and choices we create will need case-by-case consideration until the relevance of the decision to business purpose and goals is fully understood and can be made visible. As experience of the new choice situation develops, judgement criteria evolve and these can be communicated and shared widely across the organization, providing a common and consistent approach to the same set of choices. Policies and guidelines are built to inform production and, finally, the means to incorporate them into the process itself are designed. In this way, the process embodies the policies, it cannot but enact them — it is error-proofed. All the while then, as we take on the new, patterns of decision-making are rolling through the organization like waves.

The effects of poorly understood decision-making

Poor understanding and use of decision-making results in inflated operation cycle times, extended customer queues, increased indeterminateness, and crippling conflict in the delivery process. As people are coached to understand how patterns of decision-making support or undermine the business, they can progressively remove hurdles and bottlenecks and dramatically improve cycle and operation times. One difficulty is that over time, we tend to increase rather than decrease the number of decisions being made, but our individual, unaided capacity for making decisions remains more or less fixed. So what happens? We either increase resources to manage the need for more decision-making by spinning off new functions or new departments around the emerging set of choices to be made, or drop some of the old decision-making from the bottom of the pile as we take on the new. In both cases we are increasing organizational complexity without necessarily increasing organizational competency. In the latter case, because we have failed to capture well established decision-making into the process, we are creating and perpetuating a bed of shifting sand on which no stable organizational base can be built.

Assessing decision-making competency

- At the initial level, the majority of decisions are one-off, reactive, invisible, and additive. By that I mean that most of the decisions are made on a case-by-case basis as the situation, which has not been chosen, demands. The links between a decision made by this group here and its impact on that group there cannot be seen. When asked, people are unable to communicate the criteria upon which their judgements and decisions are made. Most decisions are gut feel; they depend upon individual experience and specific circumstances. No attempt is made to open up the environment and remove poor mechanisms which are the results of past decisions, instead, new decisions are plastered over to correct the old. As the delivery process is made more visible to people in the organization, the chain of dependency between decisions taken in the organization can be more easily identified. Stakeholders from the various groups who are impacted by a decision are brought together to discuss and debate the issues. But decision-making tends to be lengthy and consensus driven, depending on individuals' viewpoints and opinions rather than the needs of the process itself.
- The sign of a more managed state is when there is a visible rationalization of decision-making and a closer tie-in between decisions and process needs. Decisions are made by reference to visible purpose, goals, and stakeholder success criteria rather than the needs of the immediate moment or individual whim. Empowerment can be extended and is evidenced by a reduced need to refer decisions upwards.
- For the process to reach the repeatable stage, all necessary process decisions have well understood and consistent criteria which are readily communicable, and are used to inform either product or process design so that attention can be focused upon identifying new and emerging issues or opportunities. Routine decision-making is gradually being built into the process itself, so freeing up new decision-making capacity. In addition, it can be seen that decision-making is being made close to the action so that all feedback loops are progressively shortened and the potential for rework activity greatly reduced.
- Finally, at the optimizing level, routine decision-making is fully automated within the process and new decisions driven by technology or market changes are being channelled down the decision-making life cycle to the point where they, too, can be built into the process. The ratio of opportunity to problem-driven decision-making is vastly increased in comparison to previous stages, and in addition, past decisions

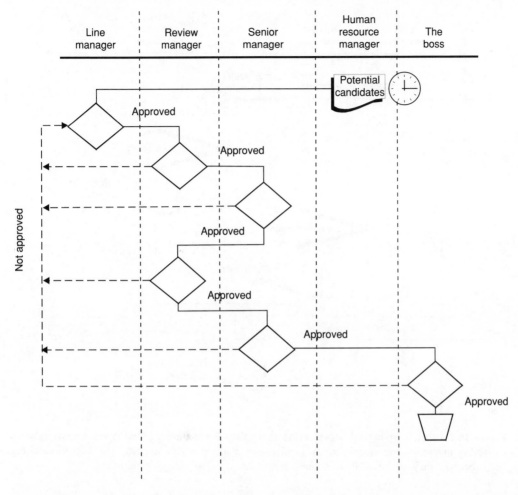

Figure 10.1 This recommendation for promotion operation occurs once a quarter. It was taking three months to complete. It need not take this long. Look at the pattern of decision-making — it is lacking in empowerment. Could the non-standard, case-by-case secret goalposts be the cause of the problem?

which were 'hard-wired' into the process are reopened, reviewed and either removed or re-engineered. See Figs 10.1 and 10.2.

10.4 INFORMATION CRITICALITY

The process of software production and delivery depends upon information logistics — the right information being in the right place at the right time. In many organizations there is information overload, frequently managed by selectively editing information according

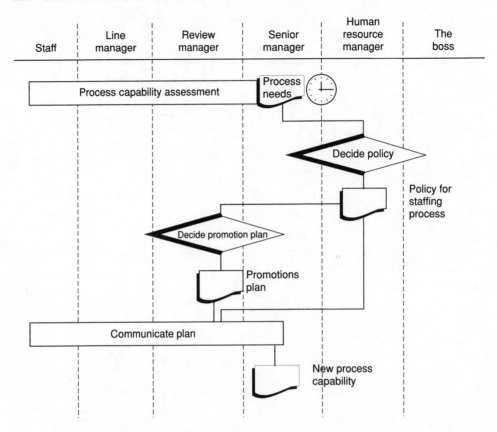

Figure 10.2 In the empowered organization the policy for manning based upon regular process capability inventory and assessment is decided and made available to staff. The decision-making rules, because they are based upon process needs, are standard and communicable.

to personal judgement before passing it on. The problem is then that information goes through numerous interpretations and translations, and valuable information is lost. The closer people are to original sources, the more effective and less costly is the process.

Life cycle deliverables — a new art form?

Because of the ready availability of standard boiler-plates for life cycle deliverables and desktop publishing packages, I now see attractive life cycle documentation which, by its very layout, suggests total credibility. But I wonder if the documents are read or just admired, and whether they contain appropriate information or information that just happens to be available, whether the documents are parrot-like cribs from existing examples or contain thoughtful, critical information destined for real people to use.

Information push creates costs and causes delays

Many people now use life cycle methodologies to govern their production cycle. Within these methodologies is scope for large bulk process and product documentation. All documentation, if the methodology is followed correctly, is subjected to stringent review and change control procedures, all of which can create potentially paralysing bottlenecks. At document reviews everyone adds their own inch of opinion, increasing size and complexity at every turn. Products are certainly more reliable, but I am regularly told of wheelbarrows of paper and the crushing burden of bureaucracy for every change request. People spend days and weeks just cogitating about what exactly should go into a particular life cycle deliverable. What should go into a quality plan? Into a feasibility study? We have all the sections and headings as prompts, but the wording itself requires thought and understanding. In many cases people do not have the information to put into the documents, and in some cases they do not know where in the organization to go for the information. Putting meaningful information into documents, then, is one thing, extracting meaning is yet another. Who is to read and sift out the relevant information in this enormous document? How is it to be used? Again, it is rare that people know. They just know that they have to create the document. Create often being the operative word.

Information pull — discovering the criticality of information

This is the real problem. Life cycle deliverables are often built with no real customer in mind. When people ask me what should be included in this or that deliverable, I always ask who is going to use the document as critical input to their work. In nine cases out of ten, the author of the document does not know who will have to use the document. Here we have a prime example of information push. Fill the document with as much information as we have and then pass it on (Fig. 10.3).

It is often the case that there will be several different downstream users of our document, all working on different delivery operations. Do we construct our documents so that each group can pull out just the information it needs in a few short pages, or does the group have to wade through the length of the whole document grasping a paragraph here and there that is relevant? Do we work as a team with the people downstream who need the information, and all of us, equally, capture the information we need for ourselves

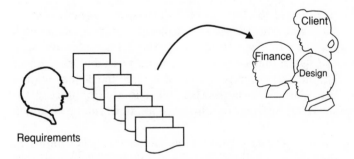

Requirements

Figure 10.3 It is usual in normal software production to throw all available information at everyone. This is unnecessary and time-consuming.

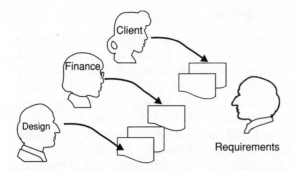

Figure 10.4 When information is designed to meet the requirements of the receiving clients you will find that you have less conflict and confusion — and considerably less paperwork to administer.

directly from source in a format with which we can work? Can we stop the paternalistic approach to information granting?

We create even more delays while we go hunting to discover who has the information we need, or while we sit through all those meetings trying to get adequate clarification. What we need is information pull (Fig. 10.4). What do I need to know to build this or that component or test? Who is going to provide that information for me? How can I ensure they know what I want and get it to me when I need it? Can I get it directly for myself?

Five levels of information management

At the initial level there is chaos. You do not have or cannot understand the information you need to do your job. You constantly need to refer to and interrupt other people. Often, you just have to make things up for yourself. Information is frequently handled like money. It is used as a reward for good behaviour, for political bribes, or for fuelling litigation.

As the delivery process becomes more defined, certain document standards are created, but it is rather like sending messages in bottles. To whom it may concern, this is what I know. Someone, somewhere should read this, it might be useful. Then we toss it into the sea. End of story. We may review the documents, but the reviews are against our document production criteria, as opposed to other people's document usage criteria.

At a more managed level, document deliverables are challenged because of the high costs of production. People quite rightly begin to challenge the value added by these documents. This is a danger point. Unless the delivery process, purpose, and stakeholder success criteria have been defined, the temptation is to arbitrarily chop the documentation and fall back into chaos or near chaos. However, when there is a clear process, the relevance to and need for documents by different production operations can be identified and evaluated.

To reach the repeatable level there has to have been a fundamental change of emphasis. Information required by operations is well defined and is collated and channelled from earlier operations. Reviews and inspections always include the people who will have to use the information, as opposed to just the peer members of the document production team who happen to be available. In all reviews, the downstream users of documents and information will feed back to the document producers their operational requirements for information and it is these requirements, rather than any theoretical requirements, which will be used to inform document design and production. Frequently used information components are presented in short forms such as a pre-established tick list.

It is hard to say what exactly happens at the optimizing level, because I have no experience of anyone working near that level. However, people who need information must be able to get their information directly from source without having to go through a number of translations. I rather like the idea of software 'agents' who can filter and search out your information needs. I also like the idea of talking to and working with people directly. Having an understanding. But perhaps that is too much of a luxury these days when everyone just wants the facts to go.

10.5 BALANCE AND SYNCHRONIZATION

Along with poor communication, the other main destroyers of value in information organizations are push-down stacks and asynchronous interrupts. Each time you come to me with urgent, unplanned work which I cannot schedule, and which I put on one side in my priority heap to look at just as soon as people stop bringing me unscheduled work, is an asynchronous interrupt feeding my push-down stack. Every time this happens an indeterminate amount of cycle time is lost, invisibly. We cannot predict when normal work will resume and, more seriously, there is no external sign of a queue or overload building up.

Ordinary queues also destroy value. However, these are easier to spot and have a constructive side, in that they flag bottlenecks for attention. That is, unless it is your policy to pretend they do not exist.

The organization is a network of activity

If you were to step back from your process to take a better view of the whole, you would in all probability see many individuals spinning round at different speeds, and from time to time their movements would coincide for a short time, perhaps just long enough for work to be transferred between them. What we need to do is to reduce all the spinning and create greater opportunities for people to work constructively with each other for longer periods.

How uncoupling operations complicated the network and increased activity

At some stage in the past, someone had the idea to break down sequences of software production work flow, believing we could obtain similar benefits from the division of labour and mass production as manufacturing. Instead of dyeing, spinning, and weaving, we have business analysis, development, and post-implementation service. Functions have become distinct specialisms. As individuals, we are encouraged to sort our work into bundles, and bus bundles in quantities that make economic sense for us, as opposed to economic sense for the organization. This is called uncoupling. Think about the times in the day when you read your mail, when you reply to mail, when you do all your paperwork, and when you talk to staff. We bus work in bundles. We can say to people, I always do budgets on Tuesday afternoons, I always hand over finished test cases at noon. The problem is that if we are passing things along, and I always hand over at noon, while you are ready to receive when you arrive in the morning before you start your meetings for the day after lunch, then between us, we are losing a half-day of cycle time. Now apply this scenario to the activities of everyone working on the delivery process. See Figs 10.5–10.7.

Improving effectiveness through synchronization

Instead of having everybody being busy, multi-tasking on concurrent jobs, we would be far more effective if we reduced the number of tasks and synchronized our work with each other better. In Japan, on production lines, an operative may be working with several machines, walking from one to the next setting them going. The rule is, because they know it to be effective, machines wait for people, people do not wait for machines. So if a machine is idling until the operative returns, there is no problem. The problem occurs if the operative is waiting and doing nothing except watching the machine finish its cycle.

In some respects, because our tools are our human intelligence and faculties, we are both operative and machine together. When someone asks us for work we are the machine or tools and they are the operative. When we do work on the critical path we are, at the same time, operative and tools. So if someone interrupts us and asks us to produce something for them and we are already working on something else, what should be our response? Some would say it depends on priorities or on objectives, and these are valid responses. But what happens if both sets of work are critical and high priority for two different customers? It is a conflict situation. One customer has to lose.

Only one critical path at a time per person

My rule of thumb is that each person works, as operative and machine, on only one critical path at a time. Most managers will say that they have to work on many critical paths at a time, it is their job. That is fine, as long as they are just operating. But when they actually take on work to do it themselves instead of delegating it, or if work is delegated back to them, then there will be problems. Ask any member of staff where the bottleneck is and they will point to their manager's office. Maybe there is some learning here.

Improving synchronization — staff allocation to work

How do balance and synchronization improve? Let us look at this practically, and consider how we allocate people to work, or work to people. The initial state is Brownian motion; people in constant movement and collision. Everybody shouting for someone else's work so they can do their job. No one knows what work there is in progress. No one knows if capacity has been reached, only that people are always busy and complaining there is too much to do. Even taking on more people does not improve delivery reliability or costs, in some cases we know the situation is made worse by adding more staff.

As people are made aware of the number and types of operation with which they are working, through process mapping or process-oriented effort management training, there is a semblance of control. However, there is still no clear understanding of the resource

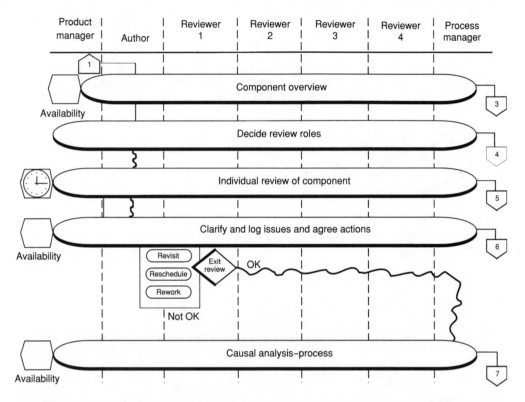

Figure 10.5 Deployment flow chart: uncoupled operations for component review inflates cycle time. This is the usual pattern for reviews. Reviewers are often people who just happen to be available. The operations are uncoupled and lack synchronization. It could take quite a time to get through the sequence of activities. So long, in fact, that it is difficult to justify the activity. If our purpose is to carry out reviews then we need to be dedicated to the product when it comes into our court and not be side-tracked by any other issues.

needs of the process. Conflict persists between activities and people caused by the clashing objectives which are used to transmit priorities to staff. Making objectives more specific, measurable, and linked to reward systems without reference to the process does not improve the situation. It makes it worse because people are working harder to do their own things, rather than the work required by the process as a whole. At the managed level, operations are reviewed and assessed and resource requirements are made more visible. At this point job descriptions and individual objectives are dispensed with. The requirements of the job are made identical to the needs of the process. Instead of job descriptions there are assignations to operations which are accompanied by work descriptions and skill profiles.

Now operations can be measured in terms of operation time, cycle time and problems. Staff changes and reorganization are rendered more flexible and safe because there is a process framework and an acquired experience base to provide training, continuity, and stability for staff. Finally, the process is optimized by managers and staff engaging in operation and process design and re-engineering. Process and operations are

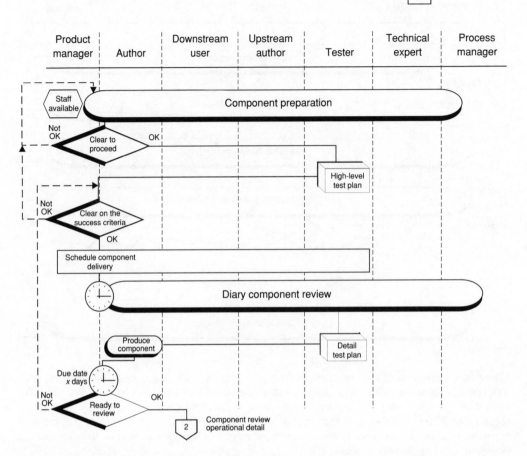

Figure 10.6 Deployment flow chart: synchronized product assurance (1). Component reviews always involve upstream and downstream stakeholders. Operational tests are agreed and documented before building the component and are available during construction. If the component is not 100 per cent complete on the planned review date, a decision to continue with the review may still be agreed. If there are complex problems still to be solved, the team can help, or if the component is almost complete a provisional go-ahead may be agreed.

self-measuring and provide immediate feedback to staff in respect of bottlenecks, delays, and errors, so that immediate action can be taken. Process capacity is visible. All new staff are wanted staff; they are engaged to work on defined operations for which they have the appropriate skill profile.

10.6 STANDARDIZATION AND AUTOMATION

The more work is standardized and automated, providing there is understanding of what is being standardized and automated and for what purpose, the greater the potential for

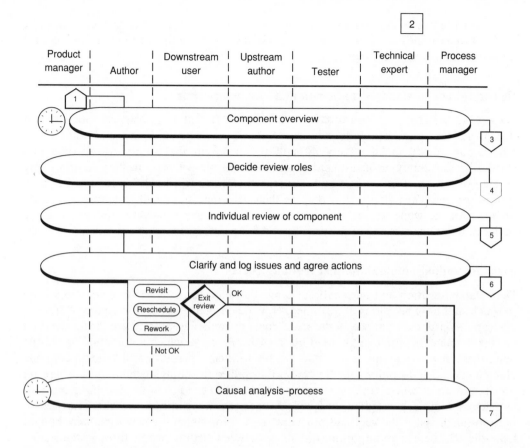

Figure 10.7 Deployment flow chart: synchronized product assurance (2). Because success criteria have been agreed and because the appropriate team is being fielded for review, sources of conflict and associated rework have been removed. There is now no reason why the whole team cannot carry out all the tasks of the review in one session. This ensures first that individual preparation is carried out and secondly, that elapsed time and paper communications are kept to a minimum.

improving cycle times and operation times. However, it is important to be aware that standardization and automation, in themselves, do not always improve the process.

Standards and automation are expensive to install and run

Standards and automation are expensive. Expensive to implement and expensive to run. Consider the costs of changing standards and tools and providing all the support and training. There is no point in investing all that time and money in standardization if there is no support at a high level for working with standards, and for allocating infrastructure resources to maintain effective standards. To give you an analogy, standards and automated tools are your process line and, in any other industry, would be considered a capital investment which could be written down against profits and would be subjected to scheduled preventive maintenance, and so on. Working in information technology, we tend not to have the luxury of that support and, instead, have to work in the chaos caused by poorly maintained and inadequately resourced production lines.

Be careful not to standardize or automate the unnecessary

What exactly is being standardized or automated? Is that task, that component, that document, that sign-off really necessary? If we are standardizing and automating bureaucracy it will make it very difficult to uproot in the future. Automation and standardization imply an investment focus which people will be unwilling to scrap and, because of that, perfectly useful and innocent operations will be deformed to fit in with this investment. Then after a time they, in their deformed state, will be hard-wired in the process. All the while we are moving away from the simple purpose and goals of the business, inflating costs and cycle times by codifying and speeding up redundant activities.

Standardization, automation, and learning curves

Does standardization and automation change the sequence of work and communication to which staff have been long accustomed? How much change is being introduced? If it is a big leap forward, can staff see all the steps from where they were to where the automation has taken them? If people are not led up the learning curve which automation has thrust upon them, if the rationale is not made visible to them, then they will want to continue ploughing the field by pulling the tractor, as they pulled the plough behind them. There are no circumstances where they will accept the increased load. I have seen all manner of automated tools subverted or tweaked in this way to continue the bad practices of previous methods — the very bad practices, in fact, for which the new tools were bought to eradicate! There is an important difference between leading people through the stages, and simply instructing in the new de facto methods. If we work to understand the process first and the relationships between the various operations, if we start to simplify and streamline before standardizing and automating, then we are better placed to make the best use of investment, and to ensure that it is appropriate investment and that it will be used to improve the process in the way it was intended.

While you will, in all probability, have made a start on standardizing and automating your software delivery process prior to process mapping, this is no problem, as long as you bear in mind the fact that you may have to make some changes. Do not let the work that you have done without process knowledge dictate the future for you. Be prepared to challenge and scrap it, if necessary. It will save you money now and in the longer term. As your process evolves, remember that existing standards and tools represent the hard-wired decisions of the past. Never let them become sacrosanct or fixed. Continually challenge.

Do not let standards undermine your responsiveness

Another pitfall to be aware of is that of oversimplifying through standardization. Once you start to examine your process, it is easy to be tempted to bundle all similar operations together and to create a single standard. In many cases this will be possible and reasonable. In other cases, it could be detrimental. Look carefully at the scale and the required responsiveness of the operations. Remember we are looking at work flow, and logistics are all. It may be important to have narrow fast-flow pipelines running parallel to bulk supply lines. Think of your financial planning operations. Some parts of your business will be comfortable with yearly plans. Other parts of the business which are required to be more dynamic and responsive may be suffering from the total inability to match standard one-year horizons. Keeping them bundled in the main pipeline may be severely undermining your business viability. Will the existence of a standard be used as a bludgeon to help them be 'better organized', or will you change the map to match the territory?

Keeping the costs of standards down

Given that standards are expensive to run, there are a number of alternatives to having large standards manuals. The first question to ask is, 'What would you have to do differently not to have this standard?' Does that leave you and your stakeholders better off or worse off? Secondly, can standards be made implicit in the process, and the process automated in such a way that people can only follow the standards? There are an increasing number of workflow management systems that are now coming on the market which can help you. See Sec. 13.5 and Appendix A. However, remember you need to determine and design a process that is suitable for your purpose, rather than take a ready-formed process that may be good, but may not match your goals. A third option is to ask if new standards can be created from existing standards. Can they be made identical? How would the process differ as seen by the customer if they were made the same? What would have to change?

Five stages of standardization and automation

How does this all develop over time as we become more expert? In the beginning there are no standards. Everyone does exactly what they think best without regard to distant members of the organization, or thought to their successors who may have to make sense of their work. Depending on the volume and simplicity of business, this informal approach may work very well. There may be the odd glitch, but not too many problems.

As work grows and the body and the scope of the work becomes more coherent it can be defined, and there will be a spontaneous move by everyone to establish some sort of standards, even if it is just checklists written in individual notebooks. Because of intergroup conflicts, there will also be pressure for managers to resolve issues by providing policies and guidelines. If this happens on a case-by-case basis, then the pattern of judgements after a while will seem incoherent, and there will be pressure to revisit the judgements. The best way to get out of this cycle is to sit down and start mapping the process. At the managed level, standards are built to reflect the needs of a defined process. In all likelihood they will be changed a number of times as the process is redesigned. The standards must not be used as an excuse to keep the process rigid. The order is: the process supports the stakeholders and standards and automation support the process. We should not be in a position of having to sell standards and automation to stakeholders.

When standards are built into the process, we can say we are at the level of repeatability, and when standards variants can be composed to meet the needs of different process pipelines, we can then say the process is approaching optimization.

Section 3

11

PERFORMANCE INDICATORS AND MEASUREMENT

In truth a good case could be made that if your knowledge is meagre and unsatisfactory, the last thing in the world you should do is make measurements. The chance is negligible that you will measure the right things accidentally.

George Miller
Psychologist
(In response to Lord Kelvin's dictum that if you cannot measure a thing then your knowledge is of a meagre and unsatisfactory kind.)

In this chapter we see how performance indicators can be derived as natural by-products of your process, and how you can bring the measurements together to create a dashboard of performance indicators against which you can measure the improvement and success of your process. There is a health warning (Sec. 11.11) at the end of the chapter. Measurement can severely damage the health of your organization. (You may feel inclined to read this section first.) Before we tackle the indicators in depth, I want to consider first the purpose behind measuring, and to reveal some in-built assumptions of which you may not be aware. We need to understand exactly what 'effectiveness' means and also that it is meaningless to consider measures outside the context of a defined process.

11.1 MEASURING UP TO SUCCESS

Performance indicators are like the dials on the flight control panel in an aeroplane. They are instrumentation to provide you with information which might concern you, such as the flight path, altitude, wind speed, engine functioning, fuel remaining, and so on. If you were designing the flight control panel for your software delivery process, what dials would it have?

There are five important facts you need to know about performance indicators.

- Most obviously, they depend upon your definition of performance.
- You need to have this definition of performance in advance, so that you can design instrumentation appropriate to your mission.
- Indicators themselves are not sensors, they are models of reality, created by people, which interpret data collected from sensors planted in the process.
- Models of reality will vary depending upon your purpose, while the sensors you use will vary depending upon your process.
- Last, but critical to achieving performance success, rather than just hypothesizing about it, you must be capable of taking decisions and acting upon the indicator readings to bring about change.

Performance indicators rely on a known definition of performance

So, what led you to choose the indicators you did? What purpose were you seeking to fulfil? It all depends on purpose and how you and your stakeholders are going to measure success given that purpose. What performance possibilities exist? Are you prepared to change performance indicators when you change or become clearer about your purpose? You may need to. If there is conflict about purpose, then there will certainly be conflict about how performance is measured. In fact, discussing performance measurement is a good way to clear up any misunderstandings about purpose. Misunderstanding and conflict do need to be resolved. I could be very happy creating so many lines of code each month, but if it is delivery reliability you want, we have a problem. What is it to you how many lines of code I can write, if I am heading in the wrong direction and cause you to miss the race to market which would have given you the biggest business breakthrough yet?

Design performance indicators to match your business purpose

A passenger-carrying car will need different instrumentation to a fighter plane which will need different instrumentation to a hot-air observation balloon. Instrumentation has to meet your specific needs. Just because measurement equipment is available does not mean that it is useful to you. Instrumentation to tell you your body temperature is 98.4°F is easy to obtain and temperature, indicating wellness, may affect how far you can travel. By all means spend time, if you have it, correlating body temperature to how far you can travel, but do not miss the fact that the distance you can travel is affected by fuel reserves. Looking back, it is obvious to us that a car needs a speedometer, and a plane, an altimeter. Looking back is easy. Looking forward, everything is still to be discovered.

Performance indicators are someone's model of reality

What instrumentation did pilots have in the first stick-and-string planes? Did they have the amount, precision, and sophistication of instrumentation pilots have now? Of course not. The pilots were the main instrumentation. They used their own vision to notice landmarks. They used their own skin to notice air movement. It was with this combination of sensory evidence and information pulled out of their mental experience banks that they calibrated their own internal models.

Now the complexity of working in the world exceeds our individual ability to model. So we rely on other people's models. Rather like using a telescope, or a pocket calculator. However, telescopes and calculators observe well-defined physical laws. Performance indicators observe rather messier human laws, and while they may be only impersonal fluctuations on a dial or a graph, they are not neutral, they embody someone else's assumptions about the world. Are we clear about those assumptions? Do those assumptions hold true? For our purpose?

Sensors vary from process to process

As planes became technologically more complex, help was needed. A spirit level provided an indication of attitude, a ribbon in the stay wires, the angle of attack. But, inevitably, a point was reached when it was no longer possible to work with the existing sensors. Instruments were needed to take account of the new process technology while rendering it transparent to the controller. The ribbon was dispensed with. Air flow round the new design of wings invalidated the ribbon as a sensor. New sensors had to be designed. How do you recognize that your sensors are no longer appropriate?

Performance indicators must help us engineer success

There is no point at all in having indicators which give you information unless you can act on that information, even if it is only to ditch or eject. It might be of interest to the insurers to learn from the black box at what altitude you were flying when you crashed into the mountain, but it is not much help to you unless you are free, there and then, to attempt actions to change your altitude and avert disaster.

As a manager, I want to see clearly from my indicators that I need to make a change and, preferably, what that change should be. Even if a change of course is too late for this particular software delivery, then I want to be able to use that information to stay on course next time. If this is not possible, then knowing that I am going in the wrong direction and unable to alter course is a frustration for me, and bad news for the client. But being able to change our course depending on the read-out from our indicators is a two-edged sword. If the indicators are not correctly designed, we could risk making change in the wrong direction and creating more problems.

11.2 SIZING THE PROBLEM

Although software metrics is now a specialism of some standing in software engineering, measurement programs which are set up in organizations suffer a high level of failure. This is largely because there is no clear purpose for measurement. Without purpose we all focus on different aspects of performance and end up on collision courses. We want proof of productivity; proof of lack of productivity; size of existing projects; predicted size of future projects; demonstration to the customer of value for money, and so on. The technical metrics devised by specialists, such as size, complexity, and reliability metrics, have been seized upon for use as performance indicators often with serious consequences.

Lines of code — a fundamental unit of measurement?

In the beginning was a line of code. A prime contender as a fundamental unit of software product. How big will it be? How much will it cost? What could be easier? In my days as a maintenance programmer, I remember source code with what looked like embedded Bob Dylan songs. 'If you want lines of code, Mr Manager, can I produce lines of code for you.' Now the Software Engineering Institute proposes in *Defining and Using Software Measures* a four-page checklist to help you define just what exactly constitutes a 'standard' line of code. Song lines are not included. Lines of code might tell us something about programmer productivity, but little else. They cannot provide you with a productivity indicator for the project as a whole, unless you intend your programmers to carry the can not only for their own problems, but also for those of the designers, analysts, managers, hardware suppliers, funny rule makers — the list is endless.

What about the other products we create? Should those be forgotten? Training, consultancy, documentation, support? How do they translate into lines of code?

As far as predicting future project costs, the argument is that if you can work out how many lines of code the new software will have, you have probably almost completed the project and can say with considerable confidence how much it has cost.

Function points — a barometer for all seasons?

Function points, although set up to enable you to measure product size in a mixed-language shop, have been used to demonstrate value to customers. More function points means more bangs per buck, or does it? Do more complex plumbing and electrics in a new house signal more value to the buyer? Not necessarily. We can just as easily generate complexity for complexity's sake. Function points are an indicator that embodies assumptions of value about the world which do not necessarily coincide with the buyer's priorities or values.

So why should this model impress the customer? It did not. Function points were never accepted as a client indicator of value. But the pressure is on us to measure and there are a lot of people selling barometers and training in the use of barometers. What other things can we do with this barometer?

How about measuring productivity? I see many organizations counting function points for new projects after the project is over, and allocating considerable time to the task. For what benefit? To know that this project scored 42 per month, and that 18, and to perform statistical correlations between samples which come from different populations. Each new project is a different population — different manager, different people, different process. Unless we gather a wealth of population data, the function point count is meaningless.

Measure completed size by capacity

People go to a lot of trouble defining 'the line of code' and establishing rules for counting function points so that they can obtain a basis for normalizing maintenance and support costs. This does not seem unreasonable, since the latest estimates are that 70 per cent of software production work is support, and the teams used here may not change to the same extent as new project teams. But would it not be less trouble and save argument to talk about capacity of object code in megabytes? While we are at it, we can also recognize all the other recurring costs, such as media storage costs. There is a precedence of sorts for this approach. I know of aerospace software suppliers who have to maintain weight control over their products: their important metric is 'How much does this functionality weigh?'

Complexity

Complexity is another well-used metric. What a pity our compilers and tools do not have in-built complexity checkers, in the same way word processors can now assess fog factors. If we want this important product information, we have to invest extra resources in tools and skills. I feel we have been let down by compiler manufacturers in terms of the lack of instrumentation they could have, but failed to, provide.

Complexity is an indicator we can act on. Once the bottleneck was creating machine efficient code. Now that machine costs and performance make human costs appear a luxury, we have a new bottleneck: human costs to retrieve, understand, and change complex code. This is why software, and all our other processes for that matter, should be designed to maximize simplicity and visibility.

Engineering to meet customer values

I am aware that I have not said anything yet about design, and it is at the design stage, when some of the most costly decisions are made, that we can act on feedback from indicators. At one stage, because a CASE tool which had the capability of providing DeMarco's function weights was being used, there was a marvellous opportunity to prototype designs. Holding design blitz sessions meant that function weight, and relative costs, could be ascertained up front. Customers would then be able to examine for themselves a number of shopping-basket options, and decide the relative value for money of this capability over that. All that we needed was a process which was under sufficient control so that the design could be enacted with similar ratios of costs and value, and that is where the problem lay. That is the main reason why I turned my attention away from my long-standing involvement with software measurement to process management and re-engineering.

How the process affects productivity

While we are under pressure to obtain more productivity, few problems actually lie with programming staff. There might be a small leak here or there, but it is nothing compared to the wide open spaces in the design of the process itself, where value gushes out. The cost of a line of code is dwarfed by the costly management decisions to work from this prestige location or that, to have so many levels of hierarchy, to prevaricate over decisions which are holding up work. All these costs are burdened on staff. If the burdened costs of programmers is so much an hour, then maybe the cost of a line of code becomes significant. But not in its own right. Only because of the decisions taken elsewhere. We ask, 'Can we afford all these people?' Pay some off and what happens? The same expensive overheads are spread over fewer people. Now they really look expensive. Is there a systemic problem here?

11.3 BITE-SIZE ELEPHANTS

Performance and productivity indicators are measures of effectiveness. If we are effective, efficiency will follow. If we concentrate on efficiencies, effectiveness will elude us.

Be effective — efficiency will follow

Your business, whatever it is, big or small, public or private sector, profit or non-profit oriented, is a total system. It has a purpose, it has goals. Become more effective at achieving your purpose and goals, and that effectiveness will permeate your organization. Focus on indicators of effectiveness, this is where you will get maximum leverage for improvement. You will also make it easier for people to do their work, and it will provide a big, initial boost to efficiency improvement. Continue to sharpen focus on purpose and goals, then waste and inefficiency will be squeezed out like water from a sponge.

Seek efficiency by itself, and effectiveness will elude you

Have efficiency indicators without indicators of effectiveness and three things will happen. First, instead of squeezing the sponge and watching the water flood out, the parts of the sponge that you cannot squeeze as hard as others will reabsorb the water. You may get a few drips out, but nothing more. Second, people will feel pinched and pained. Why are you squeezing them to get water out? Is it not the nature of sponges to absorb water? Did you not design your organization like a sponge? And lastly, are you sure your customer is not dying of thirst? Perhaps what they want is not a dry sponge, but water.

Measure yourself first, staff later

Do not start measuring your staff until at least a year after you have successfully managed to measure yourself. If you are not sure how to measure yourself, how will you know how to measure your staff? While you are learning you can limit damage and suboptimization. Pass it straight on to your staff and you will have magnified the potential for damage and suboptimization beyond your control. If you are not clear how to measure yourself, then find out what the business purpose is. Find out what your stakeholder values are, and work with your managers and peers to be clear on the exact meaning of effective performance for your business. You will be doing everybody a big favour.

Take a fortnight's holiday on the work floor

Once you have an understanding of effective performance, work to understand what operations in your process contribute to that performance, and how the operations are related to each other and to the process as a whole. If there is a client need to have speedier delivery, do not just crack the whip at the project staff, insist everyone creates more chargeable hours, and mandate weekend working from the safety of your office. Take the lead, pretend you are the request for work, map out the ground the request takes. Do it yourself. Do not delegate. Take a fortnight's holiday camping on the work floor. If you do not do it, you will always be at the mercy of operations you did not design.

Where were the bottlenecks? Where did the delays occur? Why was the request subjected to debate in all those meetings? Why were there all the interrupts along the process to ask for more information, more clarity? Understand what the process is doing so well to create the bottlenecks, the delays, the debates, and the interrupts. You may be horrified to find out how much meeting and debate there is. Be patient. Your first impulse will be to issue an edict to cut meetings. Instead, work to understand the information problems and systematically redesign and re-engineer the operations.

Start with simple indicators

When you have mapped the process, you can start to build your dashboard using some simple indicators — a spirit level, a piece of ribbon. Use no imported complex models at this stage, they will just increase the fog again. Use those indicators for a year. Watch them carefully. Understand how they might be changing for the better, for the worse. Talk to people while you tune the indicators carefully, until you know you are approaching a level of stability. Then you can start to develop the indicators and extend them.

The goal question metric approach

One of the biggest breakthroughs in software measurement came from Victor Basili and Dieter Rombach at Maryland University. They call it the *goal question metric* approach. Starting from a high-level goal, such as 'improve software reliability', you need to question how you would know that software reliability had been improved. What would be different? If you cannot answer this question, then asking for software reliability to be improved is a confusing exercise. Where are the messages of software unreliability coming from? When do they occur? With what impact? Taking the most serious problems first, what in the process gave rise to those errors? Where were they introduced? What circumstances surrounded their introduction? How did the errors succeed in being so well camouflaged that they went undetected?

This is not a witch hunt, it is just a fact-finding mission. You are looking for key points in the process to insert sensors to give you this information.

Understand the behaviour of your indicators before you automate

Before you automate the collection of the data and bury your assumptions in a model of any complexity, you first need to spend a year just working through the failures. Each one as it happens. Looking for the sources. Understand the decisions taken and the assumptions made which gave rise to the errors. Work on the ground, on the process, not on your desk, on month-old charts. Client pain is being caused in the here and now. Do not take that off-line and put it in a push-down stack. Information will be lost if you wait until you can spot a trend. Keep records. When you understand process failure points, and people have seen your commitment to searching out the reasons, when you have led them and shown them by example how to go about it, then you can start to introduce sensors for people to monitor themselves. You can move on to take the next bite out of the elephant.

11.4 RADAR

Customer key buying preferences

Customer key buying preferences are those factors customers take into account when they choose between one supplier and another. What factors influence your decision to buy from any supplier? Will they be the same as or different to your own customers' preferences?

Your set of key buying preferences may, or may not include all of the following: price, warranties and assurances, product lead times, product futures and support, and product range. Also important will be testimonies from satisfied customers concerning delivery reliability; responsiveness to change and queries; product reliability; and service-level adherence. Which of these and what others are important your customers?

Customer perceptions are all

In one organization, where mainframe response times were tracked, clients began to complain about slow response times. However, according to the indicators response service levels were being met. Nothing had happened to affect response times. There was considerable invective on both sides. The information services people shrugged it off as a case of 'perceptions'. But in our business, the client perceptions count for more than all our measures and indicators put together. When customer perceptions do not match our indicators, it is time to go out in the real world and check that we still have the right indicators, that they are still working and are not in need of recalibration.

In the above case, the customers had recently moved up a new systems learning curve and had attained a level of competence which allowed them to work faster. Now, they were having to wait for the system to catch up with them.

Framework assessment of customer preferences — the radar screen

In the assessment phase (Sec. 7.5) you will have established a regular means of using gap analyses to collect information on client preferences and perceptions. Supplement it with as much field intelligence as you can from all client interface operations. An annual survey will tell you where your customer was last year, but unless you have a particularly sluggish client who hibernates, it will not be much use. Regular soundings of stakeholder perceptions will let you know whether you are staying on track or beginning to drift off in the wrong direction — and from time to time you will drift. But the important thing is that you know quickly, before you have gone too far in the wrong direction and lose sight of clients.

11.5 JOYSTICK RESPONSE

It does not matter how well we have things under control, if our control has made us so inflexible that we are locked onto a crash course. Ideally, we should not need to make too many sudden moves, rather we should be gently correcting course all the time. However, when the need arises for rapid response, we have to know that when we turn the joystick, something will happen, not in a year's time, not next month, but quickly. All we can expect is the unexpected.

Measuring responsiveness to change

One of my clients was designing a financial process. It was working well until the boss came in and asked to have the unexpected immediately. The staff, knocked off balance, felt that was the end of process design. But a bright spark chimed, 'It is no problem. We just need to design a fast path!'

How do you respond to change? How do you measure your response to change? If an elderly customer comes and stands in the queue for their lunch but becomes alarmed and feels faint, do you have a means of responding effectively to the need to expedite this customer through your process? Do you say, 'I'm sorry dear, you'll just have to take your turn like everyone else.' Then they are taken really ill and you have to call an ambulance, and all your customers leave. Or, do you say, 'It'll cost you'? and upset all your other customers by putting them on your push-down stack? Or, are you able to communicate with all the other customers in the queue, tell them the situation and tell them how quickly you can get back to them, or what extra resources you will be bringing in so they are not unduly delayed? Or, since you are working in a district with a high proportion of infirm and elderly, do you set up a special process so that they never have to queue?

Designing process flexibility

The last option means carefully analysing and segmenting your market so that you establish appropriate value-adding processes for each segment. If you have a client group with regular and sufficient needs for different handling, then you can design a special delivery pipeline to accommodate them. If the need for urgent attention is only sporadic, but still provides high value, then a well-designed fast path is essential. Treat it in the same way as disaster recovery operations, exercise it from time to time, and ensure that it has all the necessary communication interfaces to tell people you are in rapid response mode. You may find that you can design the rapid response mode to be just as effective and safe as 'normal' response. Congratulations, you have just broken through the cycle time barrier.

Response to requests for change

What about requests for change? Will your customer be at all upset if you refuse? Will you make a charge for the change, and how will they like that? I had a colleague who depended for most of his income on his clients' requesting change. This is fine if you have the process to handle change without passing the problem onto your other clients. Will you offer last-minute change as an exciting new feature of your process which has been designed and costed to make this customer key buying preference into a new value-adding operation? You are in charge, you can design your response to meet your market needs. The measure of your response is the end-to-end process cycle time.

11.6 BLACK BOX

Although the black box is not part of the control panel, it provides vital information on what was happening at the time of a crash or failure. Much as we dislike the idea of crashes and failure, they do occur. When they do occur we need clear, objective data. Not just so we can repair the damage, but so we can remove sources of operational failure.

Linking failure data to the process

If we do not have a visible process then it is very difficult to trace back sources of problems. In fact, I would go so far as to say that it is impossible, particularly when failure occurs some time after implementation. We work with the product or service process design map (Sec. 6.8) that was produced prior to production, if the failure occurred in a new product or service, or with operations maps which describe on-going service provisions. We also need to know the skills which were available at the time, cycle times, and details of any design or production problems experienced at the time. We are often very informal in how we respond to problems in design and production, and while it is more important to sort out the issues than to write a novel about them, keeping a daily log of issues rather than remembering them in monthly progress meetings is a practise I recommend.

What to do with failure occurrences

When a failure occurs it is usually all hands on deck to restore the product and our professional credibility. That is important. And you have planned recovery operations which will reinspire confidence. Sometimes an inquest into the cause and nature of the failure is called for by senior management. The important thing to recognize is that no matter how difficult things were at the time, no matter how big the product was, how small, how complex, how new, or how old, a failure did occur. If we, as managers, seek to justify the failure, as opposed to searching out the data and looking at the process, we have created a problem for ourselves and our staff.

Sometimes, in all good faith, we assume the role of human shield between senior management and our staff. It feels brave and heroic but it does not do anyone any good. It frustrates senior management and increases antagonism, it eliminates the chance for staff to experience reality directly, we feel the pain from both sides, it certainly does not improve the process, which is the major constructive step waiting to be taken, and we lose vital data. When we say, 'I'm sorry, I'm entirely to blame, end of story', we leave the door right open for other people to go through the same pain and humiliation that we have just experienced. Before you resign, redesign the process.

Analysing fault data

I used to be greatly taken by statistical process control and we used to analyse problem reports and produce yearly rolling trends. This is another way to lose vital data. Failure, like a headache, is a symptom. The symptom may have many causes — fever, alcohol, noisy children. After monitoring my headache trends over the year, you might recommend soundproofing my study. A complete waste now, since the children have grown up and recently left home. I may also not feel very motivated to reduce my intake of alcohol. It was only once or twice I overdid it, and that was a long time ago. Do you see the problem? Process hot spots have to be worked on immediately following a failure, by a team of representatives from design, process, product, finance, capability, V&V, service, and delivery, to find out what caused the problem. Was it activities that can be error-proofed, starvation of vital resources, or faulty tools? Exactly what? Then fix it for good.

Counting failure

It is common now to keep a record of mean time to failure, mean time between failures, and mean time to recover. The other important indicators are the internal and external costs of failure. We may not feel very uncomfortable if we have become expert at fixing failures and have got cycle times and costs of fault-fixing down to a negligible sum. However, do not forget the costs to your customer whenever they lose capability. How much is your leaky process costing them? Find out. Post it high up where everyone can see. Failure should always be measured from your customers' experience.

Have you thought yet of how you could use this data as competitive advantage when you are submitting proposals? Here are our costs, here are our existing clients' losses due to our product and service failures. Unfortunately, that would mean accepting liability, and I think that is somewhere over the horizon.

11.7 SEXTANT

A sextant makes us think of horizons, and I am wondering how distant the horizons are for which you have to make your estimates. I use a crystal ball to help with estimation. It does not give me numbers, but it does focus my thoughts. When I see my distorted image reflected back at me, it reminds me to 'save face' by making promises I can keep. Having made the promises I then have to work with my environment to ensure it remains conducive to realizing the estimate.

Estimation horizons

Even for the most far-sighted, there is a limit to vision, and to how distant a horizon we can plan. I believe it is unreasonable to expect high levels of accuracy for projects with horizons over 12 months, so I break my work down into a number of project 'hops'. By that I do not mean one hop for analysis and so on. The hops I mean are tangible products I can deliver incrementally to customers.

The shorter the horizon, the greater the success

There are special times though, when planning horizons do have to stretch beyond the comfort of our vision. In that case, all you can do is to ensure there is somewhere to put down after some period that is comfortable for you, to re-establish a new horizon. It is important your customer knows where they will be landed at that stage also, and what possibilities there are for moving on, changing flight, or getting back home. Stranded customers do not pay bills.

Estimation accuracy

The true measure of estimation accuracy is that the process calls on resources as planned. There is no point in having arranged for a mid-air refuel off Labrador when you are still circling over the Bermuda Triangle. If, after a couple of turns round the triangle, you begin to suspect you will be there for some time, then you need to radio ahead and reschedule your refuelling exercise. Speed of response to estimation inaccuracies minimizes the risk to your business. Unfortunately, this is where instrumentation fails, when things get so bad that your only hope is that the instrumentation panel and not you is on the blink. The process itself needs a failsafe to message ahead, in case you are rendered incapable.

Knowing distances on the ground rather than the map improves estimation accuracy

A predictable process improves visibility and estimation accuracy. We need to know, rather than rely on assumptions and guesses, what our speed is. But as much as we need to measure progress, we need to predict cycle and operation times for producing components; they are the factors that limit our speed. When we can do that, then we can be more confident about making longer hops. If our plan is to go round the world in 80 days, and cycle times add up to 100 days, then the plan or the process needs re-engineering. If we have a variable process, and nothing is predictable, then we should make our planning horizons and delivery intervals as short as possible and not trust to fate.

11.8 TACHOMETER

I was told to say here that a tachometer is a rev counter. I was just worried that if I called it what I always call it, you might think I know nothing about cars. A rev counter is just one measure of engine efficiency.

Delivery reliability

The absolute measure of delivery reliability is simply determined by comparing the date the customer actually receives the software with both the original date requested by the customer, and the date there was agreement to deliver. I say 'original date' with considerable feeling. There are some organizations who measure their delivery reliability against the latest date negotiated with their client when the client is so far steeped in disaster and is afraid to turn back. The indicator becomes then, not a measure of delivery reliability, but a measure of manipulation and intimidation.

Listening to the engine

Delivery reliability depends on the capability to get there. This depends on fuel and resources. A starved process cannot stay the course. The ability to get there also depends on the engine lasting out, that it will not fade or stall. What is more reassuring to the traveller than the constant, controlled, and efficient pulse of the engine? What more alarming than the interruption of your concentration by a change to an off-beat, racing, or stalling sound? How can you measure the beat of software production, manage initial revving, keep your foot down, and change without stalling?

First, we must know the capacity of our engine: the cycle and operation times needed to build components. Then we can tune and synchronize our delivery system, continually reducing dissipated energy. To carry out the tuning and to make estimates based on known power output we need to know compound conformance to schedules. This is a real measure of process performance and also of how well planning systems are synchronized and integrated.

Compound conformance to schedule is the real measure of process performance

Total cycle time is the time taken for a product to flow from its entry into the process to its exit as a finished product for the customer. Each stage in component, product, and service production is measured against schedule (which has been developed upon knowledge of cycle and operation times). Conformance is then calculated by multiplying the percentage conformance of each stage. So if component design conformance to schedule is 90 per cent and component build is also 90 per cent, overall conformance to schedule is not a reassuring 90 per cent, but 81 per cent. In this way the reason for the project manager's nightmare becomes obvious. If you have just a 7-stage delivery system with every stage running at 90 per cent conformance, then really you have only 49 per cent conformance.

The corollary to this is that if you believe you have just one amorphous operation then you will always have that cosy feeling that things are 90 per cent complete, even though your heart will be waking you in the middle of the night to tell you that somehow, something is not quite right. The more stages you have all running at 90 per cent, the worse your conformance to schedule looks.

Internal conformance to schedule

So how many stages do you think you have in your delivery life cycle? If you have counted life cycle phases as stages such as analysis, design, construction, etc., please pause to think how many group boundaries the product crosses and recrosses during each phase. Please consider also the number of components the product is broken down into for purposes of work assignment. How many now? This is approaching the number of stages you have in your process. Now work out what you would expect your compound conformance to be, with each stage's internal conformance running at 90 per cent.

If you promised your client delivery of a project in one year from now, given the assessment of compound conformance you have just worked out when could you reasonably expect to deliver now?

Tuning the engine

The ultimate objective of tuning the engine is to achieve a state where the cycle time for each product delivery is the sum of the operation times for all the various stages. This is achieved when the process is balanced and synchronized and when all waste, delays, and non-value-adding activities have been eliminated. How do we know what these are?

Each stage or operation has to be analysed and understood in relation to its contribution to the delivery process as a whole. There are certain drivers which inflate schedules, and you may find it worth while to look for the impacts of some of the following common dysfunctions.

When a component is passed from one stage, one group, or one activity to another, how long does it rest while work is changed over by the receiving people? What is done to the product that does not satisfy the critical success factors of any of the stakeholders? (This means, love it or hate it, you cannot dispense with time-recording against component production; time-recording provides important business information which gives you the critical advantage of more competitive client tendering. However, you might ask, how could the job be made less time-consuming, while ensuring all the necessary information remains?) How many times is work interrupted to respond to product or component failure, and to correct the failure? What are the wait times for resources to become available? Are there bottlenecks?

Listen to the whole engine

Gathering information from operations about dissipation of energy needs to be sensitively done. It is a skill of practised listening. Do not just listen to the words, what do the sounds mean? Get to the bottom of it. But at all times remember you are working with a complex engine. As you make adjustments always keep in mind the function of the whole engine.

11.9 FUEL GAUGE

I am not alone in having had, in my younger days, to hitch home because my boyfriend's car had run out of petrol. Yes, it really had. He was so averse to putting petrol in the engine, that the poor thing, the car, choked on all the gunge in the bottom of the tank.

Everyone knows that we cannot run an engine without fuel and oil and expect it to perform well. Yet, when it comes to business, this principle seems forgotten. It is as if, by starving a thirsty engine, we expect it to change, all by itself, into a 50 miles to the gallon engine. But how do we judge how much fuel is necessary, and how much is overspill?

In our business, because human time accounts for so much of software delivery costs, we are going to be watching the rev counter as an indicator of costs. This was explained in more detail in Sec. 11.8. We also need to account for the costs to provide products and services and this is what we shall consider now.

Costs to provide products and services

Start by accumulating all costs associated with the primary transformations: the transformation of labour time and materials into finished product. How? Most organizations now have some system for collecting and accounting for project costs. However, this is not always as well integrated as it could be with their financial accounting systems. You can tell this because either massive translation exercises are involved, or people just scratch their heads and put budget reports to the bottom of their biggest push-down stack.

One organization I worked with had no less than three separate sets of books, and it was impossible to relate costs between the three. The books were kept by the accounts department, the delivery function, and the internal client requirements group. If you do not already work in harmony with your accounts department, now is the time to put all past differences behind you. Establish one set of books.

Most people cost projects by phase — so much for analysis, so much for design. Additionally, organizations, to stop project creep, close down the books for the analysis phase once it is 'complete', or has run out of budget. This means that analysis work carried out in design phases is posted to design. Whoops, they have just sprung a fuel leak. Other organizations record time, but with no defined structure. Either pre-established cost codes do not reflect actual activities, in which case arbitrary new ones are invented, or people make up their own codes. At the end of the day, an overall picture of product costs is unobtainable.

Another problem is that life cycle phases tend to be activity based, and, just to prove how active we are, we invent 'deliverables'. This was discussed in more detail in Sec. 10.4. But I need to say here that life cycle costing needs re-examination.

Component costing

What we should cost are not just life cycle phases but design components. This means that costs to design, build, and test a component should be accumulated at the component level. Let us think about this. While we are probably happy with the idea that customer manuals and training in support of new software are costed separately, what about the actual software components themselves? Well, it largely depends how you intend to quarry components for reuse. It may be that you intend to recycle user interfaces — screens, reports, etc. — to start with, then each of these would constitute a component. At an application-specific level, it may be transactions of certain classes. We need to have costs of how much it costs to design, build (or reuse), and test a report, a database, or a transaction to mail standard letters to customers. This information enables us to establish relative value for money for each component and to project costs for providing similar components in the future. If component costs are buried in the project as a whole, or are split, untraceably, across phases, then we can never hope to improve our estimation quality.

Another way of looking at the problem is to say that the cost to deliver a component in a managed process will be pretty much fixed. Compromise design time, and build and test may take longer. Compromise build, and test needs extra fuel to compensate. If we look at costs from the phase perspective alone, then reduction of design resources may give us the impression of efficiency in the design group when in fact they have just passed a problem along the line without obtaining reduced product costs.

How much does it cost to deliver an assured component?

The important questions we need to answer are not how much did the design for this project cost, but how much did each delivered and assured component cost? Not what is the design phase costing, but what is the cost of customer interfaces so far? Are we spending too much reworking report layouts compared to the value they represent to the customer? What were the costs to build the component, to review it, and perhaps, to rework it? How could those costs be managed better in the future? This method of costing links easily into incremental, evolutionary, and rapid application delivery strategies.

Total costs to supply

So far we have concentrated on petrol consumption, but now let us turn our attention to oil consumption. The oil is there not to power the engine, but to keep it in good running order. I want to focus on process costs now, or total costs to supply.

Process is designed at two levels. At the lower level we deliberately design a process, or confirm an existing process, for the delivery of each new product. We may reuse some existing process components to support the new product, or we may actively choose to make an investment decision to build a new process. In either case, in the same way as product components can be reused, so can process components. At the higher level, we are looking at overall organization design, accommodation and layout, and pay packages.

How are you going to account for new compilers, hardware to support staff in the delivery process, staff recruitment costs, property charges, and so on? How are these costs to be burdened on specific projects? I am a great believer that all costs are variable and that the biggest breakthroughs on costs occur when we shift what was once believed to be a fixed cost into the variable category. That is why I class accommodation as a variable cost. It is not variable in the sense that you may be able to lease out rooms when your staff take holidays, but you can choose the level of burden. It is a process cost, because if you shift to teleworking, and your staff work from home, you have altered your process.

Cost accounting is linked to product and process design

Cost accounting and time-recording then need to be linked to product design and process design. At the product level managers are free to break out whatever activity codes they need to accomplish the component, but at the end of the day, they can be aggregated back to component level. Because we are focusing costs on a component required by the customer, we are not side-tracked into activity for activity's sake. All activity is traceable to the support of a component. If the component is redundant or adds no value to the stakeholders, then we do not make it.

At the process level, these costly decisions should not be burdened on or buried in projects invisibly, but should be recognized for the process investment and process renewal costs that they are, and 'written down' on a standard and visible basis over time. Their efficacy can be judged with respect to rev counts. Is the oil making the engine turn more efficiently? Are we creating too rich a mixture? Can we satisfy more customers and increase market share without the same proportionate increase in capacity? Can we reduce the backlog of projects with the same capacity? In a flat market, can we maintain market share with reduced capacity? Can we break through into a new market?

This brings us to the final measure in this set: what are the total costs incurred in any period compared to the revenue earned? How many pence do you have to spend to earn a pound?

11.10 WHAT, NO SPEEDOMETER?

Yes, I have no speedometer. I know that most of you would like one and that you are probably feeling very let down and disappointed by this apparent gap. Maybe it would help you feel better to write down three ways a speedometer would help you in your business.

How speed is derived

We all know that a speedometer shows speed. How does it get the data to show speed? Well, there is usually a cable from the car road-drive which turns a magnet and induces an eddy current in a non-magnetic conductor attached to a pointer. So, basically, the data come from the number of wheel turns and the known diameter of the wheels. Which wheel, though? I was really worried by this. How do you know which wheel to attach the cable to? Then I thought, it does not really matter, does it? All the wheels travel at the same speed. Then I felt worried again. How do all four wheels travel at the same speed. What would happen if one wanted to go slower? Well it could not do it, could it? They are all linked to the same engine. No problem.

Obtaining speed from cycle times

But how many wheels have you in your delivery process? If your engine is the delivery process, which has been designed by staff and management to balance and synchronize the wheels (has it not?), the wheels are all the operations that enable work to run smoothly through the process (do they not?). So how many separate operations have you? Three? Forty-two? One hundred and twenty? Do all your operations have the same cycle time? If not, then to which operation are you going to attach the cable? To the fastest? To the slowest? To all of them? None? What information will the speedometer which you have just designed give you? And, most importantly, how will you act on that information?

How many speedometers do you need?

If you do not link the cable to any wheels, you will not get any information, and perhaps that is what you want. If you link cables to all the operations what happens then? Maybe you can handle all these dials on the dashboard and make sense of them. Perhaps there is a a computer to handle the data for you. Does average speed tell you anything useful? Do highest and lowest speeds and range help you? That might help you do some balancing. Will you balance up or down? Which of the wheels will you start with?

Let us turn back and consider what happens if you attach the cable to the fastest wheel. It will not tell you when you are going to reach your destination, unless you have allowed that fastest operation to drag all the other wheels behind it. You would not do that because you would end up with many damaged and bald wheels and a rather sick engine. So if you were travelling any distance, I suppose you might not arrive there any faster than if you had based your estimated time of arrival on the speed of the slowest wheel. If you arrived at all.

The speed of your process is determined by the slowest operation on your critical path

The speed of your process cannot be faster than the slowest operation on your critical path. Your slowest wheel is, effectively, a brake. If you want to speed up, then this is an obvious wheel to consider taking some action on. Is that wheel really necessary? What is limiting its speed? How can that limit be safely removed?

If you have only a few wheels or are able to resource the focus on many operations simultaneously, then you can work with all your operations. I suspect this might not be the case for many of you, so the other useful option is to work on the slowest operation first. How do you know it is slowest? Because you have an intuitive feel, because you have cabled it up and have started to measure its cycle time. Whatever speed changes you make to that operation, any action to cut work or to transfer work to other operations must always be preceded by identifying and cabling up the affected operations. This will stop you from just moving the problem somewhere else.

Knowing speed alone does not help you through traffic jams

Having a speedometer helps you to plan your arrival times. Knowing the speed of the slowest operation on the critical path of your process will help you assess and predict arrival times. However, even with a speedometer, while you can say that given a steady 50 miles per hour you will arrive on time, what use is it in a traffic jam? It tells you that you have stopped or are crawling below your target speed. What do you use now to help you think through alternative scenarios? You use your watch and either your knowledge of landmarks or the map to assess how far you have come and how far you have still to go. In either case, you do not put your foot down and cause an accident. You take time to see if you can see what is holding everybody up. Is it a big problem, or a small problem? Shall we tackle the problem off-line, while re-engineering the delivery process to get us round the road-block, or is it a problem that we can resolve quickly on-line and continue according to the map?

Your staff will tell you when there is a traffic jam, won't they?

You do not need to spend money on sophisticated indicators to tell you that you have stopped, do you? Or that work has come to a virtual standstill? Your staff, whom you have already paid for, will be the first to tell you. Or has someone severed the communicating cable? Maybe it is time to do some repairs.

Speedometers tell you when you are going too fast — do you need to know this?

We also use speedometers to tell us we are going over the speed limit and to slow down. Do you need a speedometer to tell you this? Or are you happy to set your own speed limits?

Speedometers tell you nothing about the cost of travelling at speed

So, a speedometer is only a measure of rate of travel. It is a mechanical link to turning wheels. By working with operation cycle times you can find out speed in a much more direct way, and also in a way that you are closer to what is happening, so your subsequent actions can be better informed. But do not forget the wheels are part of the whole transport. If you designed your car with wheels on one side only, or you have an uneconomical engine, or you do not fill the tank with fuel then, no matter how fast you are going, it is going to be a very expensive journey, and while you might arrive in time, will the customer be able to afford the cost of the journey?

11.11 TARGETS — A HEALTH WARNING

Using numerical targets for management purposes without regard to purpose and process could damage your health, the health of your company, and the health of your clients.

Deaths and discharges

In the early 1980s I was working in the UK on the design of systems to implement management information in the National Health Service (NHS). The tide was turning in the NHS. General managers from business were being recruited and productivity was the focus of everyone's attention. What did the NHS use to measure productivity? Bed statistics. Hospital accounting is geared to funding and staffing beds. So productivity was based on bed turnover rates, or to put it more clearly, patient throughput. What were the assumptions embodied in this indicator? It assumed no difference between patient discharge and patient death. That is, it was all the same, productivity-wise, whether the patient left horizontally or vertically. As a customer, I cannot subscribe to those assumptions. But, think a moment, what might be the consequence if, instead of giving hospitals brownie points for every dead patient they made, we subtracted points?

Tons make pounds

People who collect household rubbish from people's homes are rewarded in the form of bonus payments, depending upon the tonnage removed weekly. Looking at the graph which shows the weekly figures, is it not surprising that the curve looks like the ascent of Everest? Either the recession is a myth and people can afford to throw more away, or there has been an outbreak of prolonged spring cleaning. The costs of burning the refuse have also risen, but at a greater rate. Local authority waste management costs are suddenly escalating. Should they start to charge more for their services? Lay off staff? Replace vans every five years instead of every three? What do you think?

Top of the form

School league tables are enjoying considerable controversy in the press. Do we not want our schools to perform better? Do we not want them to make more academically qualified children? Do we not want to know which are the useless institutions to be avoided at all costs? Is it not important that schools are rewarded for excellence? You are a head teacher, you have little budget as it is to play with. You desperately want to improve your capability to provide better services and support for the children in your school. You can only achieve this by 'earning' performance-related awards. What would you do?

Traditional software-related targets

You are a programmer, you are paid for lines of code produced. You are a tester, you are penalized for every error that slips through your testing operations into live running. You are a manager, your chances of promotion fade with every conflict you escalate. You are a designer and you are targeted to produce 35 chargeable hours per week, but you are still waiting for client sign-off. You are a project manager, your projects have to come in within plus or minus 10 per cent of budget. You are a team manager, the company is running down staff numbers, you are asked if you have resources available for mapping your operations. What is your response going to be in these situations?

What is productivity?

Let us just stop and think what we mean by this productivity which is a number on a graph or a table or a score-chart. Productivity is not raw output divided by input. Productivity is first, a measure of effective product or service. What is meant by effective? I do not have an answer for you. But that is all right because you can easily get the answer from your stakeholders. If you do not already have that answer, and agreed it, do it now. Productivity is, secondly, a measure of resources consumed and the design of the process which consumes them. If we have yet to appreciate the systemic workings of process, or that the process can be effectively re-engineered, then the knee-jerk reaction is just to cut costs or cripple the process.

If I am rewarded for patient throughput, and it does not matter whether they are dead or not, how can it be said that a rise in throughput is necessarily an increase in effective product or service? If I am penalized for making dead patients, will I attempt to treat the frail and the critically sick? If I am rewarded for weight of waste removed, then more fools they, if they did not say whether it was dry weight or wet that was to be measured. If I am rewarded for making qualified children, maybe I find ways of excluding children whom I know would not perform well. If I am a programmer rewarded for producing lines of code, I can produce lots of lines of code. Legislate in detail what constitutes a line of code, and I can find more legal ways of producing even more lines of code. While you legislate, I will find the loopholes.

Targets can distort your purpose and your process

Are we still serving the right purpose? If we are not serving the right purpose, what is happening? What will be the consequences? If you find yourself, having set targets, going off course, do not be tempted to build even more complicated models with pages of explanations and definitions. Stop, now. Go back to your purpose. Go back to your process. Talk to your customers. Talk to your staff. Why are you measuring and rating staff morale? Why are you feeding this information into models to provide you with magic numbers which make you feel better or worse? You do not need models to tell you about staff morale and motivation. You do not need models to tell you how to improve staff morale. You just need ears, a mouth, and being with them. They will appreciate that far more than being force fed the latest brand of motivation like battery hens.

12

A LEARNING PROCESS

As soon as people come with the idea of unlearning instead of learning, you have them in the frame of mind you want.

Frederick Matthias Alexander
(originator of the Alexander Technique)

In this chapter I want to concentrate our thinking on the different skills which are needed in a process-oriented environment and on how you can introduce those skills. In particular, I would like to focus on the manager as an agent of learning.

In a process-based environment, people are assigned roles in the process, and their competencies are linked closely to process needs. Managers need to recognize the process behind their software delivery activities, and to develop strategies for making that process visible and clear to all their staff, so that staff can become members of a real team. Process management demands a team-based approach, that is, groups of people who are actively collaborating to produce group products and services, as opposed to just working together in a friendly and cooperative manner.

Let us start to think now about some of the critical competencies required in a process-oriented environment. Some of them you will already be familiar with from some of your forays in TQM, such as client or stakeholder focus. Others, such as decision-making and product knowledge are fairly obvious. But what about process awareness? What about process-oriented effort management? Most of our personal skills training is concerned with establishing and asserting our own priorities and objectives as individuals. Remember back to your time-management training. Think how inappropriate that would be in the context of a wider process. The emphasis needs to shift, so that the priorities and objectives of the team as a whole, working on the process, are served.

12.1 PEOPLE, ROLES, AND COMPETENCIES

Unlike traditional manufacturing industries, knowledge workers, in general and software producers in particular, use 'soft' process lines. While we may have tooling benches, such as our PCs and CASE tools, there is no real evidence of conveyer belts or machinery demanding that specific work be completed in a specific sequence. People, practices, procedures, and project plans and Gantt charts are our delivery line. When we become process oriented, we need to recognize the nature of our line and see it in terms of a tangible, if not tax-deductible, investment. People, their roles in the process, their competencies, and how they are empowered to use their skills, provide the dynamics of delivery success.

Recognizing investment in 'soft' production lines

In a hardware manufacturing industry we would be investing capital in a tax-deductible line and tools to support production. In software, although we invest in hardware tools, the 'line', if we can think of the delivery process in this way, is a 'soft line'. It is all the human practices, experience, and expertise gained through working in the software production environment that have been stitched together. Because it is a 'soft' line, managers either do not recognize its existence or are unwilling to invest in designing appropriate processes to meet software delivery needs. Most software managers have grown up in the software industry and few have had the opportunity to engage in and learn from manufacturing practices. When we do invest in the process, whether it is by adopting a specific life cycle or methodology, establishing a software engineering group, or simply by reorganizing, we do not recognize it as such, and when times get hard, the investment is junked. In this way, time and time again, we slip down to the bottom of the process learning curve. It is time to recognize our attempts at process definition for the investment they are, and to stick with them and learn from them.

Organizational roles come from the process not from a cookbook

I remember being asked by one information services manager if the new organizational chart he had produced for his department would be successful. He had a number of standard texts on his table and had used them to help him develop his new-look department. I had to say that an organization chart by itself does not have any special magic. Success depends, literally, on your stakeholders, the goods and services you want to produce for them, the problems you anticipate, and the process you intend to create to provide the logistics for product and service delivery. Match people to the process.

It is always easier to buy in the latest organizational template rather than to address the conflict of stakeholder needs. We have seen the rise and fall of information centres, development centres, data centres, and other organizational concepts that our advisors have been keen to sell us. Now we have division of labour and divided functions. Planning, development, and support or operations functions have been split apart and roped together, rather like a disoriented, three-piece pantomime horse. Only planning gets to see the light and value vanishes through poorly patched seams. Our job is managing logistics. We need water-tight end-to-end plumbing, not leaky functional silos.

The dangers of uncoupling staff expertise from the process

The latest trend I have encountered is the *skills centre*. The skills centre is a group responsible for administering a central pool of staff, contracting them out as needed to development projects. Staff links with managers, products, services, and process are dissolved. Staff have to advertise their services in the organization as they become free. They may be forced to become contractors and receive pay only for the time they are engaged on projects. They may even have to pay for their own skills training.

What is happening here? Employers are effectively generating staff turnover. Creating internal attrition. Product and client knowledge is being dispersed. In all other industries there has been a concerted effort to reduce staff turnover and to keep people working in teams, because this has been found to improve effectiveness and productivity. Perhaps, if we had an automated delivery line which was able to direct and produce software with minimal input from unskilled labour, then such an approach might be technically feasible. Whether you would have motivated staff working in your best interests is another matter. But in most cases, as we know, there is no visible process in software production, only people with their client and product experience, which we seem to want to downgrade to the level of an expendable commodity.

From jobs to process roles

One of the arguments put forward in support of the skills centre approach is that managers can no longer cope with administering and coaching staff while being productive in their own right. Only small spans of control can be managed and they spawn deep hierarchies. This is certainly not effective, not only in terms of lost productivity, but also in terms of massive information translation. But trying to obtain economies of scale in staff administration by having staff pools provides no advantage when the result is the destruction of the existing experience base. Before we add on another solution and more potential bureaucracy, let us look to see if we need to dispense with a past solution which has become redundant.

The question we need to ask is, 'Why do staff require so much administration by managers?' Well, there are job descriptions which have to be kept up to date and validated. There is objective setting and if not quarterly reviews, then annual reviews and appraisals to be carried out, and all the forms to be filled in for recommendations for promotion, performance and bonus awards, and training and succession plans. How much of your time is taken up competing for promotions and awards for your staff? Again, the question must be, is all this really necessary? Yes, if you have no clear purpose and process — the tasks become divorced from reality and become an end in themselves. No, if you have a visible purpose and process.

When there is a visible process, people are assigned roles in the process. The job description is simply a description of their relationship to the process, a deployment map of the operations assigned to them, and details of the activities and procedures which are to be managed. This is not altered on an annual ad hoc basis, but as and when the process requires change or to allow for planned staff succession. The process governs the amount of management and staffing required, and not the other way around. Objectives and targets are also linked to the process and are often identical for a whole team. Because of the need to balance and synchronize the process, changes to objectives and targets are under change management control. Staff receive feedback on a day-to-day basis, so much of the form-filling can be eliminated. Managers are free to do their real work, designing operations and coaching staff.

Change and staff competencies

If the process governs staffing, then what happens to promotions and career progression? Staff maintain flexibility in the team and have to be able to build, maintain, and service client products as required. But the team works with distinct product or client groups. If there is a need to move across client or product boundaries, then a planned course of training is required: an understanding of how the new product is being value-managed; the key buying preferences of a new client; and the requirements of new operations need to be gained.

Tools and techniques are also important. It is not a reasonable practice to throw staff in at the deep end and leave them to make mistakes which impact our clients and our business. We tend to hide the true costs of bringing staff on-line in a new environment; the fact is most people admit that they are not fully effective in their new jobs for six months. Is this in your capacity management plan?

The process is affected all the time by changing technology, stakeholder needs, platforms and architectures. Succession planning is based upon planned and managed changes to the process. In advance of change, new process prototypes are evaluated by teams of staff who are to work with the new operations, and they will provide the core competencies for change as it occurs, with training being timed to coincide with the introduction of the new.

Most companies keep lists of competencies for the various staff grades. Some of them are very detailed, others omit technical competencies altogether, because it is assumed that the technical competencies are already there. In truth they are omitted because no one is quite sure at a managerial or human resource level just what technical competencies are really required. Again, people look for all manner of skills, almost anything except what the process requires. Know what the process requires and suddenly skills management becomes a much more simple task.

The manager's new role

Job inflation is a tricky subject. Everybody wants promotion within two or three years of joining the organization. If they do not get promotion they think they have failed and will tend to go elsewhere to gain recognition and esteem. There is a systemic problem here. Once we stop rewarding people for how many managers they have working for them, once we stop creating managers like a New Year Honours list, we can get rid of a lot of the political tar that is clogging the process. When people express a desire to become managers, what is it they really need? They want to be able to go home to their families and not feel like a drone. It is easy to make people feel like drones: give them cheaper chairs than other people; put them in noisier work spaces; remove their right to first-hand information; undermine their ability to manage their own operations; or continually subordinate their operations and throw them out of balance because you need to rush your own work through. People just like to feel they have some say in their own destiny. In a chaotic organization with no clear process, there is no destiny. Being a manager works for a time, until the realization hits that managers are not in control of their own destinies either.

The manager's new role is to design and improve the process with the assistance of peers and staff. The manager provides coaching so that operations are carried out effectively and knowledgeably, and staff can become self-supervising. As such the manager is constantly working to improve and enable productivity. The job is that of process engineer, role model, coach, and enabler. Staff are the process. Problems with the process are staff and methods problems, and it is the manager's task to run the process problem-free. The process has to be kept running on a day-to-day basis and problems sorted out as soon as they occur. Not annually. Not quarterly. Not retrospectively. This is the value a manager brings — informed, coordinated, and immediate response.

12.2 CHALK, TALK, AND WALKING THE TIGHTROPE

Because we work with a 'soft' process line, investment in appropriate skills is necessary, and difficult. Necessary, because if we do not have the right skills available at the right time, we suffer bottlenecks with all their associated problems, dislocations, and delays. Difficult, because we have to master constantly changing and complex technology. How do we ensure that we have the right skills to manage the delivery process in our organization and remain flexible? How do we go about upgrading skills when there is change? Most importantly, how do we ensure that people have the right skills at the right time?

The skills you need depend upon the process you run

Most organizations now have a staff skills database of some sort and keep training records for their staff. This is a great step forward in resource management. However, do you know what delivery processes you have and what skills are required to manage and support those processes? Do you have a complete product portfolio detailing the resources you need to continue support for these products? In your portfolio, is there a plan for product retirement and replacement? Do you know which skills are likely to become redundant and which members of staff are affected? In your schedule for new products, is there a list of required skills? Do you know where the skill shortfalls are likely to be, and who in your organization, or possibly from outside, will fill that gap? Unless you know the answers to all these questions, training and skills maintenance is likely to be an expensive hit-or-miss operation which you cannot afford.

Many organizations allocate so many days training per member of staff on an ad hoc basis. Training has become a staff perk. People expect to have their full training quota by some means or other. In some organizations training is available from a central budget on a first-come, first-served basis. If you have an unexpected major change to hardware or software in the latter part of the year which requires upgrading staff skills, then you have problems because the budget has been spent. I am not saying that we should receive only training which is essential to the process. The more aware and skilful we are, the more responsive, innovative, and competitive we are. What I am saying is that we do need to get the training in context. In a process context.

Training in the schoolroom needs to be confined to those practices, which, if our lives depended upon them, we would be unable to carry out. Think of the tests which you might employ to check if schoolroom training is necessary. This formal training is, in general, linked to managing new hardware, new software packages, new languages, and so on. Providing we have controlled change management, training in this respect can be predicted and managed effectively.

Coaching for changes to practices

What happens when we introduce new operations, changes to the process, or new work procedures? These are all equally new, and in some cases require us to unlearn previous behaviour and habits. How do we go about training then? In the main, people can get by if their life depended on it.

Formal training can be effective when people are convinced of the need for change, but it can fail because people see practical difficulties in applying the new ways. They take the information into their heads, but their bodies will revert to old patterns when there are quite small problems. The new way does not feel right. Something more than chalk is needed in this situation, to save our wasting money.

No matter how many times we tell people that they could walk, perfectly safely, across Niagara Falls on a tightrope, we probably will not have many volunteers if we ask them to do it. But we can get them to walk across a tightrope two inches off a training-room floor, so that their bodies, in spite of all their thoughts to the contrary, know that they can do it. Then we have to lead them from the rehearsal to the real event. This is when we have to walk the rope first.

When there are changes to the process, managers in their roles of leaders, coaches, and process designers must be involved. They need to walk through the changes, to ensure staff understand the purpose and goals behind the change, to get the problems and risks in perspective, to engage staff by joining them in the changes and, most importantly, to listen. What sort of problems are staff experiencing? Is it a problem with how they are doing things, do they need help in changing their methods or is there a fundamental design problem with the new operation which has to be solved?

Staff need to see the operational changes in the context of a whole. How does it fit with this practice? With that procedure? Working alongside staff, with a visible purpose and clear goals, refinement to new practices can take place. With no understanding, and no management coaching, there is no refinement, just tinkering and tweaking which undermines the effectiveness of change. I have seen staff adding new symbols to CASE tool packages with the result that the work could not be compiled or checked. No one was on hand to understand the cause which had driven staff to make the changes, nor to advise on the consequences of the action. Managers did not think they had to be involved. Their lack of involvement meant that this investment potential was never realized.

Managers as walking role models

Whether we like it or not, all our actions are messages. Not only do we have to walk the chalk and talk, but we also have to make the purpose and goals of our actions transparent. In this way we reveal the 'big picture'. 'The reason I am doing this is because . . .'. 'I hope to achieve . . . by doing this.' Delegating tasks provides coaching. Also, walking through your tasks with people as understudies or students provides vital communication to those who are not yet ready to take on delegation.

In all training the manager is the most important asset. Without commitment to doing things differently and the active involvement of the manager, not just as signatory to the training, but also as a coach, training investment will be lost. Only train staff in what their managers are prepared to take on board and support. If the managers do not take change on board, then there is a problem which has to be resolved with them first. It could be an indication that the change is not viable in the process as they see it, it could be they do not understand the change, or it may be that they need help. Help them.

12.3 PROCESS AWARENESS

For some people in software production, the whole world of process and process management as we have talked about it is still new. There has recently been much talk about business process re-engineering, and there have been visible successes in re-engineering the work of people in non-manufacturing sectors. All this has caught the imagination, and resonated with the good common sense of managers which urges that there has to be something tangible in software delivery which can be seized upon and improved. We are now in a position to seize control, if only we knew how to pick it up.

Process awareness for managers first

The first step is to enable all managers to take an holistic approach to their organization. They need to see the business holistically in terms of purpose, goals, and aims. They need to see the business as part of a larger society, that of the market and customer values they serve, the legislation they must meet, and so on. This larger society is our stakeholders' world. The task of the manager is to ensure that their business can detect and respond skilfully to all changes in the stakeholders' world, not just division by division, but through the response of an entire end-to-end process.

The next step is to enable managers to recognize this process supporting software delivery. A process exists now, but you may not recognize it as a process. Unmanaged, it will tend to be wild and confused, but it is possible to start to make the process visible, to understand it, and to mould it as we want it to be. Managers need to develop strategies for making the process visible, and for communicating process knowledge across the management team. They need to develop their confidence in working in a process-oriented environment, and in process design and engineering. To do that, a range of management simulations and exercises such as 'Process for Managers' is available.

Managers coach staff in process awareness

Following on from management awareness training, managers work with their staff to help them understand the transition. Managers are the best people in the organization to promote process awareness for staff. It is a question of developing leadership and followership. This cannot be obtained by sending staff through some off-site training school. The staff need to work with the manager to define operations. Remember, we cannot just roll out the astroturf, the changes we sow must be firmly rooted and tended.

The role of human resources

Human resource teams need to look at how they are going to redesign their operations on this process base. What additions to their resource databases do they need? How are they going to handle changes to job descriptions, staff appraisals, and succession planning? The major support for transition is in this area, and human resource staff need to be actively working alongside managers at the outset, planning for change.

12.4 PROCESS-ORIENTED EFFORT MANAGEMENT

With the exception perhaps of team-working courses, most of our personal skills training has been concerned with establishing and asserting our priorities and objectives as individuals in the organization. We rank our work by what is important to us. We argue the case for doing things our way. We work to meet our personal objectives. However, the challenge of process-oriented software production is to achieve process balance and synchronization. This is obviously difficult if we are all furthering our own ends at the expense of the process. Individual success cannot stand by itself. Individual success must underpin delivery success, and vice versa. Process-oriented effort management (POEM) is one method of team-based time management.

Learning to manage process capacity

At the high level, there is a need for coaching in process capacity management. It is no longer acceptable to misuse project management tools and personal charm to force products along the delivery pipeline. We need an understanding of how we can gather and use information from process and operational cycle times to predict resource requirements. We also need to know how to design better planning operations so that we can work to flexible horizons which are more appropriate to specific stakeholders' needs. Different clients may demand very different planning horizons and approaches. It is unreasonable to expect your clients always to give you a year's notice of new requirements.

If, within a particular planning period, there is a need to introduce unscheduled work, staff are coached not to squeeze the work in with a large intake of breath and a prayer; they learn to reschedule resources or work dynamically by redesigning the process to create a faster path. If it is not feasible to create that faster path then maybe the honest thing is to tell the customer. Ploughing through regardless puts all work and client relations at risk. It may be tempting to pile your plate high with food, but if your plate is too small, you will only end up dropping most of it.

If there are consistent capacity problems, then the situation has to be highlighted, whether it appears politic or not. If increasing capacity makes your charges look uncompetitive, then the trained reaction is to look to your process and, using value management, systematically re-engineer operations, rather than simply make blind cuts. After all, if you were producing and delivering cars but your costs were too high for the market to bear, would you cut back on engine-making capacity and sell the car without an engine?

Learning to balance and synchronize team effort

In Sec. 3.5 the difficulties arising from suboptimizing goals and targets were described in detail. Process-oriented effort management supports the reliable delivery of products and services through team effort. No individual or group achieves its targets until the product is being successfully used by the client, and all stakeholder needs are met. There is no point in any group going faster if, overall, they disrupt the balance of production. There is a point in the team working together to design a process which will result in speedier delivery and satisfied stakeholders.

At the start of production, the delivery team, that means business analysts, designers, coders, testers, and support staff, discusses and designs together the most appropriate delivery process, making use of, and tailoring, existing operations and templates wherever there is advantage to do so. At this stage, staff need to know how to use high-level functional deployment maps to create the production plan (which includes the quality plan, cost plan, and any other plans you feel it is necessary to have). Having established the process, the objective is to meet all the requirements of the process and signal immediately when problems, bottlenecks, or delays occur. Problems are worked on as they occur and are solved. When there are problems, the remaining production plan is re-engineered to re-establish synchronization and balance. There is no reward for any group hammering through their own contribution to the product regardless, if they have created problems for other teams, or for the client.

Learning personal effort management

At the individual level, all work is process work. This approach is radically different from traditional time management. In traditional time management, I establish my own personal goals, some of which are linked to other people, but generally the other people are my staff or my manager, rather than my peers or other groups in the organization. These other people 'interrupt' me and prevent my channelling effort into furthering personal goals. I prioritize my work by what is important, that is, important to me. Urgent work is dealt with but is given short shrift, particularly if it is work that has been originated by someone else, someone I do not know, or someone I judge not to be important.

While I may have initiatives of my own that I want to pursue, if these impact other people, then I need to do some planning with them. If my new initiatives mean that planned process or operations work is mounting in my, or other people's, in-trays, then I have created a problem not only for the process but also for the clients. First, I shall be adding to delivery cycle time by delaying work on in-trays. Secondly, I shall be distorting process capacity by creating hidden queues of work. Many problems occur when we generate new work without regard to existing plans. It is difficult to resist creating new work. Planned work, after all the planning, often seems dull and unattractive, compared to the new ideas that I would like to put into practice, but the fact is that no new work can be generated until existing and scheduled workloads are complete. If there is no time available after that, then ways have to be found for improving and streamlining operations to provide the time or, failing that, justification for increased resource is needed.

I frequently meet people on training courses who say they respond to requests for work only if they receive a reminder. They work on the assumption that all requests for work are not important until someone starts to scream. While it may be the case that we are subjected to requests for work which, process wise, are unimportant, our first task has to be to understand the request with whoever has generated it. If the work really is make-work, then we can help them understand, with the aid of a process diagram, that there is a better way of achieving the same purpose. This is not the same as using influence or personal power to intimidate. If the work is important, then we are inflating product cycle times and costs by not responding professionally to the request. If the work is not necessary then help me so that I can learn and do things differently in the future.

Learning to cut corners for good

I meet people who 'break all the rules', and rush work out to clients. Breaking rules is good when you find a way to satisfy your stakeholders better, and, most importantly, when you improve the process by eliminating funny rules for good. But we need to understand that charging about like Superman or Superwoman not only is selfish and damaging to the business, but also results in no lasting change or improvement. We shall have to waste just the same amount of effort and spleen the next time we feel we have to break the rules. Do not break rules, redesign the process.

Learning value management and engineering to support negotiation

It is very interesting to watch people in workshops negotiate away value for their customers, it is almost second nature. The customer makes an urgent demand, and the team's first reaction is to see how little the customer will actually tolerate. At some stage we seem to have embedded this behaviour as good practice. Without coaching, there is no attempt to work through, map, or value process options. It is precisely by learning to look at process options that we can see how the effectiveness of our process introduces or reduces costs which are then passed on to the stakeholders.

The main problem is that we always work out costs based on the past. Most estimation tools work from an historical database. While they may provide you with useful information, people must be coached to ask, 'If our competitors were really keen to do this job, what is the lowest cost they would charge?' We then need to search for and create unobvious means to deliver the required product or service. In what process context can that delivery be achieved? What process and conditions have to be created?

Bringing about this change is fundamental to keeping business. When we know what the process options are we have a sound basis for negotiation. Negotiation as a game with no firm, or simply guessed at, process framework reduces your credibility. Either you sell yourself short, or you sell your customer short. You may not recognize that, but they certainly do, and they do not come back for more.

Learning to link roles to the process

Improving operations and the process is part of every individual's job and everyone needs training to identify and improve the process. We need to work from visible operations and process maps. Everyone should be able to map processes and operations and use them as discussion and design documents. The benefits are that everyone can map their own part of the process which will be their job description. Everyone is responsible for keeping their maps up to date, which provides input for re-engineering and for standards accreditation. Everyone can see what is being done, how their work impacts others, and how other people's work depends upon them. No bureaucracy, no fog factors, no word-smithing committees, no duplicated work, just the basis for continual improvement.

12.5 MANAGING INFORMATION CRITICALITY

Information is a major source of value and cost in software delivery, but how much do we really understand about its need, use, and timing? How many information documents do you generate for one product? How many pages? How large a readership? How much review effort? How much of this information was put to use during production? How much will be put to use actively in the next two years?

I am aware of how careful I have to be when I say that, in general, we overengineer our information and document production. Please read on before you issue a general edict to reduce product documentation by 50 per cent, or before you dismiss my statement out of hand. Let me give you some background to my thinking. If we remember our days at school, one of the important and most rewarded achievements was to be 'cleverer', that is, to know more than anybody else. It is a sad fact that most adults spend the rest of their lives with this millstone round their necks, trying to be clever, rather than being able to respond to their environment in an intelligent, and by that I mean appropriate, manner.

Learning about information

I know from personal experience that whatever information I presented to management, or whatever information my staff presented to me, there was always more that could be added. This is because we are looking at things from our own particular viewpoint, with our unique knowledge-base and personal experience. We have to consider seriously what information is critical in all our documents. This is not something we can decide for ourselves. It is for our readers, and people who need to work with the information we create.

Learning to reduce interpretation

It is important to learn how and when to create the information that is to be used by someone else to carry out their job. Often we interpret raw information, customer verbatims for example, write them down to conform to some structure of logic, either our own, or that of an existing standard, and then pass them on without a thought of the people who need the information to work with. Instead, we should be enabling them to derive their own information directly from the source and put it in a structure that is meaningful and useful to them. In so many organizations, the nearest staff get to their clients is through the proxy of a planning or marketing account manager. Is the account manager really in contact with clients themselves, or just another proxy from the customer side?

This really is a problem we must work on. Working from second-hand information leads to second-rate products and services. If we do not trust our staff to have direct contact with customers, then what training, coaching, and procedures need to be put into place so that they can take on this responsibility?

Learning to understand how information is used

Many organizations use peer reviews to validate information. The problem is that peers may not necessarily be in a position to say exactly what is required by the people who are to work on the reviewed document. Only the people who are to use it can say. One might say that using document standards should get round this difficulty. People know what to produce, in what form, and what to expect. In some cases this is absolutely necessary: when we cannot communicate directly with the users of our information, when we do not know who they are, when they are physically too far away (although this is less of a problem these days), or when they inhabit the future. However, we must not fall into the mistake of believing that all communication needs standards. This is like using Latin to enable communication between the English and French, instead of learning the target language of our listener. I expect to make as many mistakes in French as in Latin, but perhaps my French listener can help me make myself clearer. If I talk Latin and make mistakes in speaking, perhaps my French counterpart will add to those mistakes in translating, then we can really be at cross–purposes.

Standards should not be proliferated beyond necessity. When direct communication is possible it should be used. We need to spend more time with the downstream users of our information to understand how they work and what their real needs are. Reviews should always include downstream users.

Learning to tell the difference between critical and necessary information

The other aspect on which we need guidance has to do with when we produce information and documentation. Does it have to hold up the critical path, or can it be automated or done retrospectively? Again, I expect the might of standards and quality departments to come crashing on my head. But how much of the information we produce needs to be produced before the product? Can we separate out the critical from the necessary — the critical to be done now, the necessary, later? If coders do not like to document their work as they go along, and all research seems to point to this dismaying fact, then why have we continued to whip them to produce documentation instead of creating tools to produce this documentation as a by-product?

Again, if we look for an example outside our industry, then the change in procedures made by some building societies in how they issue mortgages might give us some insight. Here is a high-risk transaction. A transaction which you would like to cover with paper to save yourself from catastrophe. Well, it used to take at least a week, if not more, to obtain a mortgage after your initial request. Now you can get the mortgage the same day. Why is that? Because the critical information the mortgagers require is available from credit and property searches. The audit trail for mortgage they have extended to you is necessary, but not critical. It is completed retrospectively. It does not have to hold up the work.

There is so much we can do to improve the effectiveness and efficiency of handling information in our business, that a separate book is really required just on this topic. It is sufficient to say that we need to take this subject seriously, understand how information is being used in our organization, coach staff and listen to their ideas, and try new ways.

12.6 PRODUCT KNOWLEDGE

We do not live in a virtual reality of hardware and software technology. We do not interact with tools and compilers for the sake of interacting with tools and compilers. We are in the business of providing value-engineered products and services to real customers who need very tangible solutions to their problems. Our most valuable experience base is knowledge of the customer and knowledge of product ranges which satisfy and will continue to satisfy client needs. When this vital asset base is destroyed, lost, or ignored, no amount of ingenuity with tools and compilers can compensate for its loss.

Knowledge of the product portfolio is essential to the business

All staff need to know the product and service portfolio, and to understand the relationship between the various products and services. What point of maturity have individual products reached? What plans for retirement and new development are there? Where is the market shifting? Where is the business intending to place itself in response to the market? Most organizations are very good at providing initial skills training for new employees, but few do more than provide a cursory walk-through of their product range. As staff is turned over, what existing knowledge there is becomes diluted and lost.

When people do not know the business product strategy, many wheels are reinvented and many opportunities for rapid new product development are lost. It is not a problem unique to the software industry, other industries have been through the same pain. The point is, we can learn, and should learn from other more mature industries whatever we can to improve our advantage. I know of manufacturing companies who create many variants of products, simply because the staff do not know of existing products. Consider the enormous costs not only of devising new products from scratch, but also of creating new batteries of tests, of maintaining specialized production equipment and expertise, and of storage. It is just the same for software production.

In some software organizations I work with, there are managers and senior managers who do not know the contents of their product portfolio. In some cases there is no one person in the organization who has that knowledge. This is not particularly the fault of any single manager, but it is a failure to appreciate what is core to the business. If you do not know your product portfolio, how do you know what your service liabilities may be? How can you plan and manage capacity requirements? Can you say you are in control?

The importance of products and services as business assets needs to be transmitted as part of the organizational culture. They are the culmination of many years' investment in tools, methods, and human effort and as such need to be used to advantage and protected. We can maintain them, re-engineer them, reuse them, and use them as platforms from which we can expedite our next success.

12.7 STAKEHOLDER FOCUS

We provide products and services to real customers to enable them to be more successful in their business, whatever that may be. If we do not know who the customers are, what business they are in, what constitutes success in their business, or what their values are, then how can we be useful supplier partners? Without that knowledge, we put ourselves in a very hit-or-miss, take-it-or-leave-it position, and the chances are that eight times out of ten, the clients will leave it, thank you.

The importance of transmitting customer and stakeholder values to staff

Who in your organization is responsible for transmitting customer values to staff on a regular basis? Who in your organization is responsible for transmitting stakeholder values on a regular basis? In addition to customer values, staff need to know the legal requirements and constraints, financial constraints, security requirements, key business requirements, and so on. Without this focus on stakeholder values, how can we blame our staff for cutting corners, gold-plating, or not being business focused? Who is helping them? Who is instructing them in common company values? How can you possibly have empowerment and trust staff to make responsible decisions, if they are kept in the dark?

Without this knowledge, the way we go about software delivery in this organization, the operations and procedures, are seen by staff as just so many 'funny rules'. Rules to be broken and ignored. Rules to be followed robotically, long after they have lost their reason for existence. The consequences of this are a high spend on teaching people how to do things, high costs of policing to make sure the rules and procedures are followed, and high on-going costs to keep plugging the loopholes. It does not make very much sense.

It may be that there are policy documents passed round in a folder. You may even have statements pinned on notice-boards. In the main, this does not help. The raw facts or statements in themselves may be difficult to digest. If they are never mentioned by line management, and seem not to be taken into account by managers when they make decisions, then the message is that they are just boring bits of paper with no relevance to the real work around here.

The role of line management in transmitting stakeholder values

Stakeholder values need to be interpreted and mediated to members of the organization. Their impact on day-to-day activities has to be understood. Rules and procedures have to be linked to these values quite visibly, so that the rules can be understood and carried out correctly, and so that the rules can be challenged, broken, simplified, or replaced. Line management is the best source of this information. It can be made readily available and understandable to staff at all times when managers talk through their strategies and during day-to-day work when there are problems carrying out procedures. Line managers need coaching so that they in their turn know how to coach and transmit business values.

12.8 DECISION-MAKING

Decision-making is the engine which drives empowerment in the organization. One glance at the process and operation deployment maps of an organization will give you an indicator of how much empowerment exists, and also how effective the organization is. Informed and empowered decision-making can make all the difference between an organization that has the capability to respond athletically to shifts in stakeholder values, and an organization which never gets away from the starting block, hamstrung by its own power lines.

Decision-making and empowerment

The biggest complaint that management make about their staff is that they do not know how to make decisions and so managers have too much low-level decision-making referred to them. The biggest complaint that staff make about their senior management is their arbitrary decision-making: the way they get involved in too much detail, overturn decisions, and fail to delegate sufficient decision-making. Staff are unable to infer any coherent purposes or principles behind the decisions which managers make. For them, work and trying to carry products through to completion is like navigating through treacherous waters, not knowing when and where the next rocks or reefs, decisions and policies, will surface. They can only guess. Or second guess. And the waters are so thick with political eddies that they cannot tell whether they are making progress or getting lost.

Decisions convey goals

We are all organizational messengers, our actions are our message, and our actions are the fruit of decisions. It is only by making visible those decisions and the assumptions about the world upon which they rest that we can communicate coherent purpose throughout the organization. In Sec. 9.6 I talked about the problems of making decisions when the decision criteria are not made available to inform any preceding actions. This behaviour is to do with catching people out, not making constructive progress. If you have to make a decision, the most constructive act is to make your decision criteria public. In this way you give people a chance to satisfy your goals, and reduce the effort wasted going round and round in endless loops trying to mind-read your success criteria.

If I were to ask you now to choose between an orange and a banana which were offered to you, which would you choose? And for what reason? We do not choose the word 'banana' or 'orange'. We choose to quench our thirst or to satisfy our hunger, or, equally, to avoid or minimize displeasure or pain. All decisions are goal oriented, but a decision divorced from its goal conveys ambiguity. There could be several purposes which you might be satisfying by your choice of an orange. Only by declaring your goals and assumptions can I understand what you are trying to achieve.

It is not that staff are incapable of making decisions. As competent adults we are making decisions on our own behalf all the time, some of them very costly and risky, like who to live with, what house to buy, or how to bring up a family. Rather it is that purpose, goals, and assumptions are not made sufficiently visible, and, lacking that clarity, people either second-guess management based upon what they have experienced and seen so far, or they make decisions without sufficient or right information because it is not available. When purpose and goals are clear, decisions can be safely delegated.

Coaching for better decision-making

One way you can help people in your organization is to ensure that they are clear about how decision-making conveys information to the organization, and how important this is to organizational effectiveness and efficiency. Starting with the senior management team. It may seem for them as though they are being put back on the nursery slopes when they are coached to unpack their goals and assumptions. They will, in some cases, assume that everyone makes the same assumptions as they do. The breakthrough occurs when they find they have different sets of goals and assumptions to their peers. The conflict which arises needs to be handled skilfully until a common set of goals can be established.

Some organizations have chosen an image or metaphor to embody organizational goals, and to keep them uppermost in people's minds when they make decisions. Think of an umbrella, each section of which has a bright picture representing an important organizational goal. Now, you can turn the umbrella and ask yourself if your decision is more customer-focused, more responsive, more value for money, and so on.

When you are making decisions, there is an opportunity to coach staff in your decision-making process. Talk staff through your decision-making process. Discuss your goals and assumptions. Be like a hospital consultant working with a team of student registrars. Discover their blind spots when they form their own decisions. Learn from them how well you are communicating goals, by listening to the assumptions they make. Coach, inform, and correct whenever they miss the mark. Learn from them early news of change. Why are they suddenly assuming that this is important, or that is unimportant? When you disagree, unpack goals and assumptions and bring them altogether. What picture of the whole are they conveying? Under what conditions do all these assumptions hold true?

Talk through the decision-making patterns in the organization, in the process as a whole, and in their individual operations. Enable them to spot secret goalposts and patterns of ineffective decision referrals so that they can help you reduce the bureaucracy, and prevent outbreaks of new bureaucracy.

12.9 STEPPING UP

When you make the step up to process-oriented management, there may be a lot of change that is needed. It is all too easy to fall into the trap of trying to change everything all at once. I have worked with managers who said they wanted to generate lots of changes. What they really meant was either that they wanted to distinguish themselves by turning everything upside down and 'be seen to be doing things around here', or they wanted to bring about change and make it stick. You need to be clear in your own mind what your objective is.

Throwing everything up in the air all at once, or worse still, getting everybody else to throw things up in the air, leaves you with a statistically slim chance that everything will come down again in a workable combination. When it does not, the organization starts thrashing, and no good can come from it. Improvement can come about only by having a rational and coordinated approach grounded in process knowledge.

Coaching in goal-driven change

If you want to make change stick, then you need to go about it in a rather different manner. It is so simple you have probably heard of it before, but few people are actually shown how to implement it in practice. It is expected that change will just happen by sheer willpower, by positive thinking, or by evangelistic enthusiasm. It will not. First, take an assessment of where you are. Then, determine where you would like to be. Next, and this is new, use a state transition methodology, linked to deployment flowcharts to plot an incremental route between where you are now and where you want to be.

Each step up on the transition map represents a tenable improvement in the organization. Changes to the process or operations which are required to underpin the transition are provided as maps. This means there is a clear, coordinated, goal-driven route which is visible for everyone to see. Each step is planned and resourced. Each step can be tested or tuned. The degree of change is limited only by the horizon of your imagination. As you near the top of one map, you can start work on the next map.

Making a start to goal-driven change

You need four things to start. First, you need to work with change management because the changes you are planning may have an impact on client schedules. You will also need to work with resource management. Your changes may affect capacity, and will probably affect the training and competencies required by the process. Secondly, you need a high-level view of the process so that you can plan each transition to keep the whole process in balance. Thirdly, you need maps of the affected operations. For each transition you design a change to the process and map out how operations will function after the transition. Fourthly, you will need to work with the team who 'own' the operations.

This approach needs your understanding and design. It is very different to empowering a specialized group or an outside agency to make the change for you. You are the surgeon, not the patient. You cannot carry out the operation if you are anaesthetized. You need to be listening constantly and evaluating signs of life.

13

LEARNING FROM OUTSIDE

When anything is pointed out, our only idea is to go from wrong to right in spite of the fact that it has taken us years to get wrong: we try to get right in a moment.

Frederick Matthias Alexander
(originator of the Alexander Technique)

This chapter is called 'Learning from outside' because both benchmarking and buying-in tools give us the chance to hitch a ride on someone else's learning curve. Let us see how we can learn and transplant improved ways of working, while avoiding the pitfalls of transplant rejection.

13.1 REMOVING THE BLINKERS

We work in an industry that is fascinating, mind-stretching and rich in diversity. We can mine our personal satisfaction on a number of many different levels. My early work on compilers and machine translation was my introduction to the joy of symbolic logic, semantics, and Chomsky. Just edging sideways in a small way to handwriting recognition, I was in the world of perceptrons and Minsky and Papert. This business satisfies my interests in communication, design, and logic. Why should I ever need to look beyond its boundaries? Why look at other processes?

There is life beyond the software horizon. We need to get out more. Everywhere people are engaged in solving problems in their day-to-day lives, and not just in business either. What are they finding out? What are they discovering that I can transport and absorb into my way of working? We spend quite a lot of time, and money too, in our own industrial and professional groups, picking up information, some of which we did not know, much of which we did know, but which confirms our own beliefs and makes us feel secure. Why not take a risk and do something different? Target six different industries near you, make them as diverse as possible, and, as a substitute for your day out with the software professionals group, go and spend a day visiting them, watching how they do things.

Sources for benchmarking

We have been debating the problems of design and code reuse, repositories, and component retrieval naming conventions. Find an engineering firm that archives its drawings and reuses engineered components. What do they do? What problems do they have? What process and procedures do they employ for storing and retrieving parts? What can you learn? How do libraries store and retrieve information from articles and books? If you live near a university, you can find out how vast amounts of diverse new information from databases are sifted and communicated to staff and students. How about the software 'agents' that companies like Microsoft and General Magic are working on. These are electronic 'labradors' or 'retrievers' that go off and fetch selected information back to you, information that you have indicated you want to know. Could there be repository 'agents'?

Have you ever discussed your pension requirements with a financial advisor? Even if you have, why not go through the operation again, concentrating on their elicitation process? How are they determining your values and key buying preferences? How are they using that information? They often have very wide product portfolios. How much of what they ask is based upon knowledge of what their existing portfolio is? What do they say and do that makes you feel comfortable you will get what you want? And, importantly, what do they say and do which makes you feel you are not going to get the best deal? Ask them to explain how they are modelling your needs, what assumptions are they making, and are they taking account of risks, if so which? Who has to bear those risks if you get the requirements wrong? What happens when you change your requirements? How much does it cost? Who pays?

What about a day in a hospital? How is vital information about patients communicated to all the various staff who have to work with the patient? How are the staff organized? What are their reporting lines? To what standards and procedures do they refer? How are they learnt? Do they carry out inspections and reviews? What form do they take? What fast-path procedures are there? How does team structure vary in fast-path situations? What sort of standards govern fast paths? The patient is both the customer and the product they want. Customers do not always know what they want, they are very fuzzy about their requirements. They usually just want to be better. Is their 'betterness' ever discussed with them in terms of the functionality they want or can expect to receive? How about value analysis? Are financial options discussed? I was told a story about an American in his late eighties who was asked, after heart surgery, what sort of pacemaker he would like, a cheap one with a 25-year guarantee, or a more expensive one with a 40-guarantee. His choice was the more expensive one.

How is value added in a school? Who are the stakeholders? What sort of conflicts exist between the various stakeholder groups? How is this conflict resolved? How does conflict affect decision- and policy-making?

This is just a start for you. How are you going to go about collecting the information? What sort of process do you need to record it? How will you translate the useful things you have learnt and go about grafting them onto your process? We talk about this more in Sec. 13.3.

Bought-in tools, methodologies, and checklists embody a process and learning curve

Whenever you buy in a new tool or methodology, or make use of a recommended technique or checklist, you are grafting a different process onto your own and hitching a ride on someone else's learning curve. You may not be consciously choosing to buy a process or learning, you are usually choosing benefits of some kind, and that is where the problems occur. The tool or methodology assumes certain background experience, it forces you to do things in a certain way, and it may not be the way that you have done things in the past.

Looking beyond the frustrations, can you see the process? Can you learn from it? How is it introducing new disciplines to help you do things better? How is it introducing redundant operations which have no value to your organization?

The problems with bought-in processes

Many of the problems with CASE were that we thought we had bought a product, a tool, when in fact we had bought a process. The tool implied a certain usage and infrastructure links to a wider production process. In many cases we did not have a defined wider production process to which we could link it. Commissioning a nuclear power station makes little sense, unless there is an appropriate power grid to which it can be linked, unless power can be stored, and unless there exists sufficient demand for power to make the commissioning and decommissioning feasible. We can choose either to start at a level appropriate to our current infrastructure, say with windmills, and evolve our technology gradually, or to invest in building a grid rapidly and creating the demand for power by subsidizing sales of white goods. Who is prepared to invest in the wider process which CASE needs? Who is prepared to subsidize the systematic storage of product components for reuse? What can we learn to do differently in the future?

So here is the caveat. When you take on benchmarked processes and bought-in tools, you cannot always graft them onto your process. You may need to carry out an expensive re-engineering exercise to rebalance your existing process. You will certainly have to take account of the new learning paradigm. If you take on the new process expecting it to work its own magic, you will probably end up trashing the whole investment, but if you are prepared to spend the appropriate resources to engineer the implementation, because the costs are justified by potential benefits, you stand a far better chance of realizing your investment. The bonus is that your staff will have moved up the learning curve.

13.2 BENCHMARKING

There is no doubt that every organization, although concerned with the here and now, must have an eye on the future and what other people are doing in software production, and in other industries, which may be relevant or useful to the business. The method of comparing one's own practices against other's best practices is called *benchmarking* or, sometimes, *competitive benchmarking*.

No matter how good we are there is always every opportunity to be better, to be producing more value for clients and stakeholders. Shigeo Shingo recounts in his books how, when Toyota fell on hard times in 1973, Taichi Ohno, then managing director, asked him if they could reduce the time taken to change dies in car body production. It was taking around four hours at the time. Shigeo went off to Mercedes in Germany to watch how they handled their set-up. Mercedes managed the changeover in two hours. Shigeo went back to Japan, and soon Toyota had their changeover time down to one and a half hours. Pretty pleased with himself, he reported the good news to Taichi Ohno. Taichi's response was that he wanted changeover to take place in three minutes! We are not talking about quick fixes or cutting corners. We are talking about an outstanding achievement in process re-engineering. The Toyota team studied the process, and engineered the changeover time down to three minutes.

Benchmarking is an on-going operation

Benchmarking is an on-going change and process management operation. It needs to be well coordinated and to have clear goals. In particular, I suggest you think carefully about your policy on change. Do you want to evolve and learn incrementally (but with a fast evolution plan)? Do you want to drag your organization, kicking and screaming into the 21st century? Do you want to invest in full-scale re-engineering, providing adequate resourcing to cover progress up the learning curve? Do you want people to accept change? To understand change? To power and create change? Bringing in lots of new operations from outside without staff involvement will quickly demotivate people. You have taken their destiny out of their hands, and made them 'second-hand Roses'.

Develop your own process and operation maps before you start serious benchmarking

Until you have started to map the process and operations in your own business and have moved up that particular learning curve, I would counsel that you do no active benchmarking. However, you can start to run practice exercises and build the other branch of the benchmark operation, the watching brief and intelligence-gathering activities. Maintain a watching brief on potential areas and industries which you judge will be suitable candidates for benchmarking operations in the future. You will need to keep a watch on the news, business journals, advertisements, annual reports, conference presentations, and so on. Your library or professional body may also be able to supply you with appropriate leads. Again I would say, the more you have an opportunity to see, the more choice you have, so do consider those days out, even if, in the early stages, your visits are not targeted at any specific operations. Even when you are in a position to target your activity, some serendipity can be very fruitful.

Learn to benchmark your own process and operations first

The point of having process and operations maps before you start to benchmark is to reduce some of the passion in introducing people to different ways of working outside the organization. You can discuss and compare process maps, rather than people's competence. Once you have got some of your process and operation maps together, then I suggest you learn to benchmark using your business to start with. Bear in mind that you will have to do quite a bit of selling to make people in your organization entertain other people's ways of working. People are usually motivated by the challenge to be first, but not by the goal of catching up. If you can coach people to make their own improvements, so much the better. One way to go about this is to ask people, 'If we were the competition, how could we put ourselves out of business?'

Make a start on the gaps found in the assessment phase of your planning cycle

When you go through the assessment phase (Sec. 7.5) in your planning cycle, what obvious hot spots are there? Where are the brakes? Where are the negative gap analysis scores? Where could you gain most leverage by closing the gaps? How about your customer interface operations? This is always a good starting point for obtaining leverage. Once you have decided where you could benefit most from change, you have your point of departure. Because you are primed, and have been gathering intelligence and maintaining a watching brief, then you should have some good ideas of where to look.

It may be that it is not specific operations, such as prototyping, say, or estimation, it may be that there is a problem with communication, with decision-making, with delays. This will mean that you need to take a different angle, but the benchmarking operation will be very much the same. The operation looks like Fig. 13.1.

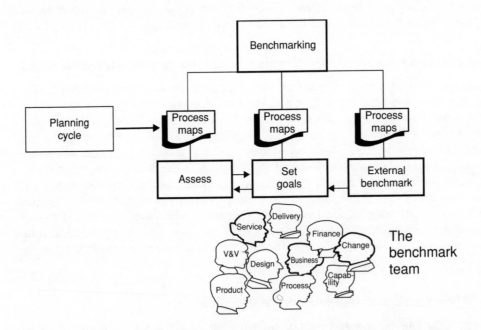

Figure 13.1 The benchmarking team work on the process maps produced by the planning cycle. An internal asessment is made and is used to refine goals. External assessments are also carried out with reference to internal process maps, and the findings are fed back into goals which will inform the next internal assessments.

Your own organization is a benchmarking resource

Can you benchmark within your organization? It may be that there are different groups, some of whom are more advanced with prototyping, some who are more effective communicators. Do not forget that your own organization is an excellent resource. You can probably get a better feel in your own organization for what is actually happening, rather than what people outside might like you to think is happening. There are probably people who can be made available on a temporary basis to act as consultant engineers when you lead in the changes.

If you are serious about benchmarking, travel

When you do have an area targeted, and you cannot seem to get it unstuck from within the organization, do not be half-hearted. Travel. Abroad. To Japan, if necessary. Depending on the size of your organization and on the cost of the brakes, a few thousand pounds for a comprehensive visit could be more than well repaid. There are Japanese delegations who come over to the West on a regular basis and perhaps you could make them welcome in your company. When you go on a benchmark exercise, ask permission to take a video. The Japanese often video their own practices for internal benchmarks. Develop a map of the process and operations as you go along. Begin with a high-level block diagram (Sec. 8.5). Look at the number of stages in their state transition diagram (Sec. 8.6). How do they achieve fewer states? Then progress down to the appropriate level of detail. This is where all your practice in the shopping queues using backs of envelopes comes into its own. It is like second nature to sketch maps quickly now.

Understand the context of other people's operations when you benchmark

The important thing to know is that you cannot and should not work from a process or operation map by itself. Remember that a process embeds purpose and goals. You need to find out what that purpose is and what the goals are. How are they similar to your own, how are they different? What is the whole context in which the operations are successful? If you are looking at a specific operation like design for reuse, then what does the pattern of decision-making look like, what does the communication map look like? What training and learning and other support activities underpin the operation? This will help you assess the possibilities and risks for re-engineering the operation into your process.

When you have completed this assessment, you will need to tune the operation before you implement it into your organization, and you may have to stage its introduction. See Sec. 12.9 for help.

You should not need standing committees for benchmarking

I have said nothing about standing committees or specialist groups to champion benchmarking. Senior management either decide to do it, and incorporate it in their plans and activities, or do not decide to do it. It is that simple. When they do decide to go ahead, it is business as usual and has planned priority in terms of time and resources the same as other scheduled work. You may need to introduce the operation to managers in the first

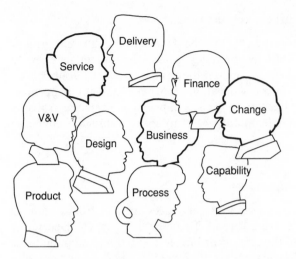

Figure 13.2 When you conduct benchmarking operations, the team needs to have representatives from these key operations

place to obtain their involvement in putting it on the agenda, but after that, it should be treated like any other work that has to be planned and completed (Fig. 13.2)

13.3 IMPLEMENTING BENCHMARKED OPERATIONS

Implementing new tools or benchmarked operations is like carrying out a transplant. You are conducting a major intervention and there are certain basic rules which need to be followed to ensure the transplant takes, and most importantly, the patient lives. Here is what the operation looks like.

Implementation change with a process map in your hand

First of all, you need to have your process and operation maps to hand. Whether you are implementing a new operation or a tool, you should also have maps which show how the operations will look and behave after the transplant. You cannot conduct this sort of organizational surgery just by generally rummaging around trying to get a feel for things in the dark.

Identify all affected process interfaces before you implement change

Compare carefully and identify the interfaces of the 'before' and 'after' operations. You would not conduct a heart bypass without knowing which veins and arteries to suture. What changes to the interfaces are needed? The affected staff will need to design and introduce those first, then you must check them out to ensure that they are sufficiently robust to handle the new cycle times or productivity increases of the transplanted operation. Sort out any problems that might occur here first. If you go ahead with the transplant, and the interfaces are not sound, you could overload the system and cause a collapse. It may not be serious, but it will certainly tie you up trying to remedy it, and everyone's confidence will take a dip. You need to know the special support requirements of the new operations or tools. Before you go into surgery, do you have to strengthen any other parts of the organization? Do you need to clear out any clogged arteries? These are the questions you should be asking.

Implement change in 'sane' periods

Most transplant surgery is carried out while the patient is resting and is not under undue strain or pressure. Planning the implementation to occur after everyone has finished rushing around trying to expedite that special project, or at the year end, if that involves a lot of activity for you, is a sane approach to take. Also, do not expect your patient to be up and running the next day, shifting heavy loads.

Many organizations make the mistake of changing staffing levels or workloads in anticipation of the change. Do not do this under any circumstance. Decide whether you want to make this change work, or whether you want to end up junking investment in tools, people's time, and their good faith. Be prepared to increase the number of staff in the short term, if necessary, so that first, people are on hand to get normal work through without stoppages and secondly, people can provide a rapid response to any problems which may arise. Do not run the operation at the planned capacity of the final state immediately. Run it in slowly, solve any problems, then move up to full speed. Parallel run if that helps.

Implementing change means moving up a learning curve quickly — do not forget to learn

Anaesthesia is not an option for anyone. Everyone involved in the new operation or any of the interface changes needs to be alerted and coached and counselled on the change. The new transplant embeds part of a learning curve that staff in your organization have not travelled up yet for themselves. If all they had to do was to press a different button in a different sequence, then maybe it would be no serious matter. However, we rely on the informed intelligence of people working in the software delivery process. It is not a case of selling or manipulating people to take on the new. We have to identify the fundamental learning which is encapsulated in the new operations and make it available and understandable to people who are affected. This learning is not of the black box type but is 'big picture' learning. By that I mean, we are not just programming people to carry out work differently, they need to know the benefits for them, and for other stakeholders. They may need to rehearse new activity patterns until they feel comfortable with them. See if you can set up some simulations to help them.

Pre-change counselling improves the chances of success

One thing we always miss out on is pre-transplant counselling. Inform staff exactly why the change is being made, what the options were, why this option was judged best, how many previous patients are still alive today, and what their state of health is. Important too, is to discuss what is going to happen, when, who will be involved, what sort of side effects will be experienced, how to spot problems and what to do, and when we expect the change to be fully effective. Lastly, ask people what contribution they can make to ensure well-being and success. If they are unsure, help them.

Monitor change after implementation — do not forget the interfaces

When surgery has been completed, the wound needs to be kept clean. Any problems have to be investigated carefully. It is not just the change which needs to be monitored regularly, but all the interfaces also. Are there impacts being detected by other parts of the business which you did not predict? You need to see if the change is really taking. When you increase speed, are you getting the productivity and improved cycle times you expected? If you are not, do not abandon it, stick with it and find out what it is that makes the difference between your environment and the benchmarked environment in which the tool or operation worked so well. Is there something you did not spot? The source of the operation or tool may be able to give you guidance.

Three key messages for implementing change

There are just three key messages I would like you to remember.

- When you introduce change think of it as surgery.
- No patient can survive a total organ transplant in one go; do it a little at a time.
- The surgeon and the patient are the most important agents of recovery, not the drugs, not the technology. There has to be a common commitment to survive.

13.4 AUTOMATING OPERATIONS

Automation needs to do more than just move the bottleneck down the road

I live in the very beautiful city of Cambridge, England, which, because of its old narrow streets, suffers from severe traffic congestion at peak times. Some time ago the council embarked upon a road-widening scheme to ease the traffic. This involved cutting across swathes of green land and taking the road right up to the classroom windows of a junior school, uprooting their trees and shrubs. The sad thing was that this widening scheme, with all the pain it involved, would move the bottleneck just half a mile down the road, unless the council was willing to plough on and demolish listed buildings. Fortunately, the scheme was abandoned after local protest. The prison-like railings were moved back from the school windows, and trees and shrubs and grass were replanted. The traffic problem remains. It is a systemic problem and not a local problem.

When we introduce automation we have to know whether we are just moving the bottleneck half a mile down the road. We need to know if we are distorting the operations and balance of other parts of the process. If we are, then maybe we need to be looking at the systemic problems of the process as a whole. What is the problem we are trying to solve? Can it be achieved by any other means. In the last decade the United States spent a trillion dollars on white-collar productivity tools, with only a one per cent increase in productivity as a result. The real benefits come through business re-engineering.

Do not do the wrong things faster, re-engineer before you automate

Use process and operation maps to help you assess, systematically, where productivity improvements can be made. You are likely to gain from streamlining and simplifying before you automate. There is no point doing more of something, or doing something faster, when you do not really need to do it all. When you are in a streamlined position and ready to go ahead and implant new technologies, then use process maps again to assess the impact of change.

Automation — buy or DIY

There is the perennial problem of do we buy in or do we tailor something for ourselves. When we choose to buy in, then we need to remember that we buy not only a tool and its benefits, but also embedded operations and learning curves. The range of tools and methodologies from a supplier may link together to provide you with a harmonious process. They may not. But if they do, is that an appropriate process for your business, will it meet the demands of your market? You may be able to benefit from the embedded learning curve in the tools, or by having a greater choice of staff available to you who are proficient in using the tools. But it may cause difficulties for your existing staff, now, because they have to change learning curves. Whether there are real benefits depends on how high your expected staff turnover is, and how easy it is for outsiders to learn your process and operations. If you have low attrition and easy-to-use tools, then it may be advantageous to build your own, rather than be locked into the tools of an outside supplier.

Another choice we have to make is when there is a conflict between the bought-in tool and our existing process. Do we throw away the tool and our investment, do we run our process in cripple mode to compensate for the poor compatibility, do we buy more tools to enable compatibility, or can we re-engineer?

The Japanese have tended to build their own tools which develop out of their process and improvements to it. Working first with very simple prototypes, they fine-tune the tools so that they are balanced and synchronized with the process. During this time, they have not only gone up the learning curve quickly, but also lived the learning, which is more valuable than any classroom instruction can be.

The need for automation

We do need to automate ourselves, there is no doubt about it. If we are to keep costs down, improve value to clients, and free ourselves to innovate, we need to be supported by tools. Tools help by restricting the freedom to introduce errors, and can embed certain standards and remove the need for tedious work instructions and checklists because personnel can only do the right thing. Tools also embed decision-making. Where once we might have had a whole function or operation devoted to taking specialist decisions, over time that can be 'digested' by the organization and transferred to a competence. From there the step to automation is short. The number of simple tools which now abound and which are found on every software developer's desk, such as spreadsheets and databases can be used to prototype automated aids.

The financial bias toward buying in process and automation

The problem that remains is the bias that persists in allocating resource for new tools. Buy off the shelf, out of capital, and there are few real problems, but build it yourself, something more appropriate and for less perhaps, then shivers run through the organizational spine. The entailed costs are revenue, personnel, and their burdened on costs, pension provisions, and so on. But when we buy in, are we not also paying for someone else's personnel, and their pension plans and more? Do we have a systemic problem here?

13.5 AUTOMATING THE PROCESS

Workflow and groupware tools provide a special kind of automation. Quite recently launched into the market, they are attracting considerable interest and support. Because of their process-orientation, and their potential support for software process design and management, they deserve their own section.

What is a workflow tool?

There are a number of varieties of tool, all with different potential, and if I were asked to supply a general description, it would be, that they are software systems for describing and controlling cooperative work processes and practices. Some are aimed specifically at software production, others are more general. Some are more sophisticated than others. Some link into CASE tools, others do not. Some are versions of electronic mail and office automation with imaging facilities for routeing documents. Some have full-blown sequencing and synchronization protocols based upon Petri nets (Sec. 8.8). This last, Process Weaver, enables you to model the dynamic interactions in your own software production process and to capture activity analysis breakdowns which are useful for costing purposes. These are obviously quite an investment, with top-of-the-range entry prices quoted at around £50,000. A list of well-known tools, their suppliers and addresses is given in Appendix A.

The benefits of workflow tools

The benefits are very variable given the range and sophistication of the tools available. The more you invest, the more potential benefits there are to be gained, if you are in a position to exploit them. I say this very carefully. There are many potential benefits to be gained from CASE, but how many people realized them? How many became simply drawing machines or tools for making very attractive design documentation?

Workflow tools, by allowing you to model and incorporate all your working practices into an automated process, take out some of the burden of remembering what to do next. The operation is mapped for you, and, on some systems, when you log in, there is an agenda ready for you, with the tasks you need to work on today. I suppose as managers, we might be tempted to say, well that sounds all right for my staff, but not for me. It all depends on how much of an important link you are in the supply chain. If your role is not important and the business does not depend on you for much intervention, then maybe you are right. But for some managers, the synchronization of their work with staff and their peers is probably more vital than that of their staff. With workflow tools we can visibly see where we might inadvertently be introducing delays into the system.

They force us to work on empowerment more. Decisions have to be moved to where people work, so they can get on and work through their agenda. There is no arbitrary linear division of labour. People can work in a natural manner as members of a cooperative team, exchanging information and routeing information even though they may be many miles distant. There are opportunities here are for tele-working, and for rerouteing work when staff are sick or otherwise unable to carry out their duties.

Importantly, staff can have access to first-hand information. You could use imaging to capture original customer verbatims. When staff need a particular document or specific information to get on with their work, it does not have to be begged from some other member of staff, nor do they have to make do with a quickly remembered verbal résumé. They can simply call it up. This means we can associate a need for very specific information with defined operations. It is possible, given some thought, that the business could take on the information criticality (Sec. 10.4) challenge and totally rationalize and reduce the amount of documentation required by the process. You could even link the workflow system into the experience base. That could be very useful.

Implementing workflow tools

If you want to implement workflow tools, then you will be making an intervention in the business at least as big as CASE, if not more so, since a wider range of personnel could be involved. In that case, you need to start moving up a learning curve as quickly as possible. The standard approach to this task is to advise you to set up a specialist process group that will design and engineer delivery processes. Given my experience with similar implementations, I have reservations about this method of attack. The way we work and the choices and decisions we make are the symbol, if not the fact, of our personal autonomy. 'Educating' people in how to do quality is one thing, 'educating' people in how to do the work which they believe they have carried out successfully for a number of years is a bigger thing. If you did set up a group, I am not sure how popular they or their offerings would be when they descended on staff and managers with new streamlined ways of working. There would have to be a long period of consensus-gathering, selling, and wheeling and dealing and probably impasse. You could be using that time more profitably.

I have my reservations, too, about the value of putting the whole organization through a training course on process modelling, although I am sure there will be people who will happily sell you this service. I have to admit my personal bias and say that the best way I have found of helping people to make the transition is simply by getting everyone to do it on a small scale, to make mistakes, and to learn from practice. Learn the difficulties, sort them out, become clearer about what you need to do, then accelerate the operation.

Start to map processes and operations now using simple tools. Introduce process and operations maps on to the agenda. Use them as starting points for discussion. Incorporate them into job descriptions. Have people work on streamlining their operations first, and then, not long after, people will start to ask for more. That is the time to make the tools available. You will not be starting from the bottom rung. You will have operations that will have been streamlined and made ready for automation, and you will have the active involvement of the majority of your staff.

13.6 MEASURING THE IMPACT

In the past it has not been easy to assess the impact of new operations or tools on the total process. We have had to rely on gut feel and people's perceptions of whether they feel they are going any faster or slower, or whether they feel they are being less productive or more. This gives us some indication of local change, but it is even more difficult to get an indication of change for the better or worse for the process as a whole.

Assessing the level of investment in new tools and operations

It is important when we decide to introduce new tools or operations, and after we have carried out the implementation, to make an assessment of benefits or otherwise. How do we decide where we are going to get the best returns, and how do we determine the appropriate level of investment to ensure we have made a value-for-money investment?

One of the things you will start to notice when you produce process and operation maps is that some operations seem to have disproportionately long cycle times compared to the time needed to process the operation. Having worked with a test team at one stage who had to put new releases through a regression cycle that simulated 13 days, it struck me as not quite right that it should take nearly 60 elapsed days. Thirteen days seemed a reasonable number to aim for, or as a half-way stage twenty-six to allow for the package to be run twice. If you could reduce the cycle time of that test operation how much would it be worth to you? There is obviously the costs of the staff involved, and machine time. Maybe you would like to reduce those costs, and redeploy some of the test team into development. That could make you more responsive in both delivering and releasing products. And what about the bottleneck, the reduction in lead time to get products to the customer? Say products could be delivered a month earlier, how much more could be earned by your customer if they got a product to market one month earlier?

Benchmarking cycle times and error rates

Knowing how long cycle times are, together with the failure rate associated with that cycle time, provides you with a useful indicator for establishing an assessment of change. You can ask your suppliers to give you an assessment of the benefits to you, in terms of reduced cycle times and errors, of their particular product in your particular environment. When you are establishing benchmarks, cycle times and failures will be on your checklist. But it is not just the changed operation itself which is measured before and after, all connecting operations need to be assessed too. Is it not reasonable that you just might increase the cycle time or effort required by an operation so that you could significantly reduce the effort and cycle times needed by related operations? By referring to newly drawn operations maps and cycle times you will be able to help people see the benefits of change, or equally the problems, if there are any.

Using an understanding of cycle times to determine the right investment

In the testing example given above, there would have been very little benefit from buying in more tools or increasing the level of automation. Looking at the operation, cycle time was taken up by waiting for the inputs to be tested and corrected. If, on the other hand, we had seen that the majority of the 60 days had been taken up by processing activities, then after validating those activities to ensure they were totally necessary, automation would have been one option to look at in more detail, but it was only by reference to an operations map that this became evident. The team always had plenty to do and would never say that they were waiting on work. They were not that secure. So the delay was effectively hidden. But asked how they could reduce cycle time to 26 days prompted some very constructive responses.

It is a simple question, 'What would have to be different for you to carry out this task in 26 days?' We can ask that same question at all points in the process, we just have to change the numbers. Then perhaps we can become the source of excellence that other people are wanting to benchmark.

Appendix A

WORKFLOW MANAGEMENT SOFTWARE AND SUPPLIERS

Process Weaver / PROWESS
Cap Gemini Innovation / Hoskyns Ltd
Hoskyns South Bank
95 Wandsworth Road
London SW8 2LX

Tel: 071 735 0800

Processwise
ICL
Kidsgrove ST7 1TL

Tel: 0782 771000

EPIC/Workflow
Computron Technologies Europe Ltd
171–175 Uxbridge Road
Ealing
London W13 9AA

Tel: 081 579 1446

ENIX Ltd
3 The Green
Richmond
Surrey TW9 1PL

Tel: 081 332 0210

QUALIWARE
Coordination Systems Ltd
3c Cornbrash Park
Bumpers Way
Chippenham
Wiltshire SN14 6RA

Tel: 0249 448870

Staffware
46 Changford Street
London NW1 6EB

Quesheet for Windows
Logical Water (UK)
Sheraton House
Castle Park
Cambridge
CB3 OAX2

Tel: 0223 846677

also:

  Olivetti   IBIsys
  BullFlowpath
  Digital   Team Route / MEGADOC
  Filenet   WORKFLO
  NCR Cooperation
  Plexus   ImageFlow

Flowcharting Tools:

ABC Flowcharter (available from any software dealer)

The FlowMap System
PO Box 281
Chislehurst
Kent BR7 5SX

Tel: 081 467 1255

Simulations and Coaching:

Process oriented effort management and process for managers
Jacqueline Holdsworth
51 Bateman Street
Cambridge
CB2 ILR

Tel: 0223 68574

BIBLIOGRAPHY

BOOKS

Ackerman, D., *A Natural History of the Senses*, Vintage Books, London, 1990.

Ackoff, R., *The Art of Problem Solving*, John Wiley, Chichester, 1978.

Ackoff, A., *Management in Small Doses*, John Wiley, Chichester, 1989.

Alexander, C., *Notes On A Synthesis Of Form*, Harvard University Press, Harvard, Mass, 1972

Alexander, F. M., *The Use Of Self*, Gollancz, London, 1983.

Argyris, C., *Organisation and Innovation*, Blackwell, Oxford, 1969.

Argyris, C., *Personality & Organisation*, Harper & Row, London, 1970.

Argyris, C., *Management and Organisational Development*, Blackwell, Oxford, 1971.

Argyris, C., et al., *Theory in Practice*, Jossey-Bass, London, 1974

Argyris, C., et al., *Organisational Learning*, Addison-Wesley, London, 1978.

Argyris, C., *Inner Contradictions of Rigorous Research*, Academic, London, 1980.

Argyris, C., *Reasoning, Learning and Action*, Jossey-Bass, London, 1982.

Argyris, C., *Strategy Change & Defensive Routines*, Pitman, London, 1985.

Argyris, C., *Action Science: Concepts, Methods and Skills*, Jossey-Bass, San Francisco, CA, 1986.

Argyris, C., *Overcoming Organisational Defences*, Allyn & Bacon, Needham Heights, MA, 1990.

Argyris, C., *Integrating the Individual and the Organisation*, Transaction, New Brunswick, NJ, 1990.

Ashby, W. R., *An Introduction of Cybernetics*, Methuen & Co. Ltd., London, 1964.

Beer, S., *Decision and Control*, John Wiley, Chichester, 1966.

Beer, S., *Platform for Change*, John Wiley & Sons Ltd., Chichester, 1975.

Beer, S., *The Heart of Enterprise*, John Wiley & Sons Ltd., Chichester, 1979.

Beer, S., *The Brain of the Firm*, John Wiley & Sons Ltd., Chichester, 1981

Bertalanfy, L., von, *General Systems Theory*, George Braziller, New York, NY, 1980.

Boehm, B., *Software Engineering Economics*, Prentice-Hall, London, 1981.

Checkland, P., *Systems Thinking, Systems Practice*, John Wiley, Chichester, 1981.

Checkland, P., *Soft Systems Methodology in Action*, John Wiley, Chichester, 1990

Churchman, W. et al., *An Introduction To Operations Research*, John Wiley, Chichester, 1957.

Clark, K. B., *The Uneasy Alliance*, Harvard Business School, Harvard, Mass, 1986.

Cooper, R., et al., *Design of Cost Management Systems*, Prentice-Hall, Englewood Cliffs, NJ, 1991.

Dale, B. G., et al., *Quality Costing*, Chapman and Hall, London, 1991.

DeMarco, T., *Controlling Software Projects*, Prentice-Hall, Englewood Cliffs, NJ, 1982.

DeMarco, T., *Peopleware*, Dorset House, New York, NY, 1988.

Deming, W. E., *Sample Design in Business Research*, John Wiley and Sons, New York, NY, 1960.

Deming, W. E., *Out of the Crisis*, Cambridge University Press, Cambridge, 1988.

Doray, B., *From Taylorism To Fordism*, Free Association Books, London, 1988.

Drucker, P., *The Effective Executive*, Heinemann, Oxford, 1988.

Espeio, R., *et al., The Viable Systems Model*, John Wiley, Chichester, 1989.

Evans, M. W., *The Software Factory*, John Wiley, New York, NY, 1989.

Evans, M. W., *et al., Software Quality Assurance and Management*, John Wiley, New York, NY, 1987.

Feynman, R. P., *What Do You Care What Other People Think?*, Unwin, London, 1990.

Ford, H., *Ford on Management*, Blackwell, Oxford, 1991.

Gabor, A., *The Man Who Discovered Quality*, Penguin, Harmondsworth, 1992.

Gilb, T., *et al., Principles Of Software Engineering Management*, Addison-Wesley, Wokingham, 1988.

Goodman, P., *Practical Implementation of Software Metrics*, McGraw-Hill, Maidenhead, 1993.

Grady, R. B., *et al., Software Metrics*, Prentice-Hall, Englewood Cliffs, NJ, 1987.

Haldane, T., *Meeting Quality Standards*, Pergamon, Oxford, 1989.

Halprin, L., *The RSVP Cycles — Creative Process*, George Braziller, New York, NY, 1969.

Hardin, H., *The New Bureaucracy*, McClelland and Stewart, Toronto, Ont, 1991.

Hay, E. J., *JIT Breakthough*, John Wiley, New York, NY, 1988.

Hayes, R., *et al., Dynamic Manufacturing*, Free Press, New York, NY, 1988.

Heisenberg, W., *Physics & Philosophy*, Penguin, Harmondsworth, 1990.

Helander, M., *et al., Design For Manufacturability*, Taylor & Francis, Basingstoke, 1992.

Hout, T. M., *et al., Competing Against Time*, Free Press, New York, NY, 1990.

Humphrey, W., *Managing the Software Process*, Addison-Wesley, Wokingham, 1989.

Imai, M., *Kaizen*, McGraw-Hill, Maidenhead, 1988.

Ishikawa, K., *What is Total Quality Control?*, Prentice-Hall, Englewood Cliffs, 1985.

Jacobson, G., *et al., Xerox: The American Samurai*, Collier Macmillan Books, NY, 1987.

James, W., *Pragmatism*, Harvard University Press, Harvard, Mass, 1947.

Jessup, P., *Continuing Process Control & Process Capability*, Dearborn, Chicago, Il, 1984.

Johnson, H. T., *Relevance Regained*, Free Press, New York, NY, 1992.

Johnson, H. T., *et al., Relevance Lost*, Harvard Business School, Harvard, Mass, 1991.

Julius, F. E., *The Winning Trainer*, Gulf, Houston, Tx, 1989.

Juran, J. M., *Managerial Breakthrough*, second edition, McGraw-Hill, Maidenhead, 1994.

Kaplan, R., *et al., Advanced Manufacturing Accounting*, Prentice-Hall, Englewood Cliffs, NJ, 1989.

Kilman, R. H., *et al., Gaining Control of the Corporate Culture*, Jossey-Bass, San Francisco, CA, 1985.

Koestenbaum, P., *Heart of the Business*, Saybrook Publishing, Dallas, Tx, 1987.

Kohn, A., *The Case Against Competition*, Houghton Mifflin, Boston, Mass, 1986.

Kuhn, T., *The Essential Tension*, Chicago University Press, Chicago, USA, 1977.

Lacy, J. A., *Systems Engineering Management*, McGraw-Hill, Maidenhead, 1992.

Laughlin, C., *et al., Brain, Symbol and Experience*, Columbia UP, 1993.

Leshan, L., *et al., Einstein's Space and Van Gogh's Sky*, Collier Books, Oxford, 1982.

Levins, R., *Evolution in Changing Environments*, Princeton University Press, Princeton, NJ, 1968.

Lewis, C. I., *The Mind and World Order*, Dover, New York, NY, 1929.

Lieberman, J., *Tyranny of Expertise*, Walker and Company, New York, NY.

Luggen, W. W., *Flexible Manufacturing Cells and Systems*, Prentice-Hall, Englewood Cliffs, NJ, 1991.

Mack, R., *Planning on Uncertainty*, Wiley Interscience, New York, NY, 1971.

Maisel, E., *The Alexander Technique*, Thames & Hudson, London, 1974.

Maturana, Humberto & Varella, *Tree of Knowledge*, Shambhala, Boston, Mass, 1988.

McCulloch, W. S., *Embodiments of Mind*, MIT, Mass, 1988.

McGregor, D. N., *The Human Side of Enterprise*, McGraw-Hill, Maidenhead, 1960.

McGregor, D. N., *Leadership & Motivation*, MIT, Mass, 1966.

McGregor, D. N., *The Professional Manager*, McGraw-Hill, Maidenhead, 1967.

Morgan, G., *Images of Organisation*, Sage Publications, London, 1986.

Musashi, M. A., *Book Of Five Rings*, Flamingo, London, 1984.

Ouchi, W., *Theory Z*, Avon Books, New York, NY, 1981.

Ouchi, W., *The M-Form Society*, Addison-Wesley, Redding, MA, 1984.

Parker, M. M., *et al., Information Economics*, Prentice-Hall, Englewood Cliffs, NJ, 1988.

Pascale, R., *et al., The Art Of Japanese Management*, Penguin, Harmondsworth, 1986.

Pinchot, G., *Intrapreneuring*, Harper & Row, London, 1986.

Pribram, K., *Brain and Perception, L Erlbaum*, USA, 1991.

Robinson, D. G., *et al., Training for Impact*, Jossey-Bass, San Francisco, CA, 1989.

Schon, D., *Beyond the Stable State*, Temple Smith, London, 1971.

Schon, D., *The Reflective Practitioner*, Temple Smith, London, 1983.

Schon, D., *Educating the Reflective Practitioner*, Jossey-Bass, San Francisco, CA, 1986.

Schonberger, R. J., *Japanese Manufacturing Techniques*, Collier MacMillan, London, 1983.

Schonberger, R. J., *et al., Operations Management — Improving Customer Service*, R. D. Irwin, USA, 1991.

Senge, P. M., *The Fifth Discipline*, Doubleday, London, 1990.

Shingo, S., *Study of Toyota Production System*, Productivity Press, USA, Cambridge, Mass., 1985.

Shingo, S., *Revolution In Manufacturing*, Productivity Press, Cambridge, Mass, 1986.

Shingo, S., *Zero Quality Control*, Productivity Press, Cambridge, Mass, 1986.

Shingo, S., *Non Stock Production*, Productivity Press, Cambridge, Mass, 1988.

Singer, E. A., *Experience and Reflection*, University of Pennsylvania Press, Philadelphia, PA, 1959.

Singh, J., *Operational Research: Great Ideas of Operations Research*, Penguin, Harmondsworth, 1971.

Sloan, A. P., *My Years with General Motors*, Penguin, Harmondsworth, 1972.

Smith, P. G., *et al., Developing Products In Half the Time*, Van Nostrand Reinhold, NY, 1991.

Stalk, G., *et al., Kaisha: The Japanese Corporation*, Basic Books, New York, NY, 1985.

Taguchi, G., *Techniques to Quality Engineering*, McGraw-Hill, Maidenhead, 1988.

Veblen, T., *The Higher Learning in America*, Hill and Wang, New York, NY, 1962.

Wheelwright, S. C., *Forecasting Methods for Managers*, John Wiley, Chichester, 1980.

Wheelwright S. C., *et al., Revolutionising Product Development*, Free Press, New York, NY, April 1992.

Wiener, N., *The Human Use of Human Beings*, Free Association Books, London, 1989.

Youll, D. P., *Making Software Development Visible*, Wiley, Chichester, 1990.

Zeithaml, V. A. *et al., Delivering quality service: Balancing Customer Performance*, Free Press, New York, NY, 1990.

ARTICLES

Abdel-Hamid, T. K., The Dynamics Of Software Project Staffing, *IEEE Trans Soft Eng*. Feb. 1989.

Abernathy, W. J., *et al.,* The New Industrial Competition, *Harvard Business Review, Harvard, Mass*, Sep./Oct. 1981.

Ackoff, R., The Future of Operational Research Is Past, *Journal of Operations Research*, 30(2), 1979.

Adler, P. S., *et al.,* Strategic Management Of Technical Functions, *Sloane Management Review*, Winter 1992.

Aggarwal, S. C., MRP, JIT, OPT, FMS?, *Harvard Business Review, Harvard, Mass*, Sep/Oct. 1985.

Akima, N. *et al.,* Industrializing Software Development, *IEEE Software*, March 1989.

Alonso, R., *et al.,* JIT Hits Home, *Sloane Management Review*, Summer 1991.

Argyris, C., Skilled Incompetence, *Harvard Business Review, Harvard, Mass*, Sep./Oct. 1986.

Argyris, C., Teaching Smart People How To Learn, *Harvard Business Review, Harvard, Mass*, May/Jun. 1991.

Argyris, C., Double Loop Learning In Organisations, *Harvard Business Review, Harvard, Mass*, Sep./Oct. 1977.

Baxter, A., Waging War Against The Paper Chase, *Financial Times*, 29 Oct. 1992.

Beatty, C. A., Implementing Advanced Manufacturing Technologies, *Sloane Management Review*, Summer 1992.

Beech, P., Cost Control, *Project Management Today*, Feb. 1990.

Bell, C. G., The Fewer Engineers Per Project, The Better, *IEEE Spectrum 'Speakout'*, Feb. 1989.

Bell, T. E., Managing Risk In Large Complex Systems, *IEEE Spectrum*, June 1989.

Bell, T. E., Managing Murphy's Law: Engineering A Minimum Risk, *IEEE Spectrum*, June 1989.

Bell, T. E., The Space Shuttle: A Case Of Subjective Engineering, *IEEE Spectrum*, June 1989.

Bell, T. E., The Limits Of Risk Analysis, *IEEE Spectrum*, June 1989.

Benjamin, R. I., *et al.,* Critical IT Issues: The Next Ten Years, *Sloane Management Review*, Summer 1992.

Berlant, D., *et al.,* How Hewlett-Packard Gets Numbers It Can Trust, *Harvard Business Review, Harvard, Mass*, Jan./Feb. 1990.

Biggerstaff, T. J., Design Recovery For Maintenance and Reuse, *IEEE Computer*, July 1989.

Blaxill, M. F., *et al.,* The Fallacy Of The Overhead Quick Fix, *Harvard Business Review, Harvard, Mass,* Jul./Aug. 1988.

Boehm, B., Industrial Software Metrics Top 10 List, *IEEE Software,* Sept. 1987.

Bower, J. L., *et al.,* Fast Cycle Capability For Competitive Power, *Harvard Business Review, Harvard, Mass,* Nov./Dec. 1988

Boynton, A. C., *et al.,* Whose Responsibility Is IT Management, *Sloane Management Review,* Summer 1992.

Cooks, F., No Silver Bullet, *IEEE Software,* 1988.

Ciss, M. D. J., Penny-wise Approach To Data Processing, *Harvard Business Review, Harvard, Mass,* Jul./Aug. 1981.

Civano, J. P., *et al.,* QA In Future Development Environments, *IEEE Software,* Sept. 1987.

Child, P., *et al.,* The Management Of Complexity, *Sloane Management Review,* Autumn 1991.

Christiansen, D., Understanding Risk, *IEEE Spectrum,* June 1989.

Cobb, R. H., *et al.,* Engineering Software Under Statistical Quality, *IEEE Software,* Nov. 1990.

Cohen, M. A., *et al.,* Out Of Touch With Customer Needs, *Sloane Management Review,* Winter 1990.

Cooper, R., You Need A New Cost System When . . ., *Harvard Business Review, Harvard, Mass,* Jan./Feb. 1989.

Cooper, R., *et al.,* Measure Costs Right, *Harvard Business Review, Harvard, Mass,* Sep./Oct. 1988.

Cooper, R., *et al.,* Profit Priorities From Activity-Based Costing, *Harvard Business Review, Harvard, Mass,* May/June 1991.

Cox, B., Planning The Software Industrial Revolution, *IEEE Software,* Nov. 1990.

Cusumano, M. A., The Software Factory: A Historical Interpretation, *IEEE Software,* Mar 1989.

Davis, A. M., *et al.,* A Strategy For Comparing Alternative Software, *IEEE Trans Soft Eng,* Oct. 1988.

Dean, J. W., *et al.,* Organising For Manufacturable Design, *Harvard Business Review, Harvard, Mass,* Jan./Feb. 1989.

DeMarco, T., Making A Difference In The Schools, *IEEE Software,* Nov. 1990.

Deutsch, C. H., Productivity: The Difficulty Of Even Defining, *Business Week,* 9 June 1980.

Dhalla, N. K., *et al.,* Forget The Product Life Cycle, *Harvard Business Review, Harvard, Mass,* Jan./Feb. 1976.

Drucker, P. F., The Emerging Theory Of Manufacturing, *Harvard Business Review, Harvard, Mass,* May/Jun. 1990.

Drucker, P. F., What Can We Learn From Japanese Management, *Harvard Business Review, Harvard, Mass,* Mar./Apr. 1971.

Eccles, R. G., The Performance Measurement Manifesto, *Harvard Business Review, Harvard, Mass,* Jan./Feb. 1991.

Francis, A. E., *et al.,* Building A Better Budget, *Quality Progress,* Oct. 1989.

Frank, L., *et al.,* The Incline Of Quality, *Harvard Business Review, Harvard, Mass,* Sep./Oct. 1982.

Garvin, D. A., Quality On The Line, Harvard Business Review, *Harvard, Mass,*

Gitlow, H. S., *et al.,* Product Defects and Productivity, *Harvard Business Review, Harvard, Mass,* Sep./Oct.1983.

Gluck, F. W., *et al.,* Strategic Management For Competitive Advantage, *Harvard Business Review, Harvard, Mass,* Jul./Aug. 1980.

Grady, R. B., Measuring And Managing Software Maintenance, *IEEE Software,* Sept. 1987.

Grant, R. M., *et al.,* Appropriate Manufacturing Technology, *Sloane Management Review,* Autumn 1991.

Griffiths, J., Honda Reaches Accord In UK, *Financial Times,* 9 Nov. 1992.

Gross, N., Now Software Isn't Safe From Japan, *Business Week,* Feb. 1991.

Gruman, G. (ed.), Early Reuse Practice Lives Up To Its Promise, *IEEE Software,* Nov. 1988.

Guest, R., Quality Of Work Life, *Harvard Business Review, Harvard, Mass,* Jul./Aug. 1979.

Hammer, M., Reengineering Work: Don't Automate, Obliterate, *Harvard Business Review, Harvard, Mass,* Jul./Aug. 1990.

Harel, D., *et al.,* STATEMENT: A Working Environment, *IEEE Trans Soft Eng,* Apr. 1990.

Hart, C. W. L., The Power Of Unconditional Service Guarantees, *Harvard Business Review, Harvard, Mass,* Jul./Aug. 1988.

Hart, C. W. L., *et al.,* Guarantees Come To Professional Service Firms, *Sloane Management Review,* Spring 1992.

Hauser, J. R., *et al.,* The House Of Quality, *Harvard Business Review, Harvard, Mass,* May/Jun. 1988.

Hayes, R. H., Why Japanese Factories Work, *Harvard Business Review, Harvard, Mass,* Jul./Aug. 1981.

Hayes, R. H., *et al.,* Why Some Factories Are More Productive Than Others, *Harvard Business Review, Harvard, Mass,* Sep./Oct. 1986.

Hayes, R. H., *et al.,* How Should You Organise Manufacturing?, *Harvard Business Review, Harvard, Mass,* Jan./Feb. 1978.

Hayes, R. H., *et al.*, Managing Our Way To Economic Decline, *Harvard Business Review, Harvard, Mass*, Jul./ Aug. 1980.

Heemstra, F. J., *et al.*, Function Point Analysis, *European Journal of Information Systems*, Dec. 1991.

Hiromoto, T., Another Hidden Edge — Japanese Management Accounting, *Harvard Business Review, Harvard, Mass*, Jul./Aug. 1988.

Hopcraft, *et al.*, Toward Better Computer Science, *IEEE Spectrum*, Dec. 1987.

House, C. H., *et al.*, The Return Map: Tracking Product Teams, *Harvard Business Review, Harvard, Mass*, Jan./ Feb. 1991.

Humphrey, W. S., Characterizing The Software Process: A Maturity, *IEEE Software*, Mar. 1988.

Jackall, R., Moral Mazes: Bureaucracy And Managerial Work, *Harvard Business Review, Harvard, Mass*, Sep./ Oct. 1983.

Jacques, E., In Praise Of Hierarchy, *Harvard Business Review, Harvard, Mass*, Jan./Feb. 1990.

Jaikumar, R., Post-Industrial Manufacturing, *Harvard Business Review, Harvard, Mass*, Nov./Dec. 1986.

Johnson, R. T., *et al.*, Made In America (Under Japanese Management), *Harvard Business Review, Harvard, Mass*, Sep./Oct. 1974.

Judson, A. S., The Awkward Truth About Productivity, *Harvard Business Review, Harvard, Mass*, Sep./Oct. 1982.

Kishida, K., *et al.*, Quality Assurance Technology In Japan, *IEEE Software*, Sept. 1987.

Klein, J., *et al.*, Good Supervisors Are Good Supervisors Anywhere, *Harvard Business Review, Harvard, Mass*, Nov./Dec. 1986.

Lee, H. L., *et al.*, Managing Supply Chain Inventory, *Sloane Management Review*, Spring 1992.

Lewis, T. G., *et al.*, The Challenge Of Software Development, *IEEE Software*, Nov. 1990.

McCoy, B. H., The Parable Of The Saddhu, *Harvard Business Review, Harvard, Mass*, Sep./Oct. 1983.

McFarlan, F. W., Portfolio Approach To Information Systems, *Harvard Business Review, Harvard, Mass*, Sep./ Oct. 1981.

Miller, J. G., *et al.*, The Hidden Factory, *Harvard Business Review, Harvard, Mass*, Sep./Oct. 1985.

Mills, H. D., *et al.*, Cleanroom Software Engineering, *IEEE Software*, Sep. 1987.

Misra, S., *et al.*, Third Generation v Fourth Generation Software, *IEEE Software*, July 1988.

Moores, T. T., *et al.*, Could Large UK Corporations & Computing Companies, *European Journal of Information Systems*, May 1992.

Musa, J. D., Tools For Measuring Software Reliability, *IEEE Spectrum*, Feb. 1989.

Parasuraman, A. B., *et al.*, Understanding Customer Expectations Of Service, *Sloane Management Review*, Spring 1991.

Parnas, D. L., *et al.*, The Modular Structure Of Complex Systems, *IEEE Trans Soft Eng*, March 1985.

Pascale, R. T., Zen And The Art Of Management, *Harvard Business Review, Harvard, Mass*, Mar./Apr. 1978.

Potosnak, K., Management: The Key To Success, *IEEE Software*, Nov. 1988.

Potosnak, K., Mental Models: Helping Users Understand Software, *IEEE Software*, Sept. 1989.

Potosnak, K., Modular Implementation Benefits Developers And Users, *IEEE Software*, May 1989.

Prieto-Diaz, R., *et al.*, Classifying Software For Reuse, *IEEE Software*, Jan. 1987.

Puxty, A., Traditional Costing And Use Of Systems Approach, *Management Accounting*, Jul./Aug. 1980.

Rehfeld, J. E., What Working For A Japanese Company Taught Me, *Harvard Business Review, Harvard, Mass*, Nov./Dec. 1990.

Rockart, J. F., *et al.*, Systems Delivery: Evolving New Strategies, *Sloane Management Review*, Summer 1992.

Senge, P., The Leader's New York, *Sloane Management Review*, Autumn 1990.

Shaw, M., Prospects For Engineering Discipline Of Software, *IEEE Software*, Nov. 1990.

Sirkin, H., *et al.*, Fix The Process Not The Problem, *Harvard Business Review, Harvard, Mass*, Jul./Aug. 1990.

Skinner, W., The Focused Factory, *Harvard Business Review, Harvard, Mass*, May/Jun. 1974.

Skinner, W., The Productivity Paradox, *Harvard Business Review, Harvard, Mass*, Jul./Aug. 1986.

Stalk, Jnr. G., Time — The Next Source Of Competitive Advantage, *Harvard Business Review, Harvard, Mass*, Jul./Aug. 1988.

Stanton, S., Organisational Learning, *Sloane Management Review*, Spring 1989.

Stix, G., Bhopal: A Tragedy In Waiting, *IEEE Spectrum*, June 1989.

Taguchi, G., *et al.*, Robust Quality, *Harvard Business Review, Harvard, Mass*, Jan./Feb. 1990.

Tajima, D., *et al.*, The Computer Software Industry In Japan, *Computer*, May 1981.

Takeuchi, H., *et al.*, The New New Product Development Game, *Harvard Business Review, Harvard, Mass*, Jan./ Feb. 1986.

Tucker, F. G., *et al.,* How To Measure Yourself Against The Best, *Harvard Business Review, Harvard, Mass,* Jan./Feb. 1987.

Varadarajan, P. R., Controlling The Uncontrollable, *Sloane Management Review,* Winter 1992.

Wheelwright, S. C., Japan Where Operations Really Are Strategic, *Harvard Business Review, Harvard, Mass,* Jul./Aug. 1981.

Wheelwright, S. C., *et al.,* Dynamics of Process Product Life — Cycles, *Harvard Business Review, Harvard, Mass,* Special Collection 6.

Wheelwright, S. C., *et al.,* Creating Project Plans To Focus, *Harvard Business Review, Harvard, Mass,* Mar./Apr. 1992.

Whitney, D. E., Manufacturing By Design, *Harvard Business Review, Harvard, Mass,* Jul./Aug. 1988.

Wiggenhorn, W., Motorola, U, When Training Becomes An Education, *Harvard Business Review, Harvard, Mass,* Jul./Aug. 1990.

Zipkin, P. H., Does Manufacturing Need A JIT Revolution?, *Harvard Business Review, Harvard, Mass,* Jan./Feb. 1991.